WHITE BACKLASH

WHITE BACKLASH

Immigration, Race, and American Politics

Marisa Abrajano & Zoltan L. Hajnal

PRINCETON UNIVERSITY PRESS

Princeton and Oxford

press.princeton.edu

Library of Congress Cataloging in Publication Control Number 2014043799

ISBN 978–0-691–16443–4

British Library Cataloging-in-Publication Data is available

This book has been composed in Electra LT Std

Printed on acid-free paper. ∞

Printed in the United States of America

1 3 5 7 9 10 8 6 4 2

Contents

Additional materials can be found in the online appendix at http://press .princeton.edu/titles/10516.html

Illustrations

Tables

Acknowledgments

We owe much to many. In the course of writing this book, we have benefited enormously from exchanges with scholars across the country. In particular, Shaun Bowler, Scott Desposato, Karen Ferree, James Gimpel, Rodney Hero, Jennifer Hochschild, Martin Johnson, David Leal, Jeff Lewis, Justin Phillips, Rene Rocha, Stella Rouse, David Sears, Jessica Trounstine, and Nick Valentino all gave generously of their time and keen insights while asking for nothing in return. All volunteered to read parts—and in some cases, large parts—of the book. Their thoughtful comments were instrumental in helping us move the project forward. We are also deeply indebted to two anonymous reviewers with Princeton University Press who not only deemed fit to accept the manuscript but also helped us expand the scope and reach of the book in critical ways.

Over the course of the last few years, we have had the privilege of presenting parts of this project at several of the nation's great universities. We are sincerely grateful to seminar participants at the University of California at Berkeley, Harvard University, Princeton University, the University of California at Davis, and the University of California at Irvine. These talks always produced lots of smart comments and questions that inevitably led to hour after hour of additional work. Admittedly, those extra hours paid real dividends.

Princeton University Press has been a joy to work with. Writing a book is hard. Working with Princeton has been anything but difficult. Eric Crahan expertly guided our manuscript from submission to completion. He nudged in the right directions and ultimately helped us craft a much better product. Our efficient, capable, and friendly production editor, Karen Carter, made sure that the final months of our work on this book progressed expeditiously. Cindy Milstein did an impeccable job of copyediting.

The two of us had one amazing intellectual home for most of this project. The faculty, staff, and students here at the University of California at San Diego (UCSD) contributed in myriad ways to the final product. By providing abundant intellectual and moral support, our colleagues in the department of political science were instrumental in this endeavor. Several went far beyond the call of duty and collegiality. Amy Bridges, Scott Desposato, Karen Ferree, Seth Hill, Gary Jacobson, Sam Kernell, Thad Kousser, Sam Popkin, and Tom Wong all offered great counsel on different parts of the project. We count them as dear, dear friends.

This book would never have been finished without Hans Hassell and Mike Rivera. They both began as research assistants on the project and became much more. Even though they were subjected to poor pay along with strange and often-incoherent instructions, they persevered and ultimately grew into full-fledged coauthors for major parts of the book. We are thankful for their time and, even more so, important insights. Six other graduate students at UCSD, Rob Bond, Francisco Cantu, Chris Fariss, Nazita Lajevardi, Lydia Lundgren, and Neil Visalvanich, also worked as research assistants, and did the project's most mundane tasks tirelessly and without complaint. We wish them all good luck, as many of them are about to go forth and prosper, or have already done so, beyond the confines of UCSD. We are also thankful to two undergraduate research assistants, Yessenia Camacho and Erica Salinas, for their coding help.

We would be remiss not to mention the significant nurturing role that the Center for Comparative Immigration Studies and the Politics of Race, Immigration, and Ethnicity Consortium played in this book as well as our broader development as scholars. Both are welcoming intellectual environments filled with like-minded scholars who continuously motivated us with their passion for understanding and helping society's most disadvantaged.

In spite of the questionable character of the two authors and their sometimes-misguided ideas, the Committee on Research at UCSD deemed the project worth funding. The committee gave both of us grants that paid for crucial research assistant support.

And finally, we would like to thank the most important people in our lives. Academic work is a selfish endeavor that requires real sacrifices from those you love the most. We are blessed that our families not only love us but also very much support and understand our work.

Marisa would like to thank Lisa Garcia Bedolla for all her support and encouragement as well as Mike Alvarez, Jane Junn, Jan Leigheley, Jonathan Nagler, Christina Schneider, and her parents and siblings. Writing a book is a long process, and without a strong group of friends and family, it would be impossible to get through it. And of course, the biggest debt of gratitude goes to Sebas, who was there from the beginning, and always provided countless help and motivation, and Marisa's daughter, Sofia, who brings such joy and happiness to life that it makes all the toils of work disappear. Marisa dedicates this book to her family.

Zoli would like to thank his sister for showing him what it really means to follow your dreams. You are absolutely fearless and truly inspirational. Mom and Dad—I could not have asked for or received better parents. With each passing year, you continue to astound me with your love, insight, and dedication. I hope that I can be half as wise and generous moving forward. Lina—you are simply amazing. When you were born, I knew that I would love you and think the world of you. But I didn't dream that you would become such a good person. Your kindness makes my heart soar. I could not be prouder of my little girl. Barb—you are not just my soul mate. You are my closest colleague. You are my best friend. You are the engine that makes my life tick. I couldn't imagine life without you.

Zoli dedicates this book to Uncle Ed. He taught me the importance of laughing and living life. He will be sorely missed.

Introduction

Immigration is unquestionably one of the most important forces shaping the United States. Since 2000, the United States has absorbed almost fourteen million immigrants, bringing the total of all documented and undocumented immigrants currently in the nation to over forty million.[1] Immigrants and their children now represent fully one in four Americans.

These raw numbers are impressive. Yet they tell only part of the story. The present wave of immigration has also wrought dramatic changes in the social and economic spheres. Large-scale immigration has produced a sea change in the racial and ethnic composition of the nation. The phenomenal growth of the Latino population has allowed Latinos to displace African Americans as the country's largest racial and ethnic group. Asian Americans, once a negligible share of the national population, are now the fastest-growing racial and ethnic group. This means that white numerical dominance is very much on the decline. By the midpoint of the twenty-first century, whites are, in fact, expected to no longer be the majority. The arrival of so many new Americans who herald from different shores has also brought cheap labor, new languages, and different cultural perspectives. There are sizable industries flourishing on low-wage migrant labor, massive Spanish-language media empires, and countless communities that have been altered almost beyond recognition. There is little doubt that US society has been transformed in innumerable, deep, and perhaps-permanent ways.

But has this changed the political sphere? What are the political consequences of such a dramatic demographic, racial, economic, social, and cultural makeover? In spite of the obvious and dramatic changes wrought by immigration, its impact on the political world is much less clear. On one level, the influence of immigration on poli-

[1] US Census Bureau 2012.

tics is obvious and already well documented. Countless studies have demonstrated the growing strength of the minority vote, particularly the Latino electorate, the largest immigrant group in the nation.[2] Many others have demonstrated the increasing attachment of immigrants and their offspring to the Democratic Party.[3] These are certainly crucial developments in the course of US political history.

A Broad Political Impact for Immigration?

We contend, however, that these changes represent only a small fraction of immigration's potential impact on US politics. Immigrants may be arriving in historically high numbers, but they account for only a relatively small proportion of the nation's population. Native-born whites still represent 63 percent of the population, and perhaps more important, some 75 percent of its voters. Thus, how nonimmigrant white Americans respond to this growing immigrant and Latino population is critical not only to the welfare of current immigrants and future of immigration policy in the United States but also relations between different racial and ethnic groups within the United States. Acceptance is likely to bring assimilation and rising economic status among immigrants. Fear and resentment is likely to bring increased efforts at border enforcement, more migrant deaths, and strained relations between the nation's white (and primarily native-born) population along with its racial and ethnic minority groups. Even more significant, if immigration leads to a backlash that not only shapes views on immigration but also alters the basic political orientation of large numbers of Americans, then the entire direction of US politics hangs in the balance. A broad backlash could lead to increasingly strict and conservative policy making, shift the balance of power between Democrats and Republicans, and advantage rightward-leaning candidates throughout the country. In short, in order to fully understand how broadly immigration is transforming US politics, we need to examine the attitudes and actions of the white population.

That is the subject of this book. We hope to delineate the different ways in which the partisan patterns, electoral decisions, and policy preferences of native white Americans are changing in response to immigration's imprint. Are whites responding with a broad backlash that

---

[2] De la Garza et al. 1992; DeSipio 1996; Alvarez and Garcia Bedolla 2003; Abrajano and Alvarez 2010.

[3] Wong et al. 2011; Alvarez and Garcia Bedolla 2003; Hajnal and Lee 2011.

results in more restrictive immigration policy, more punitive criminal justice policies, less generous public spending, and a large shift to the right politically that results in more support for the Republican Party and the candidates it puts forward? Or are whites embracing the benefits of immigration to such a degree that they seek to expand government and the services it offers to less advantaged segments of the population? Alternatively, is immigration—despite its visible effects—not deeply felt by the US public, and thus not consequential for basic political decisions like policy, party, and the vote?

On these questions, political scientists have had surprisingly little to say. Although widespread attention has been paid to the *causes* of our attitudes about Latinos and immigration, little research has focused on the *consequences* of immigrant-related views.[4] We know, for example, that cultural and racial considerations, more than personal economic interests, often seem to shape attitudes toward immigration.[5]

But we know little about how views of immigrants in turn shape core political affiliations and basic voting decisions. There is almost no direct evidence to date that the basic policy positions, partisan affiliations, or voting decisions of individual white Americans strongly reflect their views on immigration or the Latino population.[6] Studies of the white population tend to fall into one of two categories. Either they ignore immigration and race altogether.[7] Or if they focus on race, they limit the analysis to the impact of the United States' old black-white divide.[8] Only two studies that we are aware of have demonstrated a connection between immigration and the white vote in national contests, or revealed a link between immigration and white partisanship.[9] Despite the tremendous impact that immigration has had on the demographics of the nation along with the large-scale social, economic, and racial change that has ensued, there is little direct evi-

---

[4] On the causes, see Schildkraut 2010; Hainmueller and Hiscox 2010; Kinder and Kam 2010; Brader, Valentino, and Suhay 2008; Pettigrew et al. 2007; Scheve and Slaughter 2001; Quillian 1995; Citrin et al. 1997.

[5] Hainmueller and Hopkins 2014; Brader, Valentino, and Suhay 2008; Hainmueller and Hiscox 2010. See also Hanson 2005.

[6] Scholars have found clear evidence that immigration fundamentally shapes the views of Latinos, though (Hawley 2013; Nicholson and Segura 2005; but see Abrajano, Alvarez, and Nagler 2008; Alvarez and Garcia Bedolla 2003).

[7] McCarty et al. 2007; Miller and Shanks 1996; Alvarez and Nagler 1995, 1998.

[8] Lewis-Beck, Tien, and Nadeau 2010; Valentino and Sears 2005; Abramowitz 1994; Carmines and Stimson 1989.

[9] The first study is work on California alternately showing that Proposition 187 led to growing white support for the Democratic Party (Bowler, Nicholson, and Segura 2006) or that the episode had no impact on white partisanship (Dyck, Johnson, and Wasson 2012). The other is a recent study by two psychologists, Maureen Craig and Jennifer Richeson (2014), who find a relationship between changing racial demographics and white Americans' political ideology.

dence that immigration has had an enduring effect on the basic political decisions of the white majority.

Moreover, many would be skeptical that immigration could have a profound influence on the basic political choices of white Americans. The near-complete assimilation of US immigrants and their children, rapid growth of interracial marriage, increasing willingness of white Americans to support minority candidates, inexorable—if uneven—waning of white racial intolerance, and arrival of potentially more pressing issues like the United States' economic crisis, two wars, and terrorist security threats all imply that immigrant-related considerations should not weigh heavily on the political calculus of white Americans.[10]

Other skeptics would point to the immobility of partisanship.[11] Many scholars view party identification as the "unmoved mover" that colors a wide array of political perceptions and remains largely unaltered by the politics of the day.[12] Can immigration really lead to substantial changes in party identification when party identification is a deeply ingrained psychological attachment instilled early in life and largely impervious to change? From this perspective, immigration is likely to be one of many issues that fail to make much of an impact on the fortress of partisanship.

Immigration's Impact on Partisan Politics: A Theory

Nevertheless, we believe that immigration and the Latino population do impact whites' core political calculus. We offer a theory of how large-scale immigration can result in real partisan shifts in the white population. First, the sheer size of the racial and demographic change that has happened and continues to occur is impossible for white Americans to miss. All this demographic change is accompanied by the extensive presence of Latinos, Asians, and other immigrants in the media along with almost-daily interactions with nonnative speakers in the nation's streets, workplaces, and neighborhoods. It would be surprising if such a massive transformation in the makeup of the nation did not result in immigration playing a more central role in the minds of white Americans.

---

[10] Alba and Nee 2005; Bean and Stevens 2003; Hajnal 2006; Highton 2004; Sniderman and Carmines 1997; Schuman 1997.

[11] Green, Palmquist, and Schickler 2002; Campbell et al. 1960.

[12] Goren 2005.

4

Second, irrespective of the actual fiscal consequences of immigration, there is an ongoing and often-repeated threat narrative that links the United States' immigrant and Latino populations to a host of pernicious fiscal, social, and cultural consequences.[13] This narrative emphasizes cultural decline, immigrants' use of welfare, health, and educational services, their propensity to turn to crime, and their tendency to displace native citizens from jobs.[14] Each of these concerns has been spelled out repeatedly as well as in great detail in the media, political sphere, and scholarly outlets.[15] *majority? minority?*

Moreover, although many people inside and outside the political arena dispute the threat narrative, it appears that the narrative has been absorbed by a significant segment of the white population. Across the white population, attitudes on Latinos and immigration are diverse, but there is little doubt that many white Americans express real concerns about immigration and hold negative attitudes toward Latinos. Recent polls suggest that well over half of white Americans feel that immigrants are a burden on the nation, a slight majority think that Latinos add to the crime problem, and about half believe they take jobs away from Americans.[16] For many, the changes taking place in the United States represent a real threat.

Third, and critically for our account, this threat narrative has recently taken on increasingly clear *partisan* implications. Although there is still considerable variation within each party's leadership on the issue of immigration, empirical studies demonstrate growing partisan divergence on immigration between leaders of the two parties. When Republican and Democratic leaders take divergent stances on immigration and other issues of special relevance to the Latino community, and when Republicans stand more strongly against immigration, the two parties present individual white Americans with a stark choice. For those concerned about the Latino population and growth of immigration, this may be reason enough to support the Republican Party.

In short, many white Americans will see that the United States is changing, believe that immigration is driving many of the negative shifts, they see, and know that the two parties represent two different responses—one largely on the side of immigrants and one primarily in opposition to immigration.

---

[13] Pérez, forthcoming; Chavez 2008; Hopkins 2010; Brader, Valentino, and Suhay 2008; Santa Ana 2004.

[14] Huntington 2005; Borjas 2001; Gimpel and Skerry 2009.

[15] Pérez, forthcoming; Valentino, Brader, and Jardina 2013; Chavez 2008; Santa Ana 2004.

[16] CNN poll from 2010, cited in Polling Report 2014.

Why Immigration Is Different

But what about the supposed stability and immovability of party identification?[17] Can immigration shape such fundamental and stable political attachments? We believe that the answer is yes, and that in fact there are clear circumstances under which party identification can be responsive and more malleable. Even those who write forcefully about the immovability and durability of party identification note that major shifts in partisanship occur in one circumstance. When the social groups associated with each party change, mass shifts in partisanship can and have happened.[18]

Immigration today is a unique phenomenon in that it has changed the social group imagery of the parties. The growth of the Latino population and increasing support of Latinos as well as other immigrants of the Democratic Party means that a party that as late as 1980 was still 80 percent white, is now more than 40 percent nonwhite. A party that was supported by lower-class white interests increasingly became a party supported by the black community, and since the 1980s has increasingly become a party supported by Latinos and other immigrants. In other words, what it means to be a Democrat has changed. This means that even for inattentive Americans who may have little knowledge of current issues and strong attachments to a political party, immigration could still change their partisanship.

History Repeated: Partisanship and Immigration

Equally important, history provides plenty of evidence to suggest that immigration can fundamentally alter the nation's politics. The United States may be a nation of immigrants, but that does not mean it has always welcomed immigrants with open arms. Often when the number of new arrivals has been large, or the makeup of new Americans has differed from the native born in obvious racial or ethnic ways, many Americans have responded with anger, fear, and efforts to either punish immigrants who are already in the country or beat back any further influx of immigrants.[19] One of the earliest examples is the Alien and Sedition Acts of 1798. They curbed the rights of immigrants—especially radicals from France and Ireland. Nativist violence

---

[17] Green, Palmquist, and Schickler 2002; Campbell et al. 1960.
[18] Green, Palmquist, and Schickler 2002; Goren 2005.
[19] Schrag 2011; Zolberg 2009; Daniels 2004; Fetzer 2000.

and rioting reemerged in the nineteenth century when large-scale immigration from Europe reached a peak.[20] Much more recently, millions of Japanese citizens were interned in concentration camps during the course of World War II. For the vast majority of Americans (and even the Supreme Court), the threat of these immigrants—many of who were US citizens—justified the clear violation of their rights. In short, a wide-ranging backlash against immigration today would hardly be new.[21]

We have witnessed several moments in US history where immigration and partisan politics have become closely intertwined. Critically, many of these nativist episodes have had a real impact on the partisan politics of the day. In the 1850s, for example, a nativist backlash against Irish Catholic immigrants helped spur the Know-Nothings and American Party to electoral success.[22] Later in the nineteenth century, the issue of Chinese immigration spurred both the Democratic and Republican parties into action as a means to increase their voter bases. Republicans began the period internally divided on the issue, but competition from a Democratic Party strongly in favor of Chinese exclusion, the threat of their supporters' defection to the Workingmen's Party—a third party that campaigned exclusively on a platform of Chinese exclusion—and intense public sentiment against the Chinese led Republicans to support Chinese exclusion.[23]

By the 1880 presidential election, both major parties campaigned on the promise to restrict Chinese immigration to the United States, and two years later the Chinese Exclusion Act was signed into law. Again in the early 1950s, immigration exposed internal divisions in the Republican Party. More nativist members of the party hoped to place limits on the total annual inflow of immigrants, and establish preferences for immigrants from northern and Western Europe, while at roughly the same time that party's presidential nominee, Dwight D. Eisenhower, campaigned on a pledge to "strike an intelligent, unbigoted balance between the immigration welfare in America and the prayerful hopes of the unhappy and oppressed."[24] With Democratic support, the nativist wing of the Republican Party was able to enshrine both quotas and white European preference into law with the

---

[20] Schrag 2011.

[21] Pushing the analogy even further, the current backlash could be compared to any number of other historical episodes in which racial and ethnic minority efforts to attain social, economic, or political rights were actively as well as often violently rebuffed by large segments of the white population (Klinkner and Smith 1999; Foner 1984; Parker 1990; Kousser 1999).

[22] Anbinder 1992.

[23] Tichenor 2002.

[24] Quoted in ibid., 198.

passage of the 1952 Immigration and Nationality Act. Almost two decades later, in an effort to bring in more constituents who would ultimately support the party, Democrats undertook a sharp reversal of position and supported the Hart Cellars Act of 1965. The landmark immigration law that repealed national origins quotas, and replaced them with a system based on skilled workers, family reunification, and refugees, would become a critically important base for the Democratic Party over the ensuing decades.[25] As Republicans woke up to that fact in the late 1970s and 1980s, "votes in Congress on restricting legal immigration and controlling illegal immigration became increasingly easy to predict in partisan terms."[26] With the two major parties solidifying their position on immigration by the 1980s, the public was able to more easily discern where the two parties stood on immigration.

In sum, each of these historical events highlights just how interrelated immigration and partisan politics can become.

History Repeated: Partisanship and Race

Finally, there is yet another historical precedent within the arena of racial politics. Many scholars contend that the large-scale movement of whites from the Democratic to the Republican Party that occurred from the 1960s to the 1980s was mainly spurred by racial concerns. From this perspective, African American demands for increased civil rights coupled the willingness of leaders within the Democratic Party to support those demands ultimately repelled millions of white Americans from the Democratic Party and helped Republicans win nationally.[27] In this sense, our book has its intellectual origins in the "issue evolution" approach that Ted Carmines and James Stimson employed so influentially to explain how racial politics altered the nation's partisan dynamics. Just as their book was about what happens to US politics when race emerged as a political concern, our book is about what happens to US politics when immigrants and Latinos arise as a core political issue.

[25] Gimpel and Edwards 1998.
[26] Ibid., 21.
[27] Hood, Kidd, and Morris 2012; Valentino and Sears 2005; Black and Black 2002; Edsall and Edsall 1991; Carmines and Stimson 1989; Huckfeldt and Kohfeld 1989; Giles and Evans 1994. It is important to note, however, that other scholars dispute the centrality of racial considerations in the white partisan shift (Shafer and Johnston 2005; Lublin 2004; Abramowitz 1994).

Ultimately, it remains to be seen whether white worries about immigrants and Latinos mirror the concerns whites have held about African Americans. But if one minority group has triggered broad partisan reactions in the past, there is at least some reason to expect similar responses in the present. The fact that Latinos have now replaced African Americans as the nation's largest racial and ethnic minority may suggest that any current backlash is especially likely to be focused on the Latino population.

Testing Our Theory

Since our argument contends that immigration is fundamentally reshaping US politics, our data must be weighty and wide ranging. The evidence should not be limited to one election, a single survey, or a year. Instead it should span a considerable range of contests, comprehensive set of surveys, and meaningful period of time. The evidence should also not be subtle. We should see substantial movement—on the order of magnitude that could sway elections and alter the balance of power in US politics.

Demonstrating this kind of robust change is not a simple task. Thus, the bulk of this book is designed to offer a clear, systematic assessment of just how far reaching the impact of immigration is on the basic political choices and identities of the white US public. We begin this process by looking at the big picture: the overall patterns in aggregate white partisanship over the last fifty years. If immigration has had a major impact on US politics and caused the defection of substantial numbers of white Americans from the Democratic to the Republican Party, then there should be signs of a marked change in aggregate white partisanship.

Demonstrating a large partisan shift is crucial, but this kind of aggregate analysis is at most suggestive. Even if we can uncover a major change in white partisan attachments coinciding with the growth of the immigrant population, its origins will still by no means be certain. Immigration could be a fundamental driving force in the defection of so many white Americans to the Republican Party. But there are many alternative accounts for this massive movement to the right. As we have noted, some contend that African Americans have driven whites to the Republican Party.[28] Scholars and political observers also point to

---

[28] Hood, Kidd, and Morris 2012; Black and Black 2002; Carmines and Stimson 1989; Edsall and Edsall 1991; Valentino and Sears 1995.

other cultural and social factors, such as gay marriage, abortion rights, or the war on crime, as primary determinants of white Republicanism.[29] Similarly, some have claimed that Republican gains are driven by an advantage on foreign affairs and the greater willingness of Republican leaders to confront our enemies. There are, finally, perhaps even more fundamental issues like taxes, the scope of government, and the economy that are undoubtedly a central consideration for most Americans when they choose to take partisan sides.[30]

In order to tie this partisan shift to immigration, we need to undertake more fine-grained analysis to rule out these other factors. To demonstrate this causal connection, we compile several large national public opinion surveys and develop a series of statistical models of individual partisan choice that not only incorporate attitudes on immigration but also take into account each of the alternative explanations known to shape partisanship. An even more decisive test is to examine changes in individual party identification over time. If we can predict when and if a particular individual will change their partisan affiliation from Democrat to Republican based on their preexisting attitudes on immigrants, then we can be more certain that immigration is driving partisanship rather than the reverse. This kind of panel data, while not perfect, represent close to the gold standard in identifying causal connections. In addition, we assess the causal ties between immigration and partisanship at the aggregate level. We specifically look to see if the public's views on immigration at one point in time predict changes in aggregate white partisanship in future periods—a test that gets us even closer to causality.

Although party identification is generally considered to be the principal driving force in US politics, it is by no means the only measure we might care about. At its heart, democracy is about votes and elections. Who wins office and who loses? If immigration is having a basic impact on the political arena, we should also see it in the vote. Thus, we will move on to consider the role that immigrant-related attitudes play in a series of national elections. Once again using an array of public opinion surveys, we will do our best to distinguish between the effects of immigration and any number of other factors purported to shape the vote. Our focus will primarily be on the 2008 contest between Barack Obama and John McCain, but to make a more general statement about the link between immigration and US politics, we realize that we need to assess the influence of immigrant-related views

---

[29] Adams 1997; Layman and Carmines 1997.
[30] Shafer and Johnston 2005; Lublin 2004; Abramowitz 1994.

on a wide set of elections and years. Hence, we repeat our analysis of the vote going as far back as 1976 and as recently as 2012, and gauge the role of immigration not just in presidential contests but also in elections for Congress, senate, and governor.

Finally, for individual citizens, policies as opposed to parties or politicians might be the true measure by which to judge a democracy. It is not who is elected but instead what they do once in office that ultimately matters. As such, it is important to evaluate links between immigration and policy views. It would hardly be surprising to find that those Americans who hold more negative feelings toward different segments of the immigrant population favor more restrictive policies to curb the number of immigrants, reduce the benefits and services that immigrants can receive, and in different ways make life difficult for immigrants—regardless of their citizenship status. This is, in fact, a central focus of much of the immigration literature.[31]

But we suspect that the effects of immigration will extend much more broadly into a range of related policy arenas. We suspect these wide-ranging policy effects for two reasons. First, policy debates on a host of issues ostensibly not about immigration are increasingly being infused with references to both legal and undocumented immigrants, the broader Latino population, and other aspects of the immigration process. Take health care, for example. After much of the recent debate on health care reform centered on whether or not the Democratic reform package would cover undocumented immigrants, a recent Pew Research Center poll found that 66 percent of those opposed to the plan reported that they were opposed because it might cover undocumented immigrants. Welfare reform since the 1990s has similarly been permeated with discussions of Latinos and undocumented immigrants. California's Proposition 187, which sought to restrict public services to undocumented immigrants, is only the most prominent case. The fact that just under 70 percent of whites view Latinos as particularly prone to be on welfare suggests that the connection between Latinos and welfare is now firmly in place.[32] Latinos and crime is another readily available script throughout the nation.[33] Crime, terrorism, and undocumented immigration account for fully 66 percent of the network news coverage of Latinos.[34] Concerns about immigra-

---

[31] See, for example, Ha and Oliver 2010; Hood and Morris 1998; Stein, Post, and Rinden 2000; Green, Strolovitch, and Wong 1998.

[32] Bobo 2001.

[33] Ibid.

[34] National Association of Hispanic Journalists 2005.

tion therefore should be linked to attitudes on crime, welfare, education, and the like.

Second, evidence of race impacting core policy views would not be new. Research has already shown that nonracial policy can be racially coded.[35] In particular, there is evidence that individual policy preferences on welfare, education, crime, and a host of other core issue arenas have, at least at some points in the past, been shaped by attitudes toward blacks.[36]

Given the importance of race in the past along with the increasingly central role played by immigration and Latinos in the political debates of today, there is every reason to expect wide-ranging policy effects. Thus, we offer a broader study of the effects of immigration on numerous policy areas, including health, welfare, crime, and education.

All these empirical tests offer an opportunity to establish a link between immigration and US politics. But none tells us how individual Americans make that connection. How do individual Americans learn about immigration and its consequences? What is the source of their concerns and political motivations? In other words, what is the mechanism that translates demographic change into political consequences?

We explore these mechanisms in the second third of the book. Our goal here is to get at the actual mechanisms through which immigration leads to political effects. In our theory, we outline two such mechanisms: demographic change and the media. One is the direct recognition of racial change by individual residents and the sense of racial threat that this demographic change can produce. We believe that reactions to larger immigrant populations are analogous to past white responses to larger black populations. As researchers from V. O. Key to Susan Olzak to Michael Giles and Melanie Buckner have so aptly demonstrated, many individual white Americans appear to be threatened by larger black populations, and as a result have reacted in negative ways as black populations have grown or become more empowered.[37]

We test the racial threat model with an innovative research design incorporating the size of both the local and state-level Latino population. The idea is to see if whites who live in close proximity to larger Latino or immigrant populations tend to have more negative views of immigrants, favor more punitive policies, align more regularly with

---

[35] Mendelberg 2001.
[36] Winter 2008; Soss, Langbein, and Metelko 2006; Gilens 1999; Kinder and Sanders 1996.
[37] Key 1949; Olzak 1992; Giles and Buckner 1993.

the Republican Party, and more consistently support Republican candidates.

Although we believe there is a direct link between demographic change and white views, we contend that whites learn about immigration from other sources as well. Namely, we maintain that the media is a critical source of information on immigration. How whites perceive immigration, whether they think it is a widespread problem, and ultimately whether they buy into an immigrant threat narrative are all, in our opinion, likely to be shaped by what they see, hear, and learn from various media outlets. Thus, to try to further understand the underlying mechanism driving immigration's transformation of US politics, we conduct a series of tests of media coverage and its relationship to white partisanship. Specifically, using a comprehensive data set of three decades of _New York Times_ articles on immigration, we assess the tone, content, and salience of immigration coverage over time. Then we look to see if attention to negative aspects of immigration by the media leads to large-scale changes in aggregate white partisanship. In essence, when the media repeats the immigrant threat narrative, does an increasing portion of the white public identify as Republican?

Finally, we turn to an examination of the consequences of this move to the right for policy making across the states. If the majority white public has, in fact, shifted to the right in response to a growing immigrant population, we should see a robust relationship between the size of the immigrant population and policy direction. Given that states have become increasingly active in advancing immigrant-related policy and are, outside the federal government, the principal policy maker, we focus our examination on state-level policy. Our empirical tests examine whether states with large and growing Latino populations are more likely to enact policies that could negatively impact the local immigrant population. In particular, do states respond to larger Latino populations by increasing criminal punishment, reducing educational funding, decreasing welfare support, and cutting health care spending?

The Transformation of White American Politics

The results that we present over the ensuing pages will demonstrate the wide-ranging impact of immigration on the politics of white America. Our analysis shows a massive shift in aggregate white partisanship. In 1980, white Democrats dominated white Republicans numerically. Today the opposite is true. As immigration's impact on the United

States has grown, whites have fled to the Republican Party in ever-larger numbers. The end result is that the principal partisan choice of white America has been totally reversed.

At the aggregate level, we show that when media coverage of immigration uses the Latino threat narrative, the likelihood of whites identifying with the Democratic Party decreases and the probability of favoring Republicans increases. At the individual level, we will demonstrate that how we think about immigration tells us a lot about our policy preferences, partisan ties, and voting decisions. Whites who are fearful of immigration tend to respond to that anxiety with a measurable shift to the political right. Similarly, where we live and in particular whether we live in states with few or large numbers of Latinos greatly influences those same political choices. As immigration encroaches more and more on different neighborhoods, whites who live in those areas are more and more apt to want to disinvest in public spending, and less likely to offer support to less advantaged segments of the population. In short, who we are politically is driven in no small part by immigration.

One direct result of all this is the passage of a conservative policy agenda in the areas most affected by immigration. Our analysis shows a close connection between the size and growth of the state Latino population and state policy making. In states with larger and faster-growing Latino population—states where immigrants and Latinos could benefit from public support—whites have been exceptionally successful at reducing educational funding, decreasing welfare support, and cutting health care spending.

Implications

What we learn about immigration and its impact on US politics will have far-reaching implications for our understanding of how race does or does not work in the United States, grasp of the emerging place of Latinos in the hearts and minds of white Americans, knowledge of what white party identification is and how much it can change, and perhaps most obviously, predictions about the future balance of power between Democrats and Republicans in the tug-of-war that is US politics.

What is striking about the empirical patterns we will present in the following pages is not that immigration matters; it is startling just how broad the effects are. We already know that many white Americans have felt threatened by different racial/ethnic groups throughout US history.[38] What is impressive is just how wide-ranging those effects remain today, and how the presence of different minority groups can heighten or diminish those effects. In a political era in which many claim that the significance of race has faded, we find that Latino- or immigrant-related views impact the political orientation of many members of the white population. Party identification—the most influential variable in US politics—is at least in part a function of the way individual white Americans see Latinos and immigrants. So too is the vote in national contests for president and Congress. In short, who we are politically at our core is shaped substantially by deeply felt concerns about immigration and racial/ethnic change.

What is also clear from this pattern of results is that the Latino population has become a more central factor in US race relations. In US history, the issue of race has traditionally been viewed through a black-white dichotomy. That is no longer true today. The increasing visibility of immigration along with its widespread impact on the nation's economic, social, cultural, and political spheres appear to have brought forth a real change in the racial dynamics of our politics.

Our results will also speak to the long-standing debate about what partisanship is, and how much it does or does not change. The traditional and most widely held view is that party identification is a deep-seated psychological predisposition, which is both stable and drives most of the core political decisions we make.[39] An alternative notion is that party identification is both more rational and more responsive.[40] Individual Americans, from this latter perspective, survey the world and the political positions of the two parties to determine which represents a better fit. We will not attempt to argue that one of these two views is always right, but the real shifts in individual and aggregate partisanship that we will uncover along with the fact that this partisan movement can be logically tied to real-world events suggest that at least for many Americans, partisan attachments are relatively rational responses to actual circumstances.

There are also implications for the future balance of power in US politics. The pattern of results presented here suggests that at least over the short to near term, determining which party will dominate US electoral politics is very much an open question. The conventional view of pundits and prognosticators, and maybe even most social sci-

---

[38] Masuoka and Junn 2013; Tichenor 2002; Olzak 1992.

[39] Green, Palmquist, and Schickler 2002; Campbell et al. 1960; Goren 2005.

[40] Erikson, MacKuen, and Stimson 2002; MacKuen, Erikson, and Stimson 1989; Fiorina 1981; Downs 1957.

entists, is that the dramatic growth of the minority population and its strong ties to the Democratic Party portend the demise of the Republican Party. That may be true in the long term. But that prediction ignores the white population and the possibility of a widespread white backlash in the short term. Given that whites still make up about three-quarters of the voters in the nation and will likely be the clear majority for decades to come, there is every reason to believe that whites will have a real say in who governs. Indeed, the white population's rapidly growing allegiance to the Republican Party points toward a very different short-term future—one that might more likely be highlighted by Republican victory than by Democratic dominance.

Finally and perhaps most important, the dramatic surge in white support for the Republican Party has disquieting implications for the future of race relations in this nation. While many have hoped for the end of large-scale racial tensions, and some have even acclaimed Obama's election as the first sign of a postracial United States, the political impact of immigration seems to be leading the country in the opposite direction. The rightward shift of many white Americans, on the one hand, and the leftward drift of much of the racial and ethnic minority population, on the other, is exacerbating already-large racial divides.[41] The last presidential election, for example, was by some calculations the most racially divided contest in US history. Immigration and other factors appear increasingly to be pitting the declining white majority against the growing nonwhite minority. Some degree of polarization is a normal and health part of democracy, but when the core dividing line in a nation becomes closely aligned with racial and ethnic demography, larger concerns emerge about inequality, conflict, and discrimination. In short, when race becomes the primary determinant of political decision making, the nation's population is in danger of being driven apart.

Hanging in the balance is the fate of the United States' immigrants, its racial and ethnic minorities, and other less advantaged segments of the population. To this point, our results suggest that the white backlash has in many ways been successful. Our analysis of policy outcomes across the states indicates that whites have been especially effective in disinvesting in public goods in the states where immigration is most deeply felt. Precisely where the number of immigrants is largest and where the need is greatest, these public funds have become less and less available. All this has distressing implications for the welfare of these different groups. Unless the partisan poli-

[41] King and Smith 2011.

tics of immigration shift dramatically, more newcomers will simply mean a greater white backlash and greater disinvestment. Immigrants and racial/ethnic minorities themselves will have more and more of a say as they increase in size, yet they are a long way off from becoming a majority of the voting public. That means, unfortunately, that things may get worse before they get better.

Race, Immigration, or Undocumented Immigration?

Up to this point, we have been deliberately imprecise about defining exactly which immigrants or which aspects of immigration threaten white Americans. Are white Americans most opposed to some specific aspect of immigration policy (e.g., the number of immigrants, the education levels of immigrants, or border security issues) or are they more concerned about the immigrants themselves? And if immigrants are at the heart of the response, is it all immigrants or a subset of them, like undocumented or Mexican immigrants? Another possibility is that restrictive policy is directed more at a racial group most closely associated with the negative side of immigration (e.g., Latinos).

Our imprecision stems largely from the fact that we believe these different categories tend to be muddled together in the minds of individual white Americans. In theory, categories like undocumented immigrant, legal immigrant, and Latino are all distinct from each other. But in the practice of US politics, these concepts often blur together. Media coverage and the rhetoric of the two major parties as well as other political elites frequently conflate these different groups. It therefore is likely that for most individual Americans, immigration is not a precise threat but rather more of a general concern generated by the changes that immigration is bringing to the United States. In light of these muddled categories, we will begin with a series of tests that in different ways measure attitudes toward Latinos, Asian Americans, and other immigrant-related groups to try to get a clearer sense of just who or what it is that white Americans are reacting to.

What will become apparent is that reactions to immigration are highly racialized. Only one racial group—Latinos—is at the heart of white Americans' response to immigration. In this sense, our findings are more like those of Ted Brader and his colleagues, Efren Perez, and Jennifer Merolla and her colleagues, who in different ways, all find that images of Latinos spark distinctly negative reactions.[42] The flip side of this racial story is that Asian Americans do not spark nearly the

---

[42] Brader, Valentino, and Suhay 2008; Pérez, forthcoming.

same political response. Asian Americans, as we will see, are viewed quite differently from these other groups, and white reactions to proximity to large numbers of Asians are radically different from white reactions to large influxes of Latinos.

There are all sorts of reasons why whites might make this racial distinction. Fewer Asian Americans are in the United States without legal status, and they tend to fall much closer to whites than to Latinos on the socioeconomic scale and in fact surpass whites on many of these indicators. Asian Americans, at least until recently, were also much less clearly aligned with the Democratic Party than Latinos or African Americans have been.[43] Perhaps most critically, whites tend to have different stereotypes of Asian Americans than they do of Latinos or the broader immigrant category.[44] Whereas Asian Americans are often viewed as an intelligent, hardworking, law-abiding, and successful model minority, Latinos are more regularly thought of as less intelligent, welfare prone, poor, and in the United States, without legal status.[45] Whatever the root cause, it is clear that for many white Americans, Latinos—more than Asian Americans—represent an economic, social, and cultural threat that strongly shapes their partisan politics.

Book Outline

Part I: Theory

CHAPTER 1: A THEORY OF IMMIGRATION BACKLASH POLITICS

In this chapter, we offer an explanation of how immigration could lead to a broad white backlash that transforms the basic political leaning of much of white America. Specifically, we contend that the rapid and steady growth of the immigrant population with the immigrant threat narrative that dominates media coverage of immigrants work together to lead to widespread concerns about immigration. When Republican elites offer a distinctly anti-immigrant platform and Democrats counter with little support for these policies, the many Americans anxious about immigration are drawn to the Republican Party and its candidates.

---

[43] Hajnal and Lee 2011.
[44] Masuoka and Junn 2013.
[45] Bobo 2001; Lee 2001.

Part II: Views on Immigration and Defection to the Republican Party

CHAPTER 2: IMMIGRATION, LATINOS, AND THE TRANSFORMATION OF WHITE PARTISANSHIP

This chapter provides an individual-level assessment of whites' partisan preferences. Using data from the American National Election Survey (ANES) and a series of other national public opinion surveys, we show that white Americans who harbor anti-immigrant sentiments are much more likely than others to identify as Republican. This is true regardless of what other potentially relevant political factors we take into account, how we measure partisanship, or which survey we focus on. Importantly, using panel data, we find that changes in individual attitudes toward immigrants precede shifts in partisanship. Similarly, using aggregate data, we demonstrate that the public's views on immigration predict shifts in macropartisanship. Immigration really is driving individual defections from the Democratic to Republican Party.

CHAPTER 3: HOW IMMIGRATION SHAPES THE VOTE

In this chapter, we assess whether the effects of immigration extend to the electoral arena. Are concerns about immigration leading to greater support for Republican candidates across a range of elections from the presidency to gubernatorial contests? The findings reveal a strong, robust relationship between immigration attitudes and white vote choice. Whites who hold more negative views of immigrants have a greater tendency to support Republican candidates at the presidential, congressional, and gubernatorial levels, even after controlling for party identification and other major factors purported to drive the vote. The result has been a slow but steady shift of white support from Democratic to Republican candidates over the past thirty years.

Part III: Understanding the Roots of the Backlash

CHAPTER 4: THE GEOGRAPHY OF THE IMMIGRATION BACKLASH

In this chapter, we examine one of two causal mechanisms that help to explain white anxiety over immigration. Specifically, we find a strong as well as consistent link between the size and growth of the state Latino population and white attitudes on a range of immigrant-related policies and white partisan choices. All else being equal, whites who live in states with more Latinos are more punitive, less supportive of welfare and other public services, and generally more conservative than whites in other states. Whites in those same states are also significantly more likely to support the Republican Party.

CHAPTER 5: MEDIA COVERAGE OF IMMIGRATION AND WHITE MACROPARTISANSHIP

This chapter focuses on the second factor responsible for driving white fears over immigration: the mass media. In particular, we assess the relationship between media coverage of immigration and aggregate shifts in white party identification. We begin by outlining the media's profit-driven incentives to frame immigration in a negative manner. Our content analysis of immigration-related articles from the *New York Times* from 1980 to 2011 clearly demonstrates that when the issue of immigration is brought to the attention of the public, it is generally with an emphasis on the negative consequences of immigration. We then show that this negative coverage leads to important effects on white partisanship. Across this time period, we find that the reliance on the Latino threat narrative by the media is correlated with significant defection away from the Democratic Party along with increases in the proportion of the public that identifies as Republicans and Independents.

Part IV: The Consequences

CHAPTER 6: THE POLICY BACKLASH

The final empirical chapter examines the implications of this backlash on the policy decisions of state legislatures. Our analysis using the data from the National Association of State Budget Officers as well as a range of other sources reveals the impact that Latino population size has on policies tied to immigrants and Latinos. We find that in states with larger Latino populations, public goods provision drop significantly, and funds for welfare, health, and education all decline. Once the Latino population passes a threshold, however, policy outcomes become more pro-Latino.

Conclusion: Implications for a Deeply Divided United States

In the final chapter, we summarize the main findings of the book, and engage in a discussion of the book's contributions to the areas of race, immigration, and US politics. Our results, we believe, confirm the important role that immigration plays in US politics and also highlight the enduring though shifting role of race in the nation. Where African Americans once dominated the political calculus of white Americans, Latinos appear more likely to do so today. The movement of so many white Americans to the right has wide-ranging implications for both the future balance of partisan power and likely trajectory of US race relations. With a clear majority of the white population now on the Republican side and a clear majority of the minority population now on the Democratic one, political conflict in the United States is increasingly likely to be synonymous with racial conflict—a pattern that threatens ever-greater racial tension.

PART I

Theory

Chapter 1

A Theory of Immigration
Backlash Politics

The United States has a checkered history with race. At times racial discrimination has been a core element of the country's social and institutional fabric. The ownership of millions of African American slaves represents just the darkest stain on the nation's historical record. There are certainly many others. The annexation of the US west from Mexico, maltreatment of tens of thousands of Chinese laborers in the late nineteenth century, internment of thousands of Japanese during World War II, and strict color lines enforced and encoded in the Jim Crow south all demonstrate the ability of Americans to accept as well as actively engage in grossly unequal practices. Too many times in the past, the United States has displayed a woeful indifference to the rights and interests of those it views as different or somehow less deserving.[1]

At the same time, the US public seems firmly committed to the ideals of equality for all.[2] From the founders onward, Americans have expressed strong support for the inalienable rights of human beings. When questioned, the vast majority of Americans clearly and emphatically advocate for basic, universal human rights.[3] It therefore is not surprising that the United States has at times been at the forefront of movements to expand the definition and practice of equal rights.

Although these two traditions—one of racial hierarchy and another of inalienable rights—have obviously collided throughout US

---

[1] Smith 1999.
[2] Tocqeuville 1966; Hartz 1955.
[3] Hochschild 1981.

history, most would agree that the balance of power has slowly though inexorably shifted over time toward greater equality.[4] The path toward more expansive human rights has been anything but even, and there have been notable periods of regression, yet across the long arc of the nation's history, the United States has moved toward greater adherence to universal rights in both rhetoric and practice.[5]

For many, the current wave of immigration represents an opportunity to move even further on the path toward equality.[6] From this perspective, the arrival in large numbers of a motivated, energetic, and racially diverse population should serve to demonstrate the folly of racial ascription as well as institutional inequality. And at least at first glance, there are compelling signs of immigration's positive impact on the country in general and race relations in particular. With increased immigration has come rapidly rising rates of interracial marriage along with newer, more complex, and much less rigid racial categories.[7] From the relative simplicity and rigidity of the "one-drop" rule that governed the black-white divide for much of US history, we have progressed to an era where the census records mixed racial identities and the fastest-growing group, Latinos, can choose to identify with more than one racial group.

Paralleling all this is an impressive record of assimilation for present-day immigrants. Despite some immigrants, especially those from Latin America, starting on a weaker economic and educational footing than previous waves, today's immigrants have by and large been able to make substantial intergenerational strides on almost every conceivable measure of economic and social incorporation.[8] By the third generation in the United States, newcomers have come close to matching or even exceeding the average American on English-language ability, educational attainment, patriotism, and other core US values.[9] The rapid incorporation of these diverse newcomers is a strong sign of an increasingly open society and may even be an indication that the nation has reached a point where racial considerations are largely immaterial. Many have begun to ask if we are, in fact, approaching a postracial society.[10]

[4] Klinker and Smith 1999.
[5] Ibid.
[6] Hochschild, Weaver, and Burch 2012.
[7] Today, 15 percent of all new marriages are interracial or interethnic—a figure that seems well-nigh impossible given the sharp dividing lines that only recently governed the US south (Passel, Wang and Taylor 2010).
[8] Alba and Nee 2005.
[9] Ibid.; Bean and Stevens 2003; Citrin et al. 2007; de la Garza et al. 1996.
[10] King and Smith 2011; Steele 2008.

In this chapter, we argue that far from the country moving away from the use of race/ethnicity as a dividing line, immigration is actually leading to greater divisions and tensions—at least in the political sphere. As the immigrant population has grown, more and more Americans have become aware of the demographic, economic, and cultural changes taking place. For many that awareness has spurred real anxiety. The fear is driven in part by the size of the immigrant population itself, but more substantially by an immigrant threat narrative perpetuated by the media and politicians alike. As the number of immigrants coming to this country has grown over the past half century, so too has attention to this narrative. Images of immigrants clandestinely crossing the US-Mexico border, committing crimes, and accessing public services heighten anxiety among those who may already be concerned about the nation's direction. Once aroused, that anxiety seeks a political home. When the two major parties chart divergent courses on the question of immigration, with one often bemoaning the social, cultural, and economic costs associated with immigrants, and the other frequently acknowledging the benefits that immigration can provide, the political choice for Americans becomes sharp. For those who fear the changes wrought by immigration, the Republican Party provides a natural home.

The end result, we contend, is a rightward shift for a large segment of white America. As anxiety about immigration has grown, white partisanship and politics have become increasingly affected by this issue, with more and more white Americans espousing a less generous, more indignant politics that seeks to punish immigrants who violate US norms, and strives to cut off services and other public goods that could benefit them. In what follows, we outline our theory of immigration politics and detail how immigration could be reshaping the politics of white America.

Why Immigration Matters in US Politics

Immigration is undoubtedly one of the most important forces shaping the nation today. But what role does it play in the political life of this nation? Few clear answers to this question have emerged. We know much about the actions and allegiances of immigrants themselves.[11] The forty million foreign-born residents of the United States have un-

---

[11] Wong et al. 2011; Hajnal and Lee 2011; Abrajano and Alvarez 2010; Alvarez and Garcia Bedolla 2003.

doubtedly become important actors in electoral contests across the nation.[12] The immigrant voice in US politics is no longer a hope. It is very much a reality. Nevertheless, that immigrant vote still represents a small fraction of the nation's active electorate. Foreign-born residents still represent fewer than 5 percent of the voters in this country.[13] If immigration is going to have a deeper impact on the politics of the nation, it will be with the larger, native-born population.

And what of the broader US public? Is the existence of large-scale immigration changing it in any notable way? Is the nation's dramatic demographic transformation accompanied by an equally consequential political transformation for those already here? Or put more pointedly, is it impacting the core political decisions of individual Americans, and affecting the winners and losers in US democracy?

On these latter kinds of questions, we have remarkably few answers. As we will see, political scientists and other observers of US politics have done a great deal to try to assess how we feel about immigrants and immigration.[14] They have in various ways explored the *determinants* of immigration attitudes.[15] But somewhat surprisingly, we have done much less to look systematically at the *consequences* of our attitudes about immigration. Do our feelings about immigration ultimately influence how we feel about policies, parties, and candidates? Does immigration affect who we are politically?

A Theory of Immigration Politics

We contend that it does. In the following pages, we offer a theory that explains how large-scale immigration can result in core political shifts in the white population. We highlight several different aspects of immigration that we think make it a ripe candidate for generating real change in white policy views, partisanship, and vote choice. The key features of immigration are its scope (few Americans can ignore it), the widespread presence of an immigrant threat narrative that generates anxiety, the infusion of immigration into diverse policy debates ranging from welfare to health, and the growing divide between Re-

---

[12] Abrajano and Alvarez 2010.

[13] An analysis of the Cooperative Congressional Election Survey indicates that only 3.6 percent of the votes cast in the 2010 general election were by the foreign born.

[14] Hopkins and Hainmueller 2014; Cohen-Marks, Nuño, and Sanchez 2012; Schildkraut 2010; Brader, Valentino, and Suhay 2008.

[15] Wright and Citrin 2011; Hainmueller and Hiscox 2010; Brader, Valentino, and Suhay 2008; Schildkraut 2005; Scheve and Slaughter 2001; Citrin et al. 1997; Quillian 1995.

publican and Democratic elites on the issue. Immigration stirs anxiety, and the Republican Party offers a home to that unease. We then contrast this theory of immigration politics with alternate accounts that predict little to no political backlash against immigration.

Remarkable Demographic Change

The first feature of immigration that sets it apart from most other issues is its magnitude. Americans are limited political animals in many ways. They tend not to follow the minute details of the day's political debates. And they frequently show little interest in the candidates and campaigns waged for their benefit. Their knowledge of basic political facts is often sorely inadequate.[16] But immigration is no ephemeral phenomenon. Unlike many of the other political developments that US politicians debate, immigration is massive, local, and long term. We believe that one of the reasons immigration is so central in the politics of individual white Americans is its almost-overwhelming magnitude. Every year for over five decades, upward of a million immigrants have arrived on this nation's shores.[17] Immigrants and their children now represent one in four Americans.[18] The vast demographic change that has occurred and continues to do so is impossible for white Americans to miss.

What makes the change more remarkable and, for some, more menacing is its diversity. Immigrants are distinct racially and ethnically from the native population. Immigration has moved us from a primarily black-and-white world in which whites dominated numerically, economically, politically, and in almost every other sphere to a much more racially complex one. Latinos now significantly outnumber African Americans in the United States. Asian Americans are by some measures the faster-growing immigrant group in the country. And perhaps most important, whites are not far from losing their majority status.

All this demographic and racial change is, of course, accompanied by the extensive presence of Latinos, Asians, and other immigrants in the mass media. There are also the frequent interactions with nonnative speakers in the nation's streets, workplaces, and neighborhoods as well as marked, visible changes in the types of businesses springing up

---

[16] Carpini and Keeter 1996.

[17] We know, though, that the distribution of immigrants across the United States is uneven. For a more thorough discussion of these geographic variations and its impact on partisanship, see chapter 4.

[18] US Census Bureau 2005.

in towns and cities across the continent. Individual whites Americans may not be aware of many crucial developments around the world but are surely cognizant of the immense change that immigration is exacting on the nation. It would be surprising if immigration were not playing a more central role in the minds of white Americans.

The Immigrant Threat Narrative

The second key element of our account is an immigrant threat narrative that we believe, as noted earlier, fuels individual fears and insecurities about Latinos and immigrants. This wide-ranging and often-repeated narrative casts immigrants and especially Latinos in a negative light, and highlights a host of pernicious fiscal, social, and cultural consequences to immigration.[19] Within the economic sphere, there are claims that immigrants, particularly those in the country without legal status, are overly reliant on welfare, use considerable public resources in areas like health and education, and fail to pay their share of taxes.[20] The overall fiscal story, according to the narrative, is one of substantial economic loss for the nation's taxpayers.[21] Other versions of the narrative are more focused on the possibility that immigration will bring with it crime and disorder.[22] The narrative typically also underscores the cultural dissimilarity of the Latino immigrant population and likelihood that continued immigration will lead to the demise of the traditional US way of life.[23] Samuel Huntington is perhaps the best-known critic of Latino immigrants' assimilation process, but many others have lamented everything from the growing use of Spanish in US schools and public spaces to a declining national identity.[24]

This threat narrative is also fed by talk of the sleeping "Latino giant." Observers are quick to point out dramatic growth in the size of the Latino electorate—64 percent between 2000 and 2008—and equally striking increases in the number of Latino elected officials—from almost none to over five thousand nationwide in the past forty years.[25] Massive immigrants' rights protests supply fuel to suspicions

[19] Chavez 2008; Santa Ana 2004.
[20] Borjas 2001.
[21] Ibid.
[22] Gimpel and Skerry 1999.
[23] Huntington 2005.
[24] Brimelow 1995; Schildkraut 2005.
[25] Abrajano and Alvarez 2010.

about an increasingly strident immigrant population. All these add a distinctly political dimension to the threat.

There is, of course, a vigorous debate about the validity of the overall narrative. Many dispute each of the narrative's empirical claims. Nevertheless, there is little doubt that that this threat narrative has been absorbed by a large cross section of white Americans, many of who now express significant concerns about the costs of immigration. Extensive polling data reveal a depth of worry about immigrants and the immigrant population among a substantial share of white America.[26] In a range of different surveys, almost half of all Americans believe that immigrants are a "burden" or feel that immigrants "hurt the country."[27] A third to a half of the nation wants to see a decrease in the current levels of immigration, and anywhere from a third to a half thinks "immigration is a bad thing for this country."[28]

Moreover, there are large segments of the population that have bought in to each of the different elements of the threat narrative. Some 61 percent of Americans are concerned that undocumented immigrants are "putting an unfair burden on U.S. schools, hospitals, and government services." Another 87 percent are concerned or quite concerned that immigrants "making low wages might make U.S. employers less willing to pay American workers a decent wage."[29] Fully 58 percent feel that immigrants do not learn English quickly enough, and about one-third of Americans believe that Latino immigrants significantly increase crime.[30]

Attitudes toward undocumented immigrants are even more severe. When given the choice between "primarily moving in the direction of integrating illegal immigrants into American society or in the direction of stricter enforcement against illegal immigration," almost 70 percent choose stricter enforcement.[31] Two-thirds say that undocumented immigrants should not be eligible for social services.[32] Polls also show that well over 60 percent of Americans approve of Arizona's controversial SB 1070, commonly referred to as the "show me your papers" law, since it enables law enforcement officials to stop anyone who they suspect is in this country without legal status. A clear major-

---

[26] Unless otherwise indicated, all polling figures are compiled from Polling Report 2014.
[27] Pew Research Center poll in 2013 and Fox News poll 2013, cited in Polling Report 2014.
[28] Pew Research Center poll in 2013 and Gallup poll in 2012, cited in Polling Report 2014.
[29] USA Today poll in 2010, cited in Polling Report 2014.
[30] Pew Research Center 2006.
[31] Quinnipiac survey in 2010, cited in Polling Report 2014.
[32] Pew Research Center 2006.

ity would like to see a similar law requiring police to verify legal status in their state.[33] And a similarly large majority supports "building a fence along 700 miles of the border with Mexico."[34] What makes these attitudes about undocumented immigration all the more alarming is that a majority of Americans (61 percent) believe that most current immigrants are here illegally.[35] In short, immigration has *not* gone unnoticed. And for many Americans, its consequences are anything but positive.[36]

Critically, for those with concerns about immigrants, immigration is not just a minor nuisance. Few view immigration as the nation's single most important problem. Gallup polls over the years reveal that less than 10 percent of Americans usually rate immigration as the most significant problem facing the country. Yet that does not mean that immigration is a tertiary concern. In almost every survey that has asked about "illegal immigration" in the last decade, an overwhelming majority of Americans—anywhere from 80 to 95 percent—view it as a "very serious" or "somewhat serious" problem.[37] Put simply, there is a real depth to US anxiety about immigration.

None of this is to say that the United States or even white America is wholly united on immigration. Perhaps the fairest assessment of perspectives on immigration is that the public is decidedly split. Many hold positive views of immigrants, and are supportive of policies that would increase immigration and expand the rights as well as interests of immigrants.[38] Depending on the nature of the question and exact wording used, surveys can suggest reasonably widespread support for different aspects of immigration. Roughly as many Americans hold that "immigrants strengthen the United States with their hard work

---

[33] Polling Report 2014.

[34] Fox News survey in 2011, cited in Polling Report 2014.

[35] The best estimates indicate that only about a quarter of immigrants are undocumented (Pew Research Center 2006).

[36] It is worth noting that all these figures understate white fears and concerns about immigration. National polling data, of course, include large numbers of Latino and Asian American respondents who are decidedly more proimmigrant on every one of the questions that we highlight here. Typically, white views are 5 to 10 percent more anti-immigrant than these national figures suggest.

[37] CBS News surveys in 2010–14, cited in Polling Report 2014.

[38] Another almost equally large segment of the US public appears to be ambivalent about immigration. For example, roughly one-quarter of the population feels unsure whether immigrants hurt or help the country (Fox News 2010 survey, cited in Polling Report 2014). A third think we should "welcome some" immigrants but not all (*New York Times* 2010 poll, cited in Polling Report 2014). Likewise, 42 percent of Americans feel that we should pursue both increased border security and a pathway to citizenship equally vigorously (Pew Research Center 2012, cited in Polling Report 2014). For this segment of the population, in short, there appears to be real mix of admiration and concern.

and talents" as view immigrants as harming the nation.[39] Similar proportions of people see immigrants on balance as an "economic benefit" versus an "economic burden."[40] Americans appear to be especially supportive of earned legalization. In most surveys, a clear majority favors measures that would allow undocumented immigrants to remain in the country as temporary workers or eventually citizens.[41] Over all, about one-third of Americans say they are "sympathetic" to the plight of undocumented immigrants. An equal number feel that "America should always welcome immigrants."[42]

All these data indicate that immigration could represent an important dividing line in US politics. If feelings on immigration—both negative and positive—are strong enough, immigration could propel many of the core political choices that Americans make.

It is also worth noting that current patterns in US public opinion closely mirror many historical episodes of nativist reactions to growing immigrant populations. The United States is in both reality and folklore a nation of immigrants, but when the immigrants have arrived in large numbers or from distinct shores, they have often sparked widespread fear and concern among the public. Indeed, the history of the nation could be told through a series of challenging immigrant-nativist confrontations.[43] The rising tide of German and French migrants at the end of the eighteenth century sparked one of the first large-scale nativist movements. But it was just one of many. It was followed by numerous episodes of anti-Irish discrimination in the 1850s, a populist backlash against Chinese immigrants in the 1880s, prevalent anti-southern and eastern European sentiment in the early twentieth century, and a long history of animosity toward Mexicans dating back to the Mexican-American War.[44] World War II generated similarly widespread anti-immigrant concern and the internment of over a hundred thousand Japanese Americans. One could also include current-day US anxiety about and discrimination against Arab Americans in this lengthy list of nativist movements.

The larger point is that contemporary concerns about Latinos and other immigrants are not new. They represent just one example of a much larger phenomenon. If Americans have so often rallied in large

---

[39] Pew Research Center 2006.
[40] Pew Research Center 2008 survey, cited in Polling Report 2014.
[41] Polling Report 2014.
[42] *New York Times* 2010 survey, cited in Polling Report 2014. In addition, the most recent polls have shown a substantial uptick in support for immigration.
[43] Schrag 2011; Zolberg 2009; Daniels 2004; Fetzer 2000; Tichenor 2002.
[44] Higham 1985; Zolberg 2009; Fetzer 2000.

numbers against immigrants in the past, then there is a real possibility that we should expect the same kind of anti-immigrant mobilization today when the number of immigrants and the racial distinctiveness of those immigrants are at or near historical highs.

Immigration Permeates Other Issues

We already know that attitudes toward immigrants strongly shape preferences on immigration policy itself. Diverse studies have shown that whether individual Americans favor more or less immigration is closely linked to how they think about immigrants, and in particular how positively or negatively they view the Latino community. Experimental work by Brader and his colleagues clearly demonstrates that Latino images trigger opposition to immigration.[45] And several other scholars have shown that feelings toward Latinos and undocumented immigrants are one of the most important determinants of immigration policy positions.[46] Finally, several different studies have found that proximity to larger immigrant populations and especially larger Latino communities creates heightened opposition toward immigration.[47]

But do attitudes about immigrants and/or the Latino population affect views across a wider array of policy questions? Can anxiety about immigration help drive broader political outcomes? Scholars have not yet made this kind of connection, but we believe that views on immigration are likely to influence a broad range of policies.

The third critical development in our theory of immigration politics is the coupling of immigration with a range of policy debates and policy prescriptions. We contend that immigration has broad consequences for policy because concerns about immigrants are being increasingly infused into a diverse array of ostensibly nonracial- or nonimmigration-related policy areas.

This spillover of immigration into a variety of policy areas is driven in part by demographic change itself.[48] As the immigrant population

---

[45] Brader, Valentino, and Suhay 2008.

[46] Hainmeuller and Hiscox 2010.

[47] Newman 2013; Dunaway, Branton, and Abrajano 2010; Ayers and Hofstetter 2008; Hero and Preuhs 2006; Stein, Post, and Rinden 2000; Burns and Gimpel 2000; Hood and Morris 1998. See also Scheve and Slaughter 2001; Tolbert and Hero 2001. The same relationship between the size of the immigrant population and increased opposition to immigration has been found repeatedly at the cross-national level (Citrin and Sides 2008; Lahav 2004; McLaren 2003; Quillian 1995). Similarly, when Americans vote directly on immigration policy through the initiative process, greater racial diversity is often associated with support for measures that target minorities (Campbell, Wong, and Citrin 2006; Tolbert, Lowenstein, and Donovan 1998; but see Hood and Morris 2000; Citrin, Reingold, and Green 1990).

[48] Martinez-Ebers et al. 2000.

grows, immigrants almost naturally become an increasingly central focus of policy considerations. Yet we also believe that the media and political elites play a large role; both sets of actors have increasingly put immigration at the heart of a range of different policy debates. Images of Latinos and visuals of undocumented Latino immigrants are regularly inserted into articles and discussions about everything from health care to terrorism. When Americans now talk about welfare, crime, education, and a number of other important policy arenas, they often also speak about immigrants or some aspect of immigration.

Welfare is perhaps the most obvious case of a policy area colored by immigration, and in particular, the images and presumed actions of Latino immigrants. Welfare reform since the mid-1990s has been permeated with images of Latinos.[49] California's Proposition 187 is one of the leading examples, but it is certainly not the only one. Shortly after 1996, Congress, with the strong backing of President Bill Clinton, passed the Personal Responsibility and Work Opportunity Reconciliation Act, which limited federal public services to legal immigrants. Since 2005, most other states have sought to reduce immigrant access to welfare.[50]

Moreover, slightly less than 70 percent of whites view Latinos as especially prone to be on welfare.[51] Work by Martin Gilens found no clear link between attitudes toward Latinos and policy views on welfare in the 1990s, although more recent work by Cybelle Fox as well as Rodney Hero and Robert Preuhs suggests a tightening relationship.[52] Given that more Americans believe that immigrants come "primarily to use government services and welfare benefits" as opposed to "primarily for jobs," it would not be surprising to discover that attitudes on immigration are now shaping white's preferred welfare policy prescriptions.[53]

Latinos, immigrants, and crime is another readily apparent script. When Latinos are in the news, criminality is a common theme. Fully 66 percent of network news coverage of Latinos incorporates crime, terrorism, or unauthorized immigration.[54] Likewise, as we will show in chapter 5, when the news media focuses specifically on immigration, much of the coverage is negative in its tone.[55] The end result is a clear

---

[49] Chavez 2008; Fox 2004.
[50] Rivera 2013.
[51] Bobo 2001.
[52] Gilens 1999; Fox 2004, 2012; Hero and Preuhs 2006.
[53] Reason-Rupe 2013 survey, cited in Polling Report 2014.
[54] National Association of Hispanic Journalists 2005.
[55] Not only has the crime issue risen to the forefront of the national immigration debate, but it

link between crime and immigration among the public. Despite the fact that only about a quarter of the foreign-born population are undocumented, most Americans believe that the majority of immigrants are here without legal status.[56] These perceptions have influenced the stereotypes associated with Latinos. A majority of white Americans view Latinos as being particularly prone to violence.[57] Implicit attitude tests also now show a clear connection between Latinos and being undocumented.[58]

More recently, concerns about undocumented immigration have also spilled over into the issue of health care. Recall the events that transpired during President Obama's September 2009 speech to Congress regarding his proposed health care plan. When Obama stated that the Democratic plans would not include coverage for undocumented immigrants, Representative Joe Wilson of South Carolina interrupted the president's speech and shouted, "You lie!" This outburst and the overall spotlight on undocumented immigrants have made Latinos one of the main "target" groups of this policy. After much of the debate on the plan revolved around whether or not the Democratic reform package would cover undocumented immigrants, a Pew Research Center poll found that 66 percent of the opposition reported that they were against the plan because it might cover undocumented immigrants.[59]

Deliberations about the merits of different educational reforms as well as access to public education itself have also become more and more focused on Latinos. Proposition 187 began efforts to limit immigrants' access to public education. More recently, other states like Alabama, which enacted the Beason-Hammon Taxpayer and Citizen Protection Act in 2011, have attempted to restrict undocumented immigrants from attending public schools.[60] The debate continues today in a different form with arguments for and against the Dream Act.

---

has also made its way to the subnational level via a range of state and local initiatives, such as those in Arizona and other ordinances targeting unauthorized immigrants.

[56] Citrin and Sides 2008; Kaiser 2004.

[57] Bobo and Johnson 2000.

[58] Pérez 2010.

[59] Polling Report 2014.

[60] While the law does not prohibit undocumented youths from enrolling in school, immediately after its passage, the percentage of Latino students enrolled in Alabama schools dropped by 5 percent. The courts have at least temporarily blocked this provision. See http://www.nytimes.com/2011/10/04/us/after-ruling-hispanics-flee-an-alabama-town.html?pagewanted=1&_r=2&sq=alabama&st=cse&scp=3& (accessed July 13, 2014).

Similarly, images of the immigrant population at least occasionally undergird debates about broader issues like jobs and taxes as well.[61] High rates of unemployment and low wages can—and often are—linked to the flow of low-skilled, undocumented immigrants coming across the border.[62] Given that large segments of the US population believe that immigrants are hurting wages and job prospects, it seems logical that many of the proposed economic solutions would be influenced by immigration considerations. The story on taxes is analogous.[63] Worries about unauthorized immigrants not paying taxes and the long-term negative fiscal consequences of the United States' large immigrant population may already be shaping the willingness of white Americans to tax themselves to provide basic services.[64]

For those concerned about immigration and the growing Latino population, there are obvious policy implications in each of these areas. Anti-immigrant sentiment in every case should lead directly to more conservative policy preferences. Perceptions that immigrants are disproportionately using public welfare coupled with the sense that immigrants make up a larger and larger share of the welfare-receiving population could provide a strong motivation for retrenchment. The story on crime is similar. If white immigrants believe that immigrants are prone to crime and that a growing subset of the criminal population is immigrant based, then the solution is more punitive measures. More broadly, if most Americans think that immigrants are using services without paying taxes, this may lead them to be less generous toward such services. This logic may go so far as to lead to disinvestment in core areas like education and health care. The overall story is that anxiety along with resentment generated by the immigrant population should lead to less generous and more punitive policy choices.

If attitudes on immigration were tied to a range of policy debates, it would not be the first time. Past research has demonstrated a strong link between attitudes toward minority groups and nonracial policies.[65] In particular, there is evidence that individual policy preferences on welfare have been shaped by attitudes toward blacks.[66] The racialization of welfare was no accident. For almost a half century, political rhetoric and media coverage of welfare often highlighted this racial

[61] Tichenor 2002; Newton 2008.
[62] Borjas 2001.
[63] Ibid.
[64] Hopkins 2010.
[65] Winter 2008; Soss, Langbein, and Metelko 2006.
[66] Gilens 1999; Kinder and Sanders 1996.

connection. Content analysis of media coverage has confirmed the relationship.[67] Clearly, these racialized images have had an impact on the public. In experimental research by Franklin Gilliam Jr., whites' views toward blacks became more negative and their opposition to welfare increased when they were exposed to a news story featuring a black welfare recipient as opposed to a lone.[68] The end result is that attitudes toward blacks have been found to be a primary factor driving support or opposition to welfare reform.[69]

The connection between crime and the African American population is just as apparent, with news coverage disproportionately featuring African Americans and white resentment toward blacks driving criminal policy preferences.[70] Here again, experimental studies demonstrate a clear link between media coverage, racial attitudes, and policy preferences.[71] More limited research has also shown an association between attitudes toward blacks and tax policy as well as a host of other ostensibly nonracial policy areas.[72] In short, a range of policies in the United States has often been—and may continue to be—racially coded.

Given the growing prominence of immigrants and Latinos in the news and many of these different policy debates, we should expect to see an increasingly close connection between attitudes about immigrants, on one side, and white Americans' policy preferences, on the other. The implication of all this is that if we want to understand the full extent of the impact of immigration on US politics, we need to consider the effects of immigration not just on how individuals think about immigration policy itself but also on how they think about the broader array of policies that are at times implicitly linked to the issue of immigration.[73]

None of this is to say that immigration is the primary motivation whenever white Americans consider these different policy areas. In-

---

[67] Gilens 1999; Gilliam 1999; Zucchino 1997. Fully 62 percent of major newsmagazine poverty stories between 1960 and 1992 featured blacks, and nearly 100 percent of the "underclass" in these articles was black (Gilens 1999). Network television news was similarly skewed, with 65 percent of the welfare stories referencing blacks.

[68] Gilliam 1999.

[69] Gilens 1999; Hurwitz and Peffley 1998.

[70] Hurwitz and Peffley 1998; Gilliam et al. 1996; Kinder and Sanders 1996; Entman 1990, 1992.

[71] Gilliam and Iyengar 2000.

[72] Winter 2008; Soss, Langbein, and Metelko 2006; Kinder and Sanders 1996; Sears and Citrin 1982.

[73] It is also possible that the link between immigration and political views extends even more broadly as well as deeply. Indeed, if immigration is pushing Americans to the right across this range of policy questions, then it may ultimately lead to movement across the core liberal-conservative ideological line that often delineates who we are politically.

deed, immigration is unlikely to be *the* main driving force in any of the policy arenas. The coupling of immigration with each of these different policy debates nonetheless should have consequences. For many individual Americans, concerns about immigration may be strong enough to lead to a small but recognizable impact on their policy views. If these different assertions are correct, existing studies are far too narrow and have greatly underestimated the influence of immigration on US politics.

Increasingly Clear Partisan Choices

The last critical development for our immigration backlash theory is the coupling of the immigrant threat with increasingly apparent *partisan* choices. Driving this development is the growing policy gap between Democratic and Republican leaders on the immigration issue, in part fueled by intense partisan polarization among politicians and the public.[74] Although elites in both parties express a variety of views on immigration, the political entrepreneurs who have been most vocal about the immigrant threat narrative have generally come from the Republican side.[75] Republican leaders like Mike Huckabee and Tom Tancredo along with conservative commentators like Bill O'Reilly, Ann Coulter, and Rush Limbaugh have repeatedly highlighted the ills of undocumented immigration, and have urged for a range of reforms to push current immigrants out of the country and limit new immigration.[76] Even a politician like Mitt Romney who represents the more moderate faction of the party adopted an anti-immigrant platform that included self-deportation and opposition to the Dream Act in his 2012 bid for president. Some have gone so far as to say that the only things Republicans have offered Latino and Asian voters are "fear and hostility."[77] On the other hand, most Democratic leaders have either expressed support for a limited range of immigrants' rights or avoided the issue altogether.

These increasingly divergent policy stances are borne out by votes in Congress. As Gary Miller and Norman Schofield have demonstrated, there was reasonably strong Republican support for immi-

---

[74] McCarty, Poole, and Rosenthal 2008; Poole and Rosenthal 1997.

[75] Many Democratic leaders are reluctant to publicly support immigrants' rights issues while many Republicans recognize the benefits of cheap labor to business.

[76] Business interests within the Republican Party beholden to cheap immigrant labor clearly favor less regressive immigration reforms, but their views have been less and less likely to be vocalized by party leadership.

[77] http://www.nytimes.com/2013/07/08/opinion/immigration-in-the-house.html?hp&_r=0 (accessed on July 13, 2014).

grant's rights during the Reagan era and little noticeable partisan division on immigration-related legislation as late as 1990. But since that time, it is clear that "the parties have switched their positions on immigration."[78] James Gimpel and James Edwards actually trace these divisions back to the mid-1980s.[79] Votes in Congress reveal an increasingly stark contrast, with Republican legislators repeatedly supporting tougher laws against immigrants, and Democrats favoring more admission and greater immigrants' rights.[80] Tom Wong finds that across all bills and amendments that Congress voted on between 2006 and 2012, Republican house and senate members favored restrictive policies 98.4 percent of the time, while Democrats supported those measures only 66.4 percent of the time.[81] On any number of different immigration-related issues including erecting a border fence, English as the official language, amnesty, government workers reporting undocumented immigrants, and anchor babies, current Republican leadership has largely aligned itself on the opposite side of the Democratic Party.

The same pattern of partisan divergence is evident at the state level. All the infamous anti-immigrant state measures have been initiated and/or endorsed by state Republican leaders and largely opposed by Democrats. In Arizona, for example, no Democrat in the legislature supported the controversial immigrant enforcement bill, SB 1070, while all but one Republican voted for it.[82] Battle lines in California over Proposition 187 were similarly partisan in their nature, with Republican governor Pete Wilson one of the primary advocates of the "Save Our State" initiative and Democratic governor Gray Davis challenging the measure in court. There is also compelling evidence that Democratic and Republican leaders at the local level are just as sharply divided on immigration.[83]

These divergent party stances on immigration are borne out by interest group ratings. Interest groups universally rate Democratic members of Congress as distinctly liberal on immigration and Republican members as strongly conservative. The Federation for American Immigration Reform (FAIR), for example, rates current Democratic house members on average as a ten out of a hundred on its immigration legislation scale, with a hundred denoting the most restrictive po-

---

[78] Miller and Schofield 2008.
[79] Gimpel and Edwards 1998.
[80] Jeong et al. 2011; Miller and Schofield 2008; Gimpel and Edwards 1998.
[81] Wong 2013.
[82] Archibold 2010.
[83] Ramakrishnan, n.d.

sition on immigration. By contrast, Republican house members average ninety-nine. Significantly, FAIR's estimate of the partisan divide on immigration has grown sharply over time. Its ratings show little partisan divide on immigration as late as 1996, when Democrats averaged a score of forty-four on immigration and Republicans received an average score of fifty-two. But by the early 2000s, FAIR's ratings by party sharply diverge.

A similarly anti-immigrant group, NumbersUSA, gave President Obama a failing grade on immigration while offering passing grades for all the 2012 Republican presidential hopefuls. The National Latino Congreso sees the same large partisan gap, but as a decidedly proimmigrant interest group, it gave Democrats high grades—an average score of 81 percent—while labeling Republican legislators as extraordinarily poor on immigration—an average rating of 7 percent.

Especially in the current era of extreme partisan polarization, we contend that the increasing distance between Democratic and Republican leaders on matters of immigration could have real consequences for individual partisan identities. When Republican leaders criticize immigrants, condemn their actions, and bemoan the costs to the United States, and Democratic leaders either ignore immigration or offer lukewarm support for the plight of immigrants, they present individual white Americans with a compelling partisan logic. Anyone who is anxious about immigration and the growing population of Latinos has a strong incentive to favor the Republican Party. This divide over immigration is so great that in the current congressional session, the 113th Congress, little hope exists for the passage of any sort of comprehensive immigration reform, despite the strong urging of President Obama and a variety of interest groups to do so.

Party leaders are not, however, the only actors involved in this process. We believe that immigrants and Latinos are also contributing to the sorting of white Americans into pro- and anti-immigrant parties. The pro-Democratic tendencies of the growing Latino population have dramatically altered the racial group imagery of the Democratic Party. Latinos, the largest and most visible immigrant group as well as the one most often associated with the immigrant threat narrative, have overwhelmingly chosen to favor the Democratic camp. Latino Democratic identifiers outnumber Latino Republican identifiers by more than two to one.[84] When Latinos vote in congressional elections, the Democrat-to-Republican ratio is almost four to one. And in 2008 and 2012, over two-thirds of Latinos supported Obama. The end result

[84] Hajnal and Lee 2011.

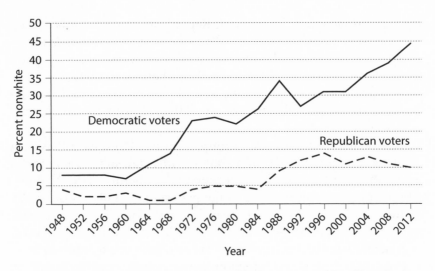

Figure 1.1 The Changing Racial Composition of the Democratic and Republican Parties: Nonwhite Share of the Presidential Vote by Party and Year
Sources: ANES 2010; National Election Pool Exit Polls.

is a dramatic reconfiguration of the racial group imagery associated with each party.

That racial reconfiguration is illustrated in figure 1.1, which details the size of the nonwhite segment of the Democratic and Republican presidential votes over time. Until the early 1960s, neither party was closely aligned with a racial minority group. Both parties received at least 90 percent of their votes from white voters. Since that time, though, the share of Democratic support coming from racial and ethnic minorities has risen dramatically, while the share of Republican support from nonwhites has been relatively flat. In 2012, almost half of all Democratic voters (45 percent) were racial/ethnic minorities. By contrast, a little less than 10 percent of Republican supporters were nonwhite. It would be hard not to notice that the Democratic Party gains a great deal of its support from racial/ethnic minorities while the Republican Party does not.

Latino elected officials have helped to reinforce this change in the racial group imagery associated with each party. Today, well over two-thirds of the Latinos in Congress are on the Democratic side. Some 83 percent of Latino state legislators are Democrats.[85] Overall, about 90 percent of Latino elected officials in partisan office across the nation

---

[85] By contrast, 97.9 percent of Republicans serving in state houses are white (Bowler and Segura 2012).

identify as Democrats.[86] The end result is that the party representatives look very different. Fully one-third of the Democratic members of the US House of Representatives are nonwhite, while less than 4 percent of Republican house members are nonwhite. If these newcomers are a threat, they are one that generally sides with the Democrats.

Immigration and the Intractability of Party Identification

But can immigration really influence partisan preferences? Party identification is, after all, one of the most stable and enduring political attachments.[87] For many of us, partisan psychological attachments begin in childhood and persist for all of our lives.[88]

There are reasons to suspect that feelings on immigration could affect partisan views, however. First, although party identification is often durable, it can and does shift.[89] Aggregate shifts in partisanship are well known and well documented.[90] Long-term panel data also demonstrate widespread and unambiguous individual-level changes in partisan attachments.[91] Indeed, diverse scholars contend that for many Americans, party identification is a standing decision that incorporates issue positions and other factors.[92] This Downsian perspective has garnered increasing support over time and is one of the two main theoretical accounts of individual partisanship.[93]

Second, if any issue can provoke change in partisan attachment, it may well be immigration. Historically, we have seen how immigration can alter the positions of the parties as well as their supporters.[94] Scholars of this Downsian perspective, moreover, do not assert that all issues are equally likely to sway partisanship. They instead suggest that partisanship is more likely to change when the issue is relatively simple or symbolic as well as stirs deep feelings.[95] Immigration conforms on both counts.

---

[86] National Association of Latino Elected Officials 2012. Latino elected officials were not always so likely to come out of the Democratic Party numbers, but over time the partisan imbalance has grown dramatically.
[87] Campbell et al. 1960; Green, Palmquist, and Schickler 2002.
[88] Niemi and Jennings 1991.
[89] MacKuen, Erikson, and Stimson 1989.
[90] Erikson, MacKuen, and Stimson 2002.
[91] Niemi and Jennings 1991.
[92] Fiorina 1981; Erikson, MacKuen, and Stimson 2002.
[93] Downs 1957.
[94] Tichenor 2002; Gimpel and Edwards 1998.
[95] Carsey and Layman 2006; Carmines and Stimson 1980.

Immigration is by most accounts a relatively easy or symbolic issue. Studies suggest that attitudes toward immigrants are at their base linked to deep, enduring attitudes like ethnocentrism and prejudice.[96] How we think about Latinos, for instance, says a lot about our policy views on immigration.[97] In this sense, immigration may be similar to racial issues. Attitudes toward immigrants and immigration may be deeply held and stable enough to sway partisan considerations.[98]

The salience of immigration certainly ebbs and flows, but it seems clear that substantial segments of the US population see it as an important issue. Polls over the last decade indicate that close to 90 percent of Americans view undocumented immigration as a serious problem, with roughly 60 percent calling it a "very serious" problem. What's more, when asked explicitly if positions on immigration would sway their partisan choices, most Americans say that immigration would win out. Fully 70 percent of Americans say they would likely vote against a political party or candidate that "took a position on immigration that you disagreed with . . . even if you agreed with that party or candidate on most other issues."[99]

But what if party identification is not really driven by issue positions and instead is a more deep-seated psychological attachment? Could partisanship still change in the face of large-scale immigration? We contend that even in this case, there is reason to expect substantial shifts in partisanship. Even those who consider party identification to be a stable and enduring political attachment admit that it can be altered under particular circumstances. One of those circumstances is a change in the group images associated with each party. Even Donald Green and his colleagues who write convincingly about the durability of party identification note that major shifts in partisanship have occurred over time as the group images associated with each party have changed.[100] Indeed, part of the seeming permanence of partisan attachments stems from the fact that those group images rarely change. Yet with immigration and growing Latino support of the Democratic Party, there is little doubt that party images have changed in recent decades. A party that once served and was

---

[96] Kam and Kinder 2012; Citrin et al. 1997.

[97] Brader, Valentino, and Suhay 2008.

[98] Another feature of the immigration issue that may make it more likely than other issues to lead to shifts in partisanship is its crosscutting nature. At least until recent decades, Americans who expressed more anti-immigrant views were found in large numbers in both political parties (Newton 2008).

[99] Fox News 2010 survey, cited in Polling Report 2014.

[100] Green, Palmquist, and Schickler 2002.

supported by lower-class white interests increasingly became a party supported by the black community, and since the 1990s has increasingly become a party supported by Latinos and other immigrant groups. In other words, what it means to be a Democrat has changed. This is precisely the kind of change that could alter enduring partisan attachments. Again, there is a precedent in US racial politics. Enormous, racially motivated shifts in partisanship have taken place in the past. That defection of whites from the Democratic Party is from another time and revolves around a different group—African Americans. Nevertheless, it is analogous to the situation today. Several studies assert that the movement of whites to the Republican Party in the 1970s and 1980s was a direct response to the civil rights movement, the increased political participation of African Americans, and growing black support of the Democratic Party.[101] As blacks joined the Democratic Party in large numbers, and as the Democratic and Republican parties diverged on the main racial policy questions of the day, white identification with the Democratic Party—especially in the South—sharply declined.[102] According to this view, whites' sentiments about blacks helped Republicans dominate national elections.[103] Gimpel and Edwards also assert that the movement of whites to the Republican Party can be explained with the passage of the Hart-Cellars Act of 1965, which resulted in a large influx of new immigrants that largely benefited the Democratic Party.[104]

If the growing strength and increasing demands of one racial minority group has triggered broad political reactions along with a widespread white backlash in the past, there is at least a possibility that the growing immigrant population could spark a similar reaction today. Given that Latinos have replaced blacks as the largest ethnic/racial minority population, it is at least plausible that Latinos and other immigrant groups have become more central in the political thinking as well as partisan choices of white America.

[101] Hood, Kidd, and Morris 2012; Black and Black 2002; Carmines and Stimson 1989; Huckfeldt and Kohfeld 1989.

[102] Many contend that attitudes toward blacks continue to strongly shape the white vote and in particular had a substantial impact on Obama's presidential bid (Lewis-Beck, Tien, and Richard Nadeau 2010; Bobo and Dawson 2009; Tesler and Sears 2010.

[103] Valentino and Sears 2005; Edsall and Edsall 1991. At the same time, it is important to note that there are several authors who dispute just how much of this partisan shift was due to attitudes about African Americans (Shafer and Johnston 2005; Lublin 2004; Abramowitz 1994). According to this alternate view, other factors like economic considerations and social issues helped drive white defection to the Republican Party.

[104] Gimpel and Edwards 1998.

Immigration and the Vote

Although party identification is generally considered to be the principal driving force in US politics, democracy at its heart is about votes and elections. Who wins office and who loses? If immigration is having a fundamental impact on the political arena, we should also see evidence of it in the vote. For all the same reasons that we believe immigration is impacting partisan identity, we expect attitudes on immigration to shape the partisan vote. As rates of immigration increase, anxiety about immigration expands, and the Democratic and Republican brands increasingly differ on immigration, it makes more sense for individual voters to use immigration to help shape their electoral choices. Strong concerns about immigration and two starkly different choices on immigration will, we contend, convince many white voters to favor Republican candidates.

Mechanisms: How Does Immigration
Impact Individual Americans?

We have suggested why large-scale immigration should shift white policy preferences and partisan affinities toward the right. But we have not yet described how that process might work. How do individual Americans see and experience immigration, and how do they learn about the Democratic and Republican parties' divergent stances on immigration? We have presented a broad theory, but we have not yet detailed a causal mechanism.

What, then, is the mechanism through which the phenomenon of immigration seeps into the political consciousness of individual Americans? Different individuals are likely to "experience" immigration in varying ways, yet we believe that two mechanisms are critical in shaping individual experiences and reactions. One is direct and geographically based. That is, living in areas where immigration is more pronounced and the visible effects of immigration are more widespread should spark stronger reactions than residing in areas with little to no immigration. The other mechanism is indirect, based on what sorts of information individuals are exposed to. Namely, the media in many cases functions as the main purveyor of information for the US public.[105] What they see and learn from the news media is likely to significantly shape their opinions about immigration along with their political reactions to newcomers to the United States.

---

[105] Iyengar and Kinder 1987; Prior 2005.

These two mechanisms are far from the only ways in which immigration could impact the public. Partisan elites, as we have already mentioned, can play a pivotal role in driving this process. There are all sorts of important and interesting strategic political decisions that these elites regularly make on the issue of immigration that we will largely ignore in this book. Likewise, interest groups and in particular organizations that strongly favor or oppose immigration in the United States can influence individual Americans through a range of activities. But we believe that geographic context and media coverage of immigration represent two of the key mechanisms helping to shift the political preferences of many white Americans to the right.

THE GEOGRAPHY OF IMMIGRATION

Individual Americans' experiences with immigration are decidedly uneven. Some live in contexts that have been overwhelmingly transformed by large numbers of newcomers, while others live in areas that have been largely untouched by the shifting demographics of immigration. We believe variation in immigrant settlement patterns has real consequences for how white Americans think about immigration and how they react politically.

Our story is essentially one of racial threat. We contend that proximity to sizable and growing immigrant populations raises the stakes of immigration. With larger numbers comes the potential for more competition for scarce resources like housing, education, welfare, jobs, and any number of other public services. Greater visibility of the immigrant population can also, in and of itself, spark stereotypes and concerns. The underlying idea is that a larger out-group increases feelings of threat—either because that threat is real or simply because it is perceived.

There is, in fact, growing evidence to suggest that this kind of racial threat mechanism is in place. A range of contextual studies has shown that concerns about immigrants and opposition to immigration both increase as the size of the local immigrant population grows.[106] More research nevertheless needs to be conducted before we can firmly connect an immigrant contextual threat to white political behavior. For one, the results, to this point, are not always consistent. Some studies have found no relationship between immigrant context and views.[107] Others have even demonstrated a positive relationship.[108]

[106] Ha and Oliver 2010; Ayers and Hofstetter 2008; Campbell, Wong, and Citrin 2006; Hood and Morris 1998; Citrin et al. 1997.
[107] Fennelly and Federico 2008; Dixon 2006; Taylor 1998; Burns and Gimpel 2000.
[108] Ha and Olivers 2010; Hood and Morris 1998, 2000; Fox 2004.

For another, existing studies of immigrant or Latino context are too narrow in scope. Not one of these contextual studies has looked at the impact of immigrant context on partisanship and other core political decisions.[109]

One other outstanding question is whether threat is driven primarily by the size of the out-group or rate at which the out-group is growing. Do white Americans feel most threatened when faced with a large number of Latinos or immigrants, or do they experience greater anxiety when confronted with a relatively small but rapidly expanding immigrant population? All the media discussion about "new immigrant destinations" where relatively small though rapidly expanding immigrant communities are sparking heated reactions suggest that the rate of growth is a critical factor.[110] A spate of recent anti-immigrant legislation in new destination states like South Carolina and Alabama reinforces this view. Moreover, several convincing academic studies have discovered a strong relationship between Latino population growth and white attitudes as well as actions.[111] But the passage of similarly stringent anti-immigrant measures in high-density Latino states like California and Arizona suggests that overall numbers may matter just as much or more. Again, as we have just noted, research that focuses on group size has frequently found evidence of a robust racial threat effect. Moving forward, we will both recognize and incorporate the distinction between group size and group growth rate in our analysis.

If in the end it turns out that we do find a broad political reaction to immigrant context, it will mirror past white reactions to the black population. Researchers including Key and Olzak have demonstrated in different ways that many whites are threatened by more sizeable black populations and have reacted negatively when the local black population has grown or sought greater empowerment.[112] Larger black populations have been associated with more resentment of blacks, violence against blacks, support for racist candidates, greater opposition to policies that might benefit blacks, and increased support for the white candidates and Republican Party.[113] If current reactions to immigrants parallel these racialized patterns of the past, whites' political

---

[109] For important exception, see Hero and Preuhs 2006. This article reveals a relationship between the size of the state immigrant population and welfare policy at the state level.

[110] Severson 2011; Sulzberger 2010.

[111] Newman 2013; Hopkins 2010.

[112] Key 1949; Olzak 1992.

[113] On resentment of blacks, see Taylor 1998; Fossett and Kiecolt 1989. See also Oliver and Wong 2003. On violence against blacks, see Corzine et al. 1983; Olzak 1992. On support for racist candidates, see Giles and Buckner 1993; Black and Black 1973. On opposition to policies that might benefit blacks, see Soss, Langbein, and Metelko 2006; Keiser et al. 2004; Fel-

behavior should be directly shaped by the immigrant context in which they live.

THE NEWS MEDIA AND ITS FRAMING OF IMMIGRATION

Although we believe that there is a direct link between demographic change and white political views, we contend that whites learn about immigration from other sources as well. Namely, we maintain that the news media is a critical source of information on immigration. How whites view immigration, whether they think it is a prevalent problem, and ultimately whether they accept an immigrant threat narrative are all, in our opinion, likely to be shaped by the new media.

We argue that the Latino or immigrant threat narrative has come to dominate media coverage of immigration, largely because of profit-based incentives.[114] The overreliance on this specific frame generates new fears about the presence of immigrants, or activates and heightens existing concerns. Ultimately, by informing individuals about the largely negative attributes of immigration as well as exposing the public to a biased perspective on this highly complex and multifaceted issue, the news media may be able to heighten concerns about immigration enough to alter core partisan attachments.

In testing these two mechanisms, we have two main goals. First and foremost, we simply want to learn more about the mechanism through which immigration works to affect US politics. How do larger national trends reach and influence individuals with respect to immigration? In addition, these tests will help us confirm the causal link between immigration and white political behavior. If we can demonstrate a link between proximity to immigrants and media coverage, on the one hand, and white views and political choices, on the other, we have yet more evidence that immigration matters in the US political arena.

The Underlying Causes of White Anxiety about Immigration

One question we have not answered is why so many white Americans feel threatened by immigration in the first place. The anxiety surrounding immigration is surprising given that most empirical studies indicate that native-born Americans should not feel any great sense of threat. The best social science data suggest that the net impact of im-

---

lowes and Rowe 2004. On increased support for white candidates and the Republican Party, see Giles and Evans 1986; Huckfeldt and Kohfeld 1989.

[114] Chavez 2008; Berry and Sobieraj 2014; Hamilton 2004.

migration is generally a positive one for most Americans.[115] With few exceptions, the documented costs of immigration are relatively small.[116] Given the overall empirical reality of immigration, few Americans should feel threatened.

Why, then, do so many Americans appear to have real concerns about immigration? One can claim—as we do—that negative media portrayals spur anxiety, politicians and other political entrepreneurs can add to the combustible mix by maligning immigrants and making them scapegoats during periods of economic downturn, and interest groups can further stoke fears among the public. Yet that still begs the question of why so many white Americans are susceptible to the message. If all or almost all the empirical evidence is to the contrary, why does the immigrant threat narrative resonate so broadly?

This is not a question that we directly address in this book. It is, however, a subject that has dominated much of the political science literature on immigration. It is also an area of research that has attracted widespread debate. Most assert that cultural and racial considerations are behind whites' responses. Views on immigration have been linked to ethnocentrism, social dominance and authoritarian personality, nationalism, and racial prejudice.[117] Indeed, there is absolutely no doubt that attitudes about immigrants are correlated with a range of different measures of cultural and racial views as well as various personality types. Whether there is a causal connection between each of these measures and attitudes on immigration is not as clear.

There is also no shortage of other hypotheses about what drives opinions concerning immigrants. Many other scholars point in particular to economic considerations. In one variation, those who are most directly in economic competition for immigrants should be the ones

---

[115] Bean and Stevens 2003.

[116] Few white Americans are in direct competition with immigrants for jobs, and wages have not been impacted for anyone but the lowest-skilled Americans (Borjas 2001; Bean and Stevens 2003). Legal immigrants do tend to use more social services than native-born whites (Borjas 2001). And while it is the case that most undocumented immigrants do not pay income tax, they do contribute to the tax base through consumption taxes. But the overall fiscal consequences are at worst slightly negative over the short term and probably positive over the long term (Bean and Stevens 2003; Borjas 2001; Smith and Edmonston 1997). On the cultural side, there is also little sign that immigrants are a real threat. Immigrants and their offspring learn English at impressive rates (Bean and Stevens 2003), are as patriotic as the native population (Citrin et al. 2007), and hold similar values to the rest of the population (de la Garza et al. 1996.

[117] On ethnocentrism, see Kinder and Kam 2010. On social dominance and authoritarian personality, see Pettigrew et al. 2007. On nationalism, see Citrin, Reingold, and Green 1990. On racial prejudice, see Pérez 2010; Schildkraut 2010; Brader, Valentino, and Suhay 2008; Burns and Gimpel 2000.

most opposed to immigration.[118] In another version, unease about immigration should reach its highest levels during trying economic times. These economic models have sometimes garnered significant empirical support. At the aggregate level, studies have linked economic conditions to immigration attitudes.[119] Others have shown that opinions about immigration are intricately connected to personal economic considerations. Unskilled, native-born Americans whose jobs and wages are most in jeopardy tend to be the most strongly opposed to immigration.[120] Likewise, taxes and public spending considerations can play a role. Hostility to immigration is especially pronounced among Americans whose taxes are most likely to be affected by immigration—high-income earners who live in states with relatively expansive social welfare benefits and large numbers of immigrants are particularly hostile to immigration.[121] At the same time, other empirical studies raise some doubt about these kinds of economic arguments.[122] More recent experimental studies strongly suggest that economic considerations play little part in structuring attitudes on immigration.[123]

In the end, we are largely agnostic about what it is that drives attitudes concerning immigrants. Each of these different theories about the underlying causes is likely to be at least partly true for some Americans. Fortunately, the story that we are presenting in this book is consistent with any of the economic, racial or cultural threat mechanisms. If white Americans feel threatened by immigration—regardless of why—it could have political consequences.

At the same time, it is important to note that our story is not simply a retelling of these earlier accounts. Even after controlling for the various factors discussed above, we find that attitudes about immigrants have a robust, direct effect on a range of political choices. Thus, there is something significant about immigration itself that matters to white Americans when they make basic political decisions.

Who Is the Threat?

Another question we have yet to address is exactly who or what whites are threatened by? Are their concerns focused on the undocumented,

---

[118] Malhotra et al. 2011.
[119] Scheve and Slaughter 2001; Quillian 1995.
[120] Hanson 2005.
[121] Ibid.
[122] Hainmueller and Hopkins 2014; Citrin et al. 1997.
[123] Hainmueller and Hiscox 2010.

or do their fears extend to the entire immigration population? Is fear concentrated on a single national origin group like Mexican Americans who represent a large share of immigrants and hail from a neighboring country with a large, porous border? Or alternatively, are concerns much broader? Do the children of immigrants and even those who appear to be immigrants spur similar anxiety? On a related point, are worries mostly centered on the growing Latino population or does the discontent that Americans feel about immigration also stem from the rapidly expanding Asian American population?

In theory, white Americans could make crucial distinctions between each of these different immigrant groups. Categories like undocumented immigrant, documented immigrant, Mexican American, and Latino all represent distinct populations with often widely divergent structural positions in the US economy and US life. In reality, we believe that most white Americans who are concerned about immigration tend not to make important distinctions between these different segments of the Latino/immigrant population. In the practice and rhetoric of US politics, these concepts frequently blur together. In surveys, Americans tend to reserve their most negative sentiments for so-called illegal immigrants, but when asked about immigrants as a whole, Mexican Americans, or even Latinos, the answers tend not to differ all that much. Indeed, most Americans, as we have already noted, incorrectly assume that most immigrants are undocumented, and their perceptions about the size of the undocumented population are strikingly similar to their estimates of the size of the Latino population.[124] What we think about undocumented immigrants seems intricately interconnected with what we think about immigrants and the broader Latino population.

All this is corroborated by a closer look at the attitudes of white Americans. In table 1.1, we shed some light on the degree of association between white attitudes toward these different categories. We present correlation coefficients in the table between different measures that together, address potentially important distinctions between undocumented immigrants, legal immigrants, and Latinos. All the data are from the 2008 ANES, a standard tool for analysis of US politics that we will return to time and again in the ensuing chapters. Four measures capture views on undocumented immigration: How warmly/coldly do you feel about undocumented immigrants as a group? How important is it to reduce undocumented immigration? Should we

[124] Kaiser 2004; Enos 2012.

TABLE 1.1
Attitudes toward Different Elements of Immigration:
Correlation Coefficients

	Illegal Immigration			
	Feelings toward	Is a Serious Problem	Allow to Work	Path to Citizenship
Illegal Immigration Feelings toward				
A Serious Problem	−0.47			
Allow to Work	0.28	−0.34		
Path to Citizenship	−0.35	−0.38	0.28	
Legal Immigration Preferred Level	0.28	−0.37	0.28	0.27
Views on Latinos Feelings toward Latinos	0.46	−0.20	0.16	0.22

Note: All correlations are significant at p < 0.001.
Source: ANES 2008.

allow undocumented immigrants to become citizens? And do you favor allowing undocumented immigrants to work in the United States before they go back to their home country? Next we include one question that gauges views on illegal immigration: Should immigration levels be increased, decreased, or kept at the same level? Finally, we incorporate feelings toward Latinos using a standard feeling thermometer that asks about feelings toward this group.

Theoretically, Americans could make important distinctions between these three different kinds of groups, but the results in table 1.1 indicate that they do not. Answers to the six questions are highly correlated (the average inter-item correlation is 0.31), and no measure stands out as being particularly divergent from the others.[125] Moreover, as we will see in the analysis that follows, it will generally not matter which question or category we use to measure attitudes. Whether we employ a question on alleged illegal immigrants, one on immigrants, or another that assesses views of the Latino population, our results will be strikingly similar. When Americans talk about undocumented immigrants, Latinos, or immigrants in general, the images in their heads are likely to be the same. In line with Brader and his colleagues, Perez, and others, we believe that white Americans' attitudes about immigra-

[125] Further tests indicated that the five measures form a coherent whole (with an alpha scale reliability of 0.73).

tion are highly racialized and concerns about immigration are largely focused on the Latino population.[126]

The one distinction that we think Americans do make is also a racial one. We believe that they see Latinos and Asian Americans in different ways. Moving forward, we maintain that Latinos and Asian Americans should be examined separately because the two groups hold quite different positions in the US racial hierarchy, and therefore are perceived in distinct ways by white Americans.[127] In terms of socioeconomic status, Asian Americans tend to fall at the top of the racial hierarchy while Latinos are disproportionately likely to fall near the bottom. Latinos are two or three times more likely than Asian Americans to be classified as living at or below the poverty line. The median Latino household income is only about half the median Asian American household income—the figures were roughly sixty thousand and thirty thousand dollars, respectively, in 2005. The differences in educational outcomes are just as stark. While only about 20 percent of Latinos currently graduate from college, almost 60 percent of Asian Americans do.

Stereotypes of the two pan-ethnic groups are also radically different. As Lawrence Bobo has documented, almost 70 percent of whites rate Latinos as especially welfare prone and almost half see them as less intelligent than whites on average.[128] By contrast, less than 15 percent of whites hold the same negative stereotypes of Asian Americans. Instead, when whites stereotype Asian Americans, it is often for being economically successful. Almost half of all whites believe that Asian Americans are especially industrious. Only 5 percent of whites feel the same way about Latinos.[129] These distinct stereotypes are also consistent with survey findings on intergroup attitudes. Most whites say they feel closer to Asian Americans than they do to Latinos.[130] In the same poll, 92 percent of whites said they get along with Asians while only 67 percent felt the same way about Latinos.

It is not immediately clear what these two patterns imply in terms of a threat to the white community. Nevertheless, it is unlikely that whites will react to the two immigrant groups in a similar fashion. If

---

[126] Brader, Valentino, and Suhay 2008; Pérez, forthcoming.

[127] Masuoka and Junn 2013.

[128] Bobo 2001.

[129] Ibid.; Lee 2001. More recent survey data concur. A Pew Research Center (2006) survey reports that whites were roughly twice as likely to believe that Latinos were prone to end up on welfare, increase crime, and do poorly in school than they were to have similar sentiments about Asian Americans.

[130] The National Conference for Community Justice sponsored the Intergroup Relation Survey in 2005.

concerns about welfare, redistribution, and criminality dominate white views, then reactions to the Latino population could be much tougher.[131] By contrast, Asian Americans, as a kind of model minority, could represent less of a threat and more of a potential partner.[132] Which of the two pan-ethnic groups represents more a threat will have to await more direct testing. But given the distinct structural locations of the two groups, both in terms of socioeconomics as well as the structure of racial hierarchy in the United States, we believe that it is critical to examine the impact of Latinos and Asian Americans separately.

At this point, however, our expectations are based largely on our beliefs and not on data. Before we can conclude that white Americans tend to make few distinctions between different aspects of immigration, but do view Latinos and Asian Americans differently, we will have to undertake a series of empirical tests of these different versions of the immigrant threat narrative. In light of these potentially muddled categories, we will empirically test several measures of Latino, immigrant, and Asian perspectives to try to get a clearer sense of just who it is that white Americans are reacting to.

[margin note: Qualification re whites Separating Latinos/Asians]

Alternative Theories

We have presented one theory of immigrant politics—one that we hope is compelling. But there are certainly alternative ways of conceptualizing immigration's impact on US politics. Many astute observers of US life and politics might suspect that immigration has a different effect on the attitudes of individual Americans.

One real possibility is that growth in the immigrant population could lead to more and more positive views of immigrants along with a greater willingness to support policies and political parties that might serve the interests of immigrants. After all, as we have already mentioned, almost all the empirical studies show that immigrants as a whole are successfully integrating into US society. Over time and across the generations, immigrants and their children tend to climb up the economic ladder, attain higher educational outcomes, and generally come closer and closer to catching up to the average American.[133]

[margin note: which? from where? How many generations?]

---

[131] Experimental research indicates that whites report much higher levels of anxiety about the costs of immigration when the images are of Latinos (Brader, Valentino, and Suhay 2008).

[132] One other possibility is that the higher socioeconomic status of Asian Americans represents *more* of a threat to members of the white community.

[133] Alba and Nee 2005; Bean and Stevens 2003.

If immigrants and their children are working hard, succeeding, and otherwise following the basic tenets of the US creed, then logically one might expect that increased contact with immigrants would effectively teach individual Americans that they have little to fear from immigration. Greater immigration could ultimately demonstrate to individual Americans that immigration could be a vital resource for the nation. This kind of contact hypothesis has been put forward for relations with African Americans and has received at least some empirical validation.[134] Systematic testing of learning from direct contact with immigrants is rare.[135] Yet there are at least tangential signs that many Americans could be learning positive lessons from immigration. As we have already highlighted, surveys show that large segments of the native population recognize the benefits of immigration and appreciate many of the qualities that immigrants bring to this country. These Americans may be eager to support policies that would open the border, or help immigrants succeed and assimilate in US society.

In this vein, any Republican strategy of targeting immigrants might backfire, and could actually enhance the willingness of individual white Americans to support more liberal, Democratic, and proimmigrant policies. If the bulk of the population is sympathetic to immigrants and views the positions of the Republican Party as an unfair attack on immigrants, then we might see a growing segment of the white population defecting to the Democratic Party. Indeed, there is evidence that just a shift occurred on a small scale in California in response to the Republican Party's support of Proposition 187.[136]

Still others might contend that immigration is simply not important enough in the minds of individual Americans to generate the kinds of broad political consequences that we have envisioned in our theory of immigrant politics. Two classes of data might support this latter perspective. First, the US public has rarely viewed immigration as the na-

[134] Allport 1954; Jackman and Crane 1986; Pettigrew et al. 2007; Dixon and Rosenbaum 2004. Studies that assess contact with African Americans generally find that it does have positive effects. White Americans who have close ties to racial and ethnic minorities either through work, social activities, or friendship tend to have more favorable views of these groups (McClain et al. 2006; Dixon and Rosenbaum 2004; Pettigrew et al. 2007). But one real concern with many studies of self-reported contact is that it is usually unclear whether contact breeds understanding or whether individuals with more favorable views of the out-group tend to spend more time with members of the out-group. Other studies that assess geographic context and proximity to minorities or immigrants are much more likely to find that proximity is associated with more negative views of the out-group (Newman 2013; Dunaway, Branton, and Abrajano 2010; Ayers and Hofstetter 2008; Hero and Preuhs 2006; but see Scheve and Slaughter 2001; Tolbert and Hero 2001).

[135] In contrast, see Lay 2012.

[136] Bowler and Glazer 2008. See also Dyck, Johnson, and Wassen 2012.

tion's most significant problem. Rarely have more than 10 percent of Americans cited immigration as the most pressing concern facing the country.[137] Furthermore, over the last few decades the nation has faced any number of other issues that have captured the lion's share of the public's attention. Many scholars would argue that war, economic woes, emerging social issues, and a number of other worries have dominated recent political debates, and therefore probably have dominated the decision-making calculus of individual Americans.[138] Finally, some scholars would contend that even if immigration were on par with these other issues, it still would have little impact on core partisan decisions. Regardless of how compelling our theoretical account may or may not have been, there are those who believe that party identification is largely impervious to change.[139] Concerns about immigration, however widespread, will simply not be enough to substantially alter deep-seated psychological attachments to a political party formed early in life. If anything, attitudes on immigration will fall in line with preexisting partisan attachments.[140]

Immigration and White Backlash: What Do We Know?

We have outlined what we think is a compelling theory of immigration and its impact on the politics of white America. But as we just noted, our story is not the only possible version of reality and could be wrong. Which of these different accounts is accurate? One obvious place to look for answers is in the existing literature. What do scholars have to say about the broad consequences of immigration for US politics?

The answer is precious little. Although we believe that there are valid reasons to suspect that immigration has wide-ranging consequences for the politics of white America, we have to admit that few of these effects have been documented. Almost all the literature on immigration and US political behavior focuses on one of two subjects. Either scholars concentrate on immigrants themselves and their political choices, or they seek to understand underlying attitudes about immigration. They rarely aim to understand the implications of our views on immigration.

---

[137] Gallup 1990–2013.
[138] Adams 1997; Layman and Carmines 1997; Miller and Shanks 1996.
[139] Campbell et al. 1960; Green, Palmquist, and Schickler 2002.
[140] Green, Palmquist, and Schickler 2002.

In the first case, there is ample evidence that immigrants themselves have had an impact on US politics. Numerous studies have illustrated the growing strength of the minority vote and ability of Latinos, the largest immigrant group in the nation, to sway electoral outcomes.[141] Other research has highlighted different partisan patterns among the immigrant population, and in particular the increasing attachment of immigrants and their offspring to the Democratic Party.[142] These are certainly important developments in the course of US political history. As we have mentioned, though, immigrants are only a small fraction of the population.

What about research on whites and immigration? Here the overwhelming focus has been on understanding and explaining what drives our attitudes toward immigrants, and what motivates our preferences on a range of polices related to immigration.[143] Why is it that we do or do not like immigrants? What leads us to favor or oppose policies that would open or close the border?

These various studies can be incredibly helpful, but the end result is an important gap in our understanding of immigration and its impact on US politics. Scholars have helped us to develop an understanding of the underlying *causes* of attitudes on immigration and our views toward Latinos, but they have done much less to assess the broader *consequences* of immigrant related views. We know little about how views of immigrants shape core political affiliations and basic voting decisions. To date, there is scant evidence that the partisan affiliations or voting decisions of individual white Americans strongly reflect their views on immigration or the Latino population.[144]

The existing research that examines partisan trends has generally overlooked the role of immigration and race.[145] The few studies that have done so exclusively center on the black-white divide, without any recognition of the nation's burgeoning immigrant population.[146] No study that we know of has demonstrated a connection between immigration and the white vote in national contests, or revealed a direct test

---

[141] De la Garza et al. 1992; DeSipio 1996; Alvarez and Garcia Bedolla 2003; Abrajano and Alvarez 2010.

[142] Wong et al. 2011; Alvarez and Garcia Bedolla 2003; Hajnal and Lee 2011.

[143] Schildkraut 2010; Hainmueller and Hiscox 2010; Ha and Oliver 2010; Kinder and Kam 2009; Brader, Valentino, and Suhay 2008; Pettigrew et al. 2007; Campbell, Wong, and Citrin 2006; Scheve and Slaughter 2001; Quillian 1995; Citrin et al. 1997.

[144] For exceptions that examine the link between immigration and welfare, see Fox 2004; Hero and Preuhs 2006. For a look at the relationship between immigration politics and white partisanship in California, see Bowler, Nicholson, and Segura 2006.

[145] McCarty et al. 2006; Miller and Shanks 1996; Alvarez and Nagler 1995, 1998.

[146] Lewis-Beck, Tien, and Nadeau 2010; Valentino and Sears 2005; Abramowitz 1994; Carmines and Stimson 1989.

between immigration and white partisanship across the nation.[147] Despite immigration's tremendous impact on the demographics of the nation along with the large-scale social, economic, and racial change that has ensued, there is little direct evidence that immigration has had an enduring impact on the basic political decisions of the white majority. Comparative studies in Europe have identified clear links between the size of the national immigrant population and support for right-wing parties.[148] But the same has not been done in the United States. Ultimately, compelling evidence is missing that immigration is a core element of US politics.

This all means that more research needs to be done. There is, we would argue, every reason to expect that immigration will have a broad partisan impact on the politics of white America. Yet there is little to no available study of that impact. In the pages that follow, we seek to provide systematic, empirical evidence that assesses the broader political consequences of immigration.

---

[147] An experimental study conducted by Craig and Richeson (2014), however, shows the relationship between racial demographic change and whites' ideological preferences.

[148] Arzheimer 2009; Lubbers, Gijsberts, and Scheepers 2002.

PART II

Views on Immigration and Defection
to the Republican Party

Chapter 2

Immigration, Latinos, and the Transformation of White Partisanship

with Michael Rivera

The people who are coming across the border—as far as I'm concerned, they are common criminals.

—*Bill Storey, sixty-eight, retired civil engineer from Greenville, SC*

What we need to do is put them [unauthorized immigrants] on a bus.

—*Ken Sowell, sixty-three, lawyer from Greenville, SC*

S torey and Sowell are far from alone in expressing concerns about immigration. As we have already seen, systematic public opinion surveys indicate that large segments of the US public articulate deep reservations about a range of different aspects of immigration. Up to two-thirds of all Americans think immigration is a "serious problem," and a little over half feel that undocumented immigrants are "mostly a drain on American society."[1] In response, 80 percent of Americans favor more border enforcement agents, 60 percent would allow "police to question anyone who they think may be in the coun-

[1] Univision 2010 poll, cited in Polling Report 2014.

try illegally," half favor building a fence along the entire length of the Mexican border to limit immigration, and a little over a third would revise the US Constitution to prevent children of undocumented immigrants from automatically becoming citizens.[2] Moreover, among whites, opposition to almost every aspect of immigration is higher than these nationwide figures suggest. In short, it is apparent that immigration looms large in the minds of many white Americans. For these individuals, there is real fear and anxiety about what immigration and immigrants are doing to the United States. The Republican Party along with its policies of exclusion, punishment, and retrenchment should be an attractive option for these uneasy Americans.

But do sentiments about immigration really drive the politics of large numbers of white Americans? Are concerns about immigration sharp, widespread, and politically relevant enough to shift appreciable segments of the white public to the right on the most profound political decisions they make—their party affiliation and votes?

Although we contend that immigration is central to the politics of white Americans, we readily admit that there are reasons to suspect otherwise. First, as we have already documented, many segments of the white population hold positive or at worst ambiguous views of the immigrant population. CNN reports, for instance, that some 33 percent of Americans claim to be "somewhat" or "very sympathetic" to undocumented immigrants and their families, and a *New York Times* poll found that a third believe that "America should always welcome all immigrants."[3] Second, despite relatively widespread concern about immigration, it usually does not rank as the most significant problem confronting the nation. Figures vary, but generally less than 10 percent of white Americans place immigration as the single most important issue facing the country. Finally, and most crucial, even when immigration does generate intense feelings, it may still not be enough to lead to substantial shifts in partisan attachments. For many in political science, party identification is the unmoved mover—a remarkably durable and impressively potent element in US politics.[4] From this perspective, Democrats and Republicans are defining identities in the political realm that shape everything else from one's issue positions to candidate preferences. The party that we are socialized into as children or young adults is the one that we are likely to remain attached to for the rest of our life. Can immigration really affect large-scale change on this near-permanent substructure of US politics?

---

[2] CNN 2012 poll, cited in Polling Report 2014.
[3] CNN 2011 and *New York Times* 2010 polls, cited in Polling Report 2014.
[4] Campbell et al. 1960; Green, Palmquist, and Schickler 2002.

Tying Immigration to Partisanship: A First Step

Demonstrating the role that immigration plays in shaping partisanship and other political orientations will be a multistep process. Yet we begin with the simplest, most direct, and at least for some, most convincing test. We show that how we think about immigrants is strongly correlated with how we think about the parties.

That task starts by considering how we should measure our attitudes about immigration. Defining and operationalizing attitudes toward immigration is not straightforward. It is complicated by the fact that we do not yet really know who or what it is that white Americans are reacting to. Are they most concerned about undocumented immigrants, or do their fears extend to the entire immigrant population? Likewise, are anxieties more focused on the growing Latino population, or does the disquiet that Americans feel about immigration also stem from the growing number of Asian Americans? The alarm, alternatively, may be linked to a specific national origin group such as Mexican Americans.

In theory, categories like undocumented, legal, Latino, and Mexican American are all distinct. But as we noted earlier, in the practice and rhetoric of US politics, these categories largely overlap with one another. When politicians talk about immigrants, their discussions seem to highlight concerns about undocumented migrants, and whether the conversation is explicitly about legal or undocumented immigrations, the accompanying images are generally of Latinos and Mexican Americans.[5] Similarly, when members of the US public think about immigration, they are likely to have a picture of a Latino or Mexican American coupled an impression that they are in this country without legal documentation.[6] In the minds of many white Americans, these different categories simply blur together.

In light of these muddled categories, we will incorporate a series of different measures of immigrant views to try to get a clearer sense of which group most troubles white Americans. But since public opinion surveys are clear on one point—Americans express the most negative sentiments to undocumented immigrants—we begin by concentrating on attitudes toward them.

We turn to the ANES—the standard tool of US survey research on politics—and 2008, because it is relatively recent and more critically

[5] Pérez, forthcoming; Chavez 2008.
[6] Pérez 2010.

because it contains a fine array of questions on undocumented immigrants—a stipulation that rules out most other years covered by the ANES. Specifically, the survey asks white Americans four questions that explicitly address this segment of the immigration population: a standard feeling thermometer that asks how one feels about "illegal immigrants" and ranges from zero (meaning extremely cold or negative feelings) to one hundred (for extremely warm or positive feelings); "Should controlling and reducing illegal immigration be a very important [or] . . . not an important foreign policy goal?"; "Do you favor/oppose the US government making it possible for illegal immigrants to become US citizens?"; and "Do you favor, oppose, or neither favor nor oppose allowing illegal immigrants to work in the United States for up to three years, after which they would have to go back to their home country?"

To reduce error in measurement and get an overall measure of attitudes toward undocumented immigration, we combine the four questions and create an alpha factor score for each respondent. The scale ranges from -2.8 to 1.7, with higher values representing more positive views of immigration. The four items cohere well with a scale reliability of 0.70 and an average inter-item correlation of 0.36. In practice, it matters little how we combine these questions, or whether we look at a subset of these questions or just one of these questions.[7] A simple additive scale performs likewise in the analysis that follows. Also, in alternate tests when we substitute each single question or combinations of two or three of these questions, the pattern of results is similar.

Our main measure of partisanship is the standard seven-point party identification scale. Respondents place themselves on a scale that ranges from strongly Democratic (one) to strongly Republican (seven). To assess the robustness of our results, in alternate tests we also direct our attention to party feeling thermometers, dummy variables isolating Democratic and Republican identifiers, and unordered party identification models (utilizing multinomial logistic regressions).

Figures 2.1–2.2 show a simple bivariate relationship between feelings, or affect, toward undocumented immigrants and two different measures of partisan attachments: Democratic and Republican

---

[7] The consistency across alternative specifications is important as each of these different questions taps into different aspects of the debate over undocumented immigration. Many would argue, for example, that support for a guest worker program that could condemn workers to permanent second-class status is not in fact proimmigrant and should be viewed quite differently than support for large-scale legalization.

A

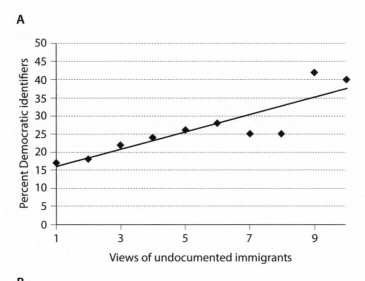

B

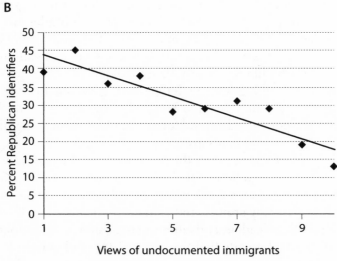

Figure 2.1 Immigrant Views and Partisan Choice: (a) Democratic and (b) Republican

Party identification.[8] The idea is to see whether a plausible connection exists between views of undocumented immigrants and partisan attachments.

As the patterns from these figures illustrate, how whites think about undocumented immigrants is linked significantly and substantially to their attachments to the Democratic and Republican parties.

---

[8] For the figures, we divide respondents into ten evenly split groups based on their views on the undocumented immigration scale.

What is impressive is not that there is a correlation but rather the magnitude of it. Fully 45 percent of those whites who have more negative views toward undocumented immigrants identify as Republicans. In contrast, only 13 percent of whites who feel more warmth toward undocumented immigrants choose to align with the Republican Party. Similarly, as white attitudes shift from less to more negative to more positive views of undocumented immigrants, the probability of identifying as a Democrat increases from 17 to 40 percent. The relationship between views on immigration and partisanship is also pronounced if we focus on feeling thermometers for the Democratic and Republican parties.[9]

The figures above suggest a close connection between attitudes on immigration and partisanship.[10] But before we make stronger causal claims about that relationship, we need to consider two possibilities. First, it is possible that the correlation between views on immigration and partisanship is spurious. It may be that attitudes on immigration are correlated with party identification only because attitudes on immigration are correlated with some other factor that is itself driving our partisan attachments. On this point, there are several possibilities. The culprit could be liberal-conservative ideology, or more specific issue positions on anything from preferences on government's role in the economy to social morality and race. The way to deal with this concern is to incorporate and control for all the other main factors that have been known to shape partisanship.

Second, we must also consider the possibility that the reason party identification and immigration-related views are correlated is because our partisan attachments are propelling our attitudes on immigration rather than the other way around. Individual Americans could be taking cues from partisan leaders, and adjusting their stances on immigration to match those of a party that they know, trust, and believe in. If

[9] As affect toward undocumented immigrants goes from cold to warm, the average level of affect toward the Democratic Party increases by more than twenty points on the zero to one hundred scale. Feelings about undocumented immigrants, however, do not have as substantial of an effect on white Americans' affect toward the Republicans. Going from the most positive to the most negative feelings toward immigrants shifts feelings about the Republican Party by approximately ten points on the zero to one hundred scale.

[10] Pew Research Center (2012, 86–88) data reveal a similarly strong connection between immigration and partisanship. This poll shows that immigration is now one of the issues that most distinguishes Democrats from Republicans. Six in ten Republicans feel that "newcomers threaten traditional American custom and values" compared to just 39 percent of Democrats. Likewise, most Republicans (55 percent) state, "It bothers me when I come in contact with immigrants who speak little or no English," while the majority of Democrats say it doesn't bother them (69 percent).

party identification is the unmoved mover that many claim, individual perspectives on immigration could easily be swayed by elite partisan influences.[11]

To help address this second concern, we perform a series of different tests. In this chapter, we offer two direct tests of the causal story. We will employ individual-level panel data to determine if individual positions on immigration at one point in time help to shape future changes in individual partisanship. And we examine the aggregate level to see if the public's views of immigration at one point in time predict subsequent changes in aggregate partisanship.

Then in the next chapter, we move on to focus on the vote. Assessments of the vote are critical because we can evaluate the impact of immigration views *after* controlling for party identification. In other words, we can see if attitudes toward immigrants have a relationship with the vote that goes beyond partisanship. In related tests, we also assess the effects of immigrant-related views on the vote separately for Democrats, Independents, and Republicans, and explore the role of views on immigration in party primaries. The goal once again is to try to demonstrate that immigration matters when party does not. We now turn to this range of tests.

A More Comprehensive Model of Partisanship

Before we can offer confident conclusions about the importance of immigrant-related views on US politics, our analysis needs to incorporate a range of other factors that have been shown to influence core decisions like party identification and the vote. Thus, in table 2.1, we display a series of regressions that control for numerous factors from sociodemographic characteristics to issue positions, ideological views, and racial attitudes—all purportedly central to partisan choice in the United States. Each model is an ordinary least squares (OLS) regression with the standard seven-point party identification scale as the dependent variable.[12]

We start with a basic model (model 1) that includes a traditional set of socioeconomic characteristics and other demographic variables. Given claims about class- and religious-based support for each party, we include conventional markers of class (education, income, em-

---

[11] Campbell et al. 1960.
[12] Ordered logit regressions lead to the same conclusions.

TABLE 2.1
Views on Immigration and White Partisanship

	Party identification (high = strong Republican)			
	Model 1	Model 2	Model 3	Model 4
Immigration				
Positive views toward undocumented immigrants	−0.61 (0.09)**	−0.24 (0.09)**	−0.22 (0.09)*	−0.19 (0.09)*
Demographics				
Education	−0.01 (0.03)	0.02 (0.03)	0.01 (0.03)	0.01 (0.03)
Income	0.04 (0.01)**	0.03 (0.01)**	0.03 (0.01)**	0.03 (0.01)**
Unemployed	0.16 (0.33)	0.22 (0.29)	0.25 (0.29)	0.29 (0.29)
Age	−0.08 (0.04)*	−0.05 (0.03)	−0.03 (0.03)	−0.07 (0.04)
Female	−0.20 (0.14)	0.06 (0.12)	0.04 (0.12)	0.03 (0.12)
Married	0.57 (0.14)*	0.14 (0.12)	0.14 (0.11)	0.16 (0.12)
Union member	−0.53 (0.21)*	−0.51 (0.16)**	−0.52 (0.17)**	−0.54 (0.17)**
Jewish	−1.30 (0.52)*	−0.23 (0.42)	−0.14 (0.42)	−0.31 (0.42)
Catholic	0.16 (0.18)	−0.09 (0.16)	−0.05 (0.16)	−0.11 (0.16)
Protestant	0.80 (0.16)	0.17 (0.14)	0.21 (0.14)	0.11 (0.14)
Ideology				
Conservative		0.62 (0.05)**	0.60 (0.05)**	0.61 (0.05)**
Issue positions				
War and terrorism				
Expand war on terror		0.02 (0.03)	0.02 (0.03)	0.02 (0.03)
Support war in Iraq		−0.02 (0.04)	−0.02 (0.04)	−0.02 (0.04)
Support war in Afghanistan		−0.08 (0.04)*	−0.08 (0.04)*	−0.08 (0.04)*
Economy/retrospective				
Economy improving		−0.10 (0.09)	−0.09 (0.09)	−0.10 (0.09)
Approve president		−0.43 (0.05)	−0.42 (0.05)	−0.43 (0.05)
Redistribution				
Favor higher taxes on rich		−0.14 (0.06)*	−0.12 (0.06)*	−0.15 (0.09)*
Increase welfare spending		−0.01 (0.03)	−0.02 (0.03)	−0.01 (0.03)
Morality/religion				
Favor gay rights		−0.05 (0.04)	−0.06 (0.04)	−0.05 (0.04)
Religion important		0.05 (0.03)	0.06 (0.03)	0.06 (0.03)
Racial resentment to blacks				
Blacks deserve less			0.17 (0.07)*	
Blacks get special favors			0.12 (0.06)*	
Little discrimination			−0.02 (0.06)	
Blacks should try harder			0.03 (0.06)	
Other racial considerations				
Warmth toward blacks				−0.81 (0.52)
Warmth toward Asians				1.18 (0.52)*
Warmth toward whites				0.59 (0.43)
Constant	4.39 (0.50)**	3.36 (0.69)**	2.46 (0.74)**	3.36 (0.69)**
N	803	581	578	569
Adjusted R^2	0.12	0.60	0.61	0.61

*p < 0.05
**p < 0.01

Note: Entries not in parentheses are OLS coefficients and entries in parentheses denote the corresponding standard errors.

Source: ANES 2008.

70

ployment status, and union membership) and a series of dummy variables measuring religious affiliation.[13]

Model 1 suggests that many of these measures are crucial for partisanship, but more important, it shows that net basic demographic controls, attitudes toward undocumented immigration are closely linked to partisan attachments. The estimates indicate that all else being equal, non-Hispanic whites who have more negative feelings toward undocumented immigrants are just over one point more Republican on the seven-point party identification scale than are whites with less negative views.[14] Given that a one-point shift equals the difference between a strong versus weak Democrat, immigrant views have the potential to reshape US politics.[15]

Political choices in the United States are obviously about much more than immigration. In recent years, the two parties have squared off over the United States' ongoing economic recession, wars in Iraq and Afghanistan, and enduring terrorist threat facing the nation.[16] Also, few would contest the relevance of moral values issues like gay rights and abortion in explaining the partisan divide.[17] In addition, the core ideological dimension—liberalism versus conservatism—undoubtedly helps to shape partisan choice. Lastly, research on US partisanship regularly highlights the role of retrospective evaluations of the president and economy.[18] As such, if we want to show that the relationship we see between immigration and party identification is not spurious, we have to incorporate these other factors.

In model 2, we do exactly that. We specifically include measures for *basic ideology*—the standard seven-point liberal-conservative self-placement scale (from "extremely liberal" to "extremely conservative"); *war, terrorism, and security*—"Do you approve/disapprove of the way the US federal government has handled the war in Afghanistan?" "Do you approve/disapprove of the way the US federal government

[13] McCarty et al. 2006; Adams 1997; Layman and Carmines 1997.

[14] These estimates are based on a one standard deviation shift in views on immigration—a practice we follow throughout the rest of the book for estimating the magnitude of effects.

[15] We attempted to assess variation in the effects of immigration across different kinds of individuals. One might expect immigration to be especially threatening for the less well educated, those who are racially intolerant, or those who face more direct economic competition with low-skilled immigrants. Our tests revealed few clear and consistent interaction effects between immigration perspectives and any of these different individual characteristics. We did find significant variation in the effects of immigration across different geographic contexts, though. As we will detail in chapters 4 and 6, the level of immigration one faces greatly shapes how individuals react to immigration.

[16] Abramson et al. 2007.

[17] Adams 1997; Layman and Carmines 1997.

[18] Fiorina 1981; MacKuen, Erikson, and Stimson 1989.

has handled the war in Iraq?" and "Should federal spending on the war on terrorism be increased, decreased, or kept about the same?"; *the economy and retrospective evaluations*—"Do you approve/disapprove of the way George W. Bush is handling his job as president?" and "Would you say that over the past year the nation's economy has gotten better, stayed about the same, or gotten worse?"; *redistribution*—"People who make more money should pay a larger percent of their income in taxes to the government than people who make less money" and "Should federal spending on the welfare be increased, decreased, or kept about the same?"; *morality and religion*—"Do you strongly favor [or] . . . strongly oppose laws to protect homosexuals against job discrimination" and "Is religion an important part of your life?"

What we find confirms much of what we know about US politics. Most of these issues, the basic ideological orientation, and retrospective evaluations greatly influence which party individual Americans choose to support. What is striking, however, is that the inclusion of all these different elements of US politics does not eliminate the impact of immigration. Views of undocumented immigrants still significantly shape white partisanship after controlling for a range of measures of issues, ideology, and retrospective evaluations.

Moreover, alternate tests indicate that it matters little which issues we include, or how we measure issues, ideology, and retrospective evaluations. When policy questions on health care, crime, foreign aid, schools, women's rights, the environment, and science are added to the model, the impact of immigrant-related views on partisan attachments is largely unaffected.[19] Further, immigrant-related views remain significant when we substitute in alternate measures of economic policy preferences or retrospective evaluations. Regardless of one's opinions on the economy, war, abortion, and other factors, views of undocumented immigrants are strongly associated with being a Republican.

Immigrants/Latinos or Blacks
and Ethnocentrism?

One element of US politics that we have largely ignored to this point is the black-white divide. When race has mattered in US national elections, the main issue has usually been the rights and interests of Afri-

---

[19] These "other issues" are not included in the main model because they are only asked of half of the respondents.

can Americans.[20] Especially in 2008, with Obama, the nation's first black presidential nominee, on the ballot and evidence that racial resentment played a role in the white vote, these kinds of racial attitudes need to be integrated into the analysis.[21] Thus, in model 3, we add four different questions from the racial resentment scale that have been developed by Donald Kinder and Lynn Sanders and are included in most biannual editions of the ANES.[22] All four measures explicitly ask about attitudes toward African Americans, and combined, they have been shown to play a critical role in white public opinion.[23]

The results in model 3 indicate that the black-white divide remains significant in shaping white partisanship. Whites who are more racially resentful of blacks are, all else being equal, 1.1 points more Republican on the party identification scale than are whites who are less resentful of blacks.[24] But the results also suggest that immigration represents a distinct dimension that helps to shape white partisan ties. Even after considering the effects of racial resentment toward blacks, those who have more negative views of undocumented immigrants continue to be significantly more apt to identify as Republican.[25]

The ongoing significant of views on immigration indicate that attitudes on immigration are not merely proxies for racial attitudes. We can test this more directly by looking at the correlation between white attitudes toward African Americans and their attitudes toward Latinos

---

[20] Klinkner and Smith 1999; Carmines and Stimson 1989; Key 1949.

[21] Lewis-Beck, Tien, and Nadeau 2010; Bobo and Dawson 2009; Tesler and Sears 2010. See also Ansolabehere and Stewart 2009.

[22] Kinder and Sanders 1996.

[23] Ibid. The four standard racial resentment questions are: "It's really a matter of some people not trying hard enough; if blacks would only try harder they could be just as well off as whites"; "Irish, Italian, Jewish and many other minorities overcame prejudice and worked their way up. Blacks should do the same without special favors"; "Over the past few years, blacks have gotten less than they deserve"; and "Generations of slavery and discrimination have created conditions that make it difficult for blacks to work their way out of the lower class." In each case, respondents were asked whether they agreed or disagreed with the statement, and how strongly. According to Kinder and Sanders (1996), these four questions all focus on the central element of US race relations: the extent to which blacks face barriers in US society.

[24] When we replaced the four different racial resentment questions with an additive racial resentment scale or racial resentment alpha factor scale, the basic pattern of results did not change.

[25] Given the historical significance of Obama's candidacy in 2008, in alternate tests we also controlled for feelings about African American candidates. Specifically, we included the following three measures: Does the idea of black person being president make you feel uncomfortable?; Do you think most white candidates who run for political office are better suited to be an elected official than most black candidates?; and, Do you think most white candidates are better suited in terms of their intelligence than most black candidates? Being uncomfortable with a black person as president was closely tied to partisanship, but the inclusion of these measures did not affect the impact of immigration on white partisanship.

and immigration. Looking across these two types of question in the 2008 ANES, it is apparent that the attitudes toward the two groups are related yet also distinct. Feelings toward blacks are often significantly correlated with measures of attitudes toward immigrants and Latinos, but the correlations are typically well below the average 0.31 inter-item correlation that exists within all the questions on immigrants and Latinos. Immigration appears to be a new, distinct, and highly relevant dimension of US politics.

In our final regression analysis, captured by model 4, we further investigate the role of race along with the possibility that immigrant-related perspectives stand in for some deeper aspect of US racial dynamics like racial prejudice or ethnocentrism.[26] We incorporate whites' views of African Americans, white Americans, and Asian Americans.[27] Specifically, we use a basic feeling thermometer toward each group.[28] Despite the inclusion of feelings toward the three different racial groups in the model, we still find that immigrant-related views are important for white partisanship. Whites with the most negative views of undocumented immigrants are one-third of a point higher on the seven-point party identification scale than are whites with the most positive views of undocumented immigrants. The incorporation of traditional measures of stereotypes and ethnocentrism cannot wholly reduce the impact of immigration on US politics.

One other interesting result emerges when we incorporate attitudes toward other racial and ethnic groups. There is some suggestion that whites react differently to Asian Americans than they do to undocumented immigrants. In contrast to what we see with attitudes toward immigrants, whites who hold more positive views of Asian Americans are more likely to identify as Republicans. The estimated difference between those with positive views of Asian Americans and those with negative ones is roughly half a point on the party identification scale.

There are, as we noted earlier, a range of reasons why white Americans make distinctions between Asian Americans and Latinos. There are fewer Asian Americans in the United States without legal status, relative to Latinos. Socioeconomically, Asian Americans tend to fall much closer to whites than to Latinos. They have also been less clearly

---

[26] Kam and Kinder 2012; Kinder and Kam 2009; Brader, Valentino, and Suhay 2008; Burns and Gimpel 2000.

[27] Since we believe that attitudes toward immigrants and Latinos are closely linked, we do not include a Latino feeling thermometer in the basic model.

[28] The feeling thermometer ranges from zero to one hundred. The end points are labeled with zero, indicating cool feelings toward the group in question, and one hundred, indicating warmth for the group.

aligned with the Democratic Party than Latinos.[29] Stereotypes of the two groups differ dramatically as well. Almost half of all whites see Latinos as "less intelligent" and "more welfare prone," but only about 10 percent of whites feel the same way about Asian Americans.[30] By contrast, whites tend to view Asian Americans as particularly intelligent and especially diligent.[31] It may be that the stereotype of successful, hardworking Asian Americans resonates with the individualism that runs at the core of the Republican philosophy. Thus, those who feel warmly toward Asian Americans may also tend to identify with the Republican Party. Whatever the reason, Asian Americans do not evoke the same kinds of partisan reactions as undocumented immigrants do.

While these divergent effects for Asian Americans may be surprising to some, our results parallel what others have found in the literature on contextual effects. Proximity to Asian Americans has often had the opposite effect as proximity to Latinos or blacks.[32] Although firm conclusions about the root of this divergent reaction require further investigation, it seems clear that Asian Americans hold a unique place within the dynamics of US racial politics. In short, race and partisanship are tied together in complex as well as important ways.

Robustness Checks

To help ensure that the results in table 2.1 measure the underlying relationships between immigration-related views and white partisan choices, we performed a series of additional tests. First, we repeated the tests in table 2.1 with a range of different measures of immigrants and Latinos. When we replaced our main measure of immigrant attitudes with a measure of feelings toward Latinos (a Hispanic feeling thermometer), a measure of feelings toward legal immigration (Should immigration levels be increased or decreased?), and a simpler measure of feelings toward undocumented immigrants (an undocumented immigrant feeling thermometer), all were significant in most of the regression models. Regardless of how we measure attitudes toward immigrants or Latinos, these attitudes are closely connected to party identification.

Second, we also assessed different party-based dependent variables. That is, instead of relying on the standard seven-point party identification scale, we used feeling thermometers toward each party,

---

[29] Hajnal and Lee 2011.
[30] Bobo 2001.
[31] Lee 2001; Bobo et al. 2000.
[32] Ha and Oliver 2010; Hood and Morris 1998; Hero and Preuhs 2006.

a dummy variable for Republican identity, a dummy variable for Democratic identity, and an unordered three-point party identification scale.[33] Views toward undocumented immigrants in each case remained statistically significant and the effects were generally substantial. For example, all else being equal, those with more positive views of immigrants were six points to the right on the Democratic Party feeling thermometer than those with more negative stances. These alternative specifications suggest that regardless of how partisanship is measured, it appears to be closely linked to perspectives on immigration.

We realize that if we want to make a more general statement about US politics, however, we need to assess the role of immigration-related views across a wider range of data sets, years, and contexts. To do this, we repeated as much of the analysis as possible with a number of different data sets. That process began with the 2010 Evaluations of Government and Survey, a survey that replaced the ANES series in 2010. The 2010 evaluations closely mirrored the results we present here. After controlling for a similar set of electoral factors, whites who felt that "immigration was a burden" were significantly and substantially more apt to identify as Republican, as opposed to Democrat. Using the 2000 and 2004 National Annenberg Election Surveys (NAES), we examined the link between party identification and immigrant-related views (Should the federal government do more to restrict immigration, and is immigration a serious problem?) in 2000 and 2004. Once again, attitudes on immigration proved to be a robust and significant factor predicting white party identification. We then repeated the analysis with the 2010 and 2012 Cooperative Congressional Election Survey (CCES).[34] Results from these large, Internet-based surveys demonstrate that there is an ongoing robust relationship between views on immigration and white partisanship. The General Social Survey (GSS) cumulative file provided us yet another opportunity to reexamine the link between immigration and partisan choice. The GSS only includes viewpoints on immigration and partisan choice in a select number of years. Furthermore, in any given year it has a much more limited set of political covariates. Nevertheless, in 2004, 2000, and 1996, we were able to assess the impact of immigration on partisan-

---

[33] For the latter variable, we estimate the model using multinomial logit analysis, given the unordered nature of this variable.

[34] The CCES has three immigration-related questions. The analysis is robust to using an alpha factor score of the three questions or simply inserting a question about increasing border patrols.

ship and in each case found a significant relationship. Whites who felt that immigration is a "cost to Americans" (2004), those who felt "bilingual education should be abolished" (2000), and those who believe it is "important to be born in America" (1996) were significantly linked to a Republican Party identification.[35]

The fact that views on Latinos and immigration mattered across different data sets, different elections, different measures of immigration-related views, different methods of measuring partisanship, and different sets of control variables greatly increases our confidence in the role that Latinos and immigration play in white partisan politics.[36]

Addressing Causality

One concern with the analysis that we have presented to this point is the potential of reverse causation. It is possible that party identification may impact rather than be impacted by immigrant-related views. Indeed, much of the literature in US politics suggests that party identification stands near the beginning of a funnel of causality that drives factors like issue positions and the vote.[37] From this perspective, party identification is a "durable attachment not readily disturbed by passing events and personalities."[38] We generally do not dispute that contention. There is little doubt that party identification is among the most stable elements of US politics.[39]

But none of this rules out the possibility of issue-based change in party loyalties. There is, in fact, little doubt that partisanship can and does shift.[40] Although few dispute the deep childhood origins of partisanship, there is a second well-supported account of partisanship that sees it at least in part as a product of issue positions and experiences.[41]

---

[35] For all these results, see the online appendix at http://pages.ucsd.edu/~zhajnal/styled/index.html.

[36] We also performed a series of tests in which we added a range of different individual characteristics into our model. Specifically, we delved deeper into religious attachments (the frequency of church attendance and whether the respondent identified as born again), class ties (self-identified class position), and mobility (years in current residence). As well, given that region and race have at times been intricately linked at different points in US history, we included controls for region. These additional controls did little to affect the results.

[37] Campbell et al. 1960; Layman and Carsey 2002; Bartels 2002; Miller and Shanks 1996.

[38] Campbell et al. 1960, 51.

[39] Green, Palmquist, and Schickler 2002.

[40] Erikson, MacKuen, and Stimson 2002; Niemi and Jennings 1991.

[41] Downs 1957; Fiorina 1981; Achen 2002.

Indeed, there is irrefutable evidence that partisanship changes and slowly aligns with issue positions over the course of one's lifetime.[42] There are also signs that in recent decades, policy preferences have become more consequential in shaping partisanship.[43] Ultimately, few would dispute the notion that issue positions and partisanship can and do influence each other under certain circumstances.[44]

Along with others, we believe that race and by extension immigration is one of those cases where issue attitudes can be consequential.[45] Race and immigration are not like other issues. They are relatively simple, symbolic, and emotional ones.[46] Moreover, both are closely linked to core psychological predispositions like ethnocentrism and authoritarianism.[47] As such, attitudes on immigration and race are likely to be particularly stable as well as influential for the US public. Ultimately, we suggest that deep-seated attitudes on immigration and race can shift the partisan leaning of some members of the population.

Assertions and logic aside, we have to stake our case on hard empirical evidence. For our first causality test, we focus on the most recent ANES panel. The basic idea is to determine if past views on immigration predict current partisanship net the effects of past partisanship. In other words, do past views on immigration help predict future changes in party identification? As the estimates presented in table 2.2 illustrate, there is a clear, temporal link between immigrant views and partisanship. Views on immigration (measured by a question about whether undocumented immigrants should be given a chance to become citizens) in 2008 have a significant effect on party identification measured in 2009 after controlling for party identification measured in 2008. Or to put it another way, individuals with anti-immigrants views in 2008 were more likely than individuals with pro-immigrant views to move their party identification toward the Republican Party. The causal link between immigrant-related views on partisanship even persists when we control for a range of other major issues typically linked to partisanship.[48]

---

[42] Niemi and Jennings 1991.

[43] Highton and Kam 2011; Carmines and Stimson 1989; Nie, Verba, and Petrocik 1979.

[44] Carsey and Layman 2006; Dancey and Goren 2010; Fiorina 1981; Page and Jones 1979; Markus and Converse 1979.

[45] Attitudes on race have been shown to affect partisanship in various ways (Carmines and Stimson 1989; but see Abramowitz 1994).

[46] Carmines and Stimson 1980.

[47] Kinder and Kam 2010; Schildkraut 2005.

[48] For estimates, see the online appendix at http://pages.ucsd.edu/~zhajnal/styled/index.html.

TABLE 2.2
Assessing Causality: Immigration's Temporal Impact on
Party Identification in 2009

Party identification, 2008 (high = Republican)	0.89 (0.01)**
Views on undocumented immigrants, 2008 (high = pro-immigration)	–0.03 (0.01)*
Constant	0.21 (0.06)**
N	1,171
F	2,603**

Small... for 1 year margin...

*p < 0.05
**p < 0.01
Source: ANES 2008.

The size of the effects, although not dramatic, is large enough to play some part in the aggregate shift of white Americans to the Republican Party. After controlling for past partisanship, a one standard deviation shift in views of undocumented immigrants is associated with about a one-quarter-point shift on the seven-point party identification scale. Attitudes on immigration are not leading to a wholesale shift from strong Democrat to strong Republican over the course of a year, but feelings about immigrants do appear to be leading to some real changes in partisanship.[49] Just as Carmines and Stimson have argued about resentment toward blacks as well as Adams has contended on the issue of abortion, we suggest that these small shifts could accumulate over time to help account for the large-scale partisan changes that we see in recent decades.[50] Small changes at the microlevel can be associated with considerable shifts in the aggregate, as Robert Erikson and his colleagues have shown.[51]

Importantly, our findings about the causal relationship between views of immigration and party identification persist when we look at other panel data. Immigration continues to shape partisanship if we instead perform the Granger causality test on the other two recent ANES panels from 2000–2004 and 1992–93.[52]

---

[49] It also is important to note that by the same test, party identification does cause changes in immigrant-related views. The relationship between party identification and immigrant-related views is reciprocal.

[50] Carmines and Stimson 1989; Adams 1997.

[51] Erikson, MacKuen, and Stimson 2002.

[52] For estimates, see the online appendix at http://pages.ucsd.edu/~zhajnal/styled/index.html.

The Transformation of White Partisanship over Time

Time is a key element underlining our story about immigration. Each of the different factors tying immigration to partisanship is increasing over time. There is an increase over time in the number of immigrants, the salience of immigration, the divide between Democratic and Republican elites on the issue of immigration, and the association of the Democratic Party with Latino voters. If all this represents a threat pushing white Americans to the right politically, then we should find a slow but reasonably steady shift in white party identification over time. That is exactly what we see in figure 2.2, which presents white partisan ties from 1950 to 2008. Crucially, we focus only on non-Hispanic whites—a restriction that greatly impacts the trend that emerges. The data are from the ANES cumulative data file, and report the proportion of all non-Hispanic white respondents that identify as Democrats and as Republicans over time.[53]

Between 1952 and 2008, there is a slow, steady, and ultimately massive shift in white partisan attachments. In the 1950s, Democrats dominated the white population. Almost half of all white Americans identified as Democrats compared to a little less than 30 percent who identified as Republicans. But that margin declines slowly over time to the point where in the twenty-first century, white Republicans sub-stantially outnumber white Democrats. This is, by any estimation, a remarkable and important change in the core contours of US political identity.

Much has been made of the defection of whites from the Democratic to Republican Party in the 1960s and 1970s in response to the civil rights movement, Republican Southern strategy, and growing participation of blacks in the Democratic Party.[54] Whether or not one believes that racial resentment toward blacks was responsible for the white exodus from the Democratic Party during this early period, that era of change has been well documented.

What is new here is that the shift in white partisanship continues to occur well after the waning of the civil rights movement.[55] There

---

[53] In figure 2.2, leaners are not included with partisans. The same trend is evident if we include leaners.

[54] Carmines and Stimson 1989; Hood, Kidd, and Morris 2012; Black and Black 2002. But see Abramowitz 1994; Shafer and Johnston 2005; Lublin 2004.

[55] Not surprisingly, given the magnitude of the change, we find the same pattern when we analyze the GSS cumulative file or Gallup poll series. In all three of these time series, after 1980 there is a dramatic defection of whites from the Democratic to Republican Party.

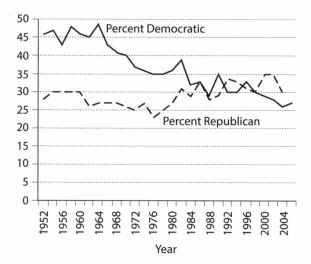

Figure 2.2 White Partisanship over Time
Source: ANES 2010.

is a sharp turn to the Republican Party even after 1980.[56] In 1980, according to the ANES, white Democratic identifiers dominated white Republican identifiers (39 versus 28 percent). But that Democratic advantage has been totally reversed over the ensuing thirty years. By 2010, white Republicans greatly outnumbered white Democrats (36 versus 29 percent)—a remarkably large and largely overlooked shift.[57] And while Obama's candidacy seemed to stem that tide for a period of time, in recent years the Republican advantage among whites appears to be growing. Pew Research Center reports that by 2012, the Republican advantage among whites had grown to 13 percentage points.[58]

---

[56] It is difficult to imagine that attitudes toward blacks are driving the more recent changes in white partisanship. By 1980, black voter registration and participation in the Democratic Party had peaked, and by most accounts, the centrality of African Americans and debates over pro-black policies in the politics of the United States was declining (Abramowitz 1994). Until an African American ran on the ballot in 2008, many thought that whites' attitudes toward blacks had become largely irrelevant (Abramowitz 1994; Miller and Shanks 1996; Sniderman and Carmines 1997; but see Valentino and Sears 2005).

[57] The same reversal occurs over the same period for the white vote. In the 1980s, Democratic congressional candidates dominated the white vote, but by 2010 Republicans won 56 percent of the white vote.

[58] This ongoing shift in white partisanship is generally overlooked because racial and ethnic minorities have grown in number, and have tended to align with the Democratic Party. If we look at everyone in the nation, Democrats are not losing to Republicans. In fact, when non-whites are included in the trend analysis, the Democratic advantage has only partially been eroded since 1980.

This kind of massive partisan shift is significant, but does it have anything to do with immigration? Given a limited number of years along with an almost-endless array of events and issues that could be responsible for shifts in white partisanship over time, a comprehensive test of immigration's role is close to impossible. Nevertheless, we can offer a preliminary test that gets a little closer to the causal link between attitudes on immigration and shifts in aggregate white partisanship. Specifically, we look to see if aggregate views on immigration at one point in time predict changes in white macropartisanship in subsequent periods.

To do so, we combine data from the two different data sets that most regularly ask about attitudes on immigration (Gallup poll) and partisanship (CBS/*New York Times* poll). To measure views on immigration, we use the question, "Should immigration be kept at its present level, increased, or decreased?" Gallup has asked this question twenty-one times between 1993 and 2011. To get an aggregate opinion, we subtract the portion that favors an increase from the portion that favors a decrease. Thus, higher values represent more support for immigration. We utilize the CBS/*New York Times* standard five-point party identification scale with higher values equal to Republican identity to measure white macropartisanship. In line with Michael Mackeun and his colleagues as well as others who study macropartisanship, we average the party identification score for all respondents in a given survey and then average across surveys in a given quarter of a given year.[59] Given this, the unit of analysis is the quarter.

As illustrated in table 2.3, aggregate attitudes on immigration significantly predict future shifts in white macropartisanship. After controlling for past macropartisanship, we find that greater opposition to increased immigration nationwide is significantly linked to increases in Republican Party identity. The size of the effect is far from massive, but it is meaningful. A shift from the minimum level of support for immigration to the maximum level is associated with a little over one-tenth-point shift on the five-point macropartisanship scale. Immigration is certainly not the only factor driving changes in white party identification, yet it appears to be an important contributing one.

Over-time analysis serves a second purpose in that it can help us establish the direction of the causal relationship between immigration attitudes and partisanship. When we reverse the test, we discover that

---

[59] MacKuen, Erikson, and Stimson 1989. We have included 169 CBS/*New York Times* polls. The average sample size per quarter is 3,729. Due to space limitations, we describe other details of the Gallup and CBS/*New York Times* time series in the online appendix at http://pages .ucsd.edu/~zhajnal/styled/index.html.

TABLE 2.3

The Impact of Aggregate Immigration Views on White Macropartisanship

Lagged macropartisanship (high = Republican)	0.39 (0.15)*
Lagged immigration views (high = pro-immigration)	−0.22 (0.09)*
Constant	1.81 (0.45)**
N	21
Adjusted R^2	0.43

*$p < 0.05$
**$p < 0.01$

Source: Immigration views from Gallup series, cited in Roper 2014; macropartisanship from CBS/*New York Times* series, cited in Roper 2014.

macropartisanship does not significantly predict changes in attitudes on immigration. Hence, we can conclude that immigration views drive macropartisanship.[60]

It is also worth noting that we see the same pattern if we focus separately on the proportion of whites who identify as Republicans and proportion who identify as Independents. More negative attitudes on immigration greatly predict increased Republican identity and increased independence. All these relationships persist if we control for presidential approval and unemployment—the two factors viewed as most important in shaping macropartisanship.[61] Finally, since we were concerned about the limited number of data points, we reran the analysis after incorporating data from every question in the Roper Center Archives that asks about the preferred level of immigration. Combining all the different survey houses doubles the number of quarters for which we have immigration attitudes (forty-two quarters), but it also introduces considerable error as each survey house uses different question wording and different samples. The results for this larger data set roughly mirror the results we see here.[62]

Obviously, much is going on in US politics over this time and there is little doubt that many factors are contributing to the shift. But one can make a plausible case that the ongoing transformation of the country by immigrants and Latinos helps to explain the partisan transformation of white America. And if that conjecture is true, one of the most significant developments in the last half century of US politics

[60] For the results, see the online appendix at http://pages.ucsd.edu/~zhajnal/styled/index.html.

[61] MacKuen, Erikson, and Stimson 1989. Alternative Prais-Winsten AR(1) and vector autoregressive models lead to similar results. Table 2.3 has a one-quarter lag. Longer lags were insignificant.

[62] For the results, see the online appendix at http://pages.ucsd.edu/~zhajnal/styled/index.html.

can be linked to the demographic and political changes that immigration has brought to the nation.

More Over-Time Analysis

Given the growing importance of immigration, we also examined the predictive power of immigration over time at the individual level. In short, do attitudes on immigration predict partisanship more today than they did in the past? That effort was hampered by relatively severe data limitations. No public opinion exists with questions about immigration and other potentially relevant issues that are consistently repeated for more than a decade. The next best thing is the ANES, which has asked respondents intermittently since 1980 for their overall feelings toward Hispanics. Many years are missing in that sequence, and the question itself is not ideal, but when we analyzed different years of the survey, we found a pattern that at least marginally reflected our hypothesis about the increasing significance of immigration.

For many of the recent versions of the ANES surveys, our results parallel the 2008 ANES results that we presented above. In the years prior to 2000, however, the impact of feelings toward Hispanics often fades away. The Hispanic feeling thermometer is sometimes significantly correlated with partisan identification, but the impact that feelings toward Hispanics has on party identification generally disappears when we include a feeling thermometer for blacks. This may suggest that although immigration has been crucial in recent years, it has not always been the case. For much of US history and indeed until relatively recently, whites' racial sentiments were dominated by feelings toward African Americans and not immigrants. This appears to be changing.[63]

Discussion

Party identification is, by almost all accounts, the primary driving force in US politics. Few would disagree that "the psychological attachment to one or the other of the major parties . . . reveals more about political attitudes and behaviors than any other single opinion."[64] Party identifi-

[63] Other data from Pew Research Center (2012) also suggest that immigration is becoming increasingly central in shaping partisan choice. Although party polarization has grown on almost every issue in the past decade, according to the Pew Research Center data it has grown much faster on immigration than on any other issue except the environment.

[64] Keefe and Hetherington 2003, 169.

cation is also by many accounts a durable attachment that is extremely difficult to sway. Thus, what is noteworthy about this chapter is that we find major shifts in white partisanship. Whites' partisan ties were closely aligned with the Democratic Party—even as late as the mid-1980s. But that is no longer the case. White Republicans now far outnumber white Democrats. Given the centrality of party identification in almost every explanation of US political behavior, this shift is vital in the contours of US politics.

What is perhaps even more remarkable is that the increasing attachments of so many white Americans to the Republican Party appear to be in no small part a consequence of immigration. How white Americans feel about immigration and immigrants is, by all our tests, closely linked to how they feel about the two major parties. The more refined tests indicate that changes in partisan attachments often follow from attitudes on immigration. This rightward shift in the face of racial diversity is, of course, not new. It harks back to earlier periods in US history when whites mobilized against different forms of black empowerment.[65] It also very much parallels the more recent defection of so many whites from the Democratic Party in light of demands from the civil rights movement and the Republican's Southern strategy.[66] Yet whether this kind of racial reaction is new or not, the movement of so many whites away from the party generating more and more minority support is a real concern because it means that just when the United States is become more racially diverse, it is becoming more racially divided.

These patterns have far-reaching implications for our understanding of US politics, and in particular how race does or does not work in that context. Our analyses highlight both the enduring nature and changing impact of race on US politics. Race clearly persists. What we see here is that race still very much matters for whites' core political decisions. Party identification—the most influential variable in US politics—is at least in part a function of the way individual white Americans view Latinos and undocumented immigrants.

Our findings also underscore the changing nature of race in the United States. Race—throughout the twentieth century—was primarily understood through the divide between blacks and whites. In the aftermath of slavery and institutionalized segregation, blacks demanded greater rights and resources, and whites either relented or resisted. For individual white Americans, racial considerations in the

---

[65] Klinkner and Smith 1999; Foner 1984; Parker 1990.
[66] Carmines and Stimson 1989; Edsall and Edsall 1991.

political arena were generally dominated by their attitudes toward blacks. What was once a black-white dichotomy is, though, no longer so. The increasingly visible nature of immigration along with the enormous social, economic, and cultural transformations that immigrant has wrought on the United States appear to have also brought forth real change in the racial dynamics of US politics. How white Americans think about African Americans still greatly matters—as many of our results suggest—but so does attitudes toward Latinos, Asian Americans, and immigrants in general. There should be little doubt that the growing Latino population has become more central in the minds and thoughts of white Americans. The negative thoughts associated with Latinos in decisions about partisanship attests to the growing role that Latinos and immigrants play in the story lines of US politics. The patterns we see here also posit a role for Asian Americans—although a quite different one. Asian Americans may represent less of a threat and more of a model minority for conservative whites to herald as well as work with. Those on the political right have generally positive feelings toward Asian Americans. Put simply, concerns and hopes about these emerging groups now provoke strong reactions while helping to sway core political identities.

Finally, these results speak to the long-standing debate between adherents of the Michigan school who believe that party identification is a strong psychological attachment that is developed early in life, colors one's views on almost every other political object, and remains rigidly stable in most circumstances, and on the other side, supporters of a Downsian view that sees partisanship as a rational choice that stems from a running tally of issue positions, party performance, and other real-world events.[67] We are not so naive to believe that our findings will settle the debate, but we would say that our results strongly suggest that party identification is both more malleable and rational than the Michigan school often contends. Not only do we see massive aggregate shifts in white partisanship over time, but those changes also appear to be logically and reasonably linked to salient moments. Party identification is still assuredly one of the most stable and predictive elements of US politics, yet it can and does change when circumstances warrant. When the major parties maintain consistent positions on the issues of the day, little changes at the individual partisan level. But when new issues like immigration take center stage, and the two parties take increasingly divergent positions on those new issues, there is

---

[67] For the Michigan school, see Campbell et al. 1960. For the Downsian model, see Fiorina 1981; Erikson and Wlezien 2012.

likely to be substantial and predictable change for individual partisan choice. In that sense, the key question should not be, Is party identification stable? Rather, the core questions should be, When and why should we expect substantial shifts in party identification?

Still, much remains to be uncovered and explained. Decisions about partisan attachments are certainly a primary element of US politics, but they are, in essence, an interim stage in the electoral calculus of individual Americans. Ultimately what we care about is the outcome of the vote. If immigration really has an impact on US politics, we should see its imprint on the vote as well. In the next chapter, then, we move on to an examination of a range of national electoral contests. We will see whether attitudes about immigrants and Latinos also influence the decisions whites make in the voting booth.

Chapter 3

How Immigration Shapes the Vote

Americans are presented with two different narratives on immigration. On the one side, a range of anti-immigrant voices underscore the immigrant threat narrative, and regularly oppose initiatives to try to aid immigrants or expand immigration. That narrative is epitomized by the sentiments of these two presidential candidates.

> We all know Hillary Clinton and the Democrats have it wrong on illegal immigration. Our party should not make that mistake. As Governor, I authorized the State Police to enforce immigration laws. I opposed driver's licenses & in-state tuition for illegal aliens. As president, I'll oppose amnesty, cut funding for sanctuary cities and secure our borders.
> — Mitt Romney, 2012 Republican presidential candidate

> We're not just talking about the number of jobs that we may be losing, or the number of kids that are in our schools and impacting our school system, or the number of people that are abusing our hospital system and taking advantage of the welfare system in this country—we're not just talking about that. We're talking about something that goes to the very heart of this nation—whether or not we will actually survive as a nation. . . . What we're doing here in this immigration battle is testing our willingness to actually hold together as a nation or split apart into a lot of Balkanized pieces.
> — Tom Tancredo, 2008 Republican presidential candidate

The other side of the immigration debate can be equally fervent. A series of proimmigrant voices highlight the benefits of immigration and often favor policies that help secure immigrants a better, more normalized life. Again, the words of two presidential candidates typify this more positive perspective.

> America can only prosper when all Americans prosper—brown, black, white, Asian, and Native American. That's the idea that lies at the heart of my campaign, and that's the idea that will lie at the heart of my presidency. Because we are all Americans. Todos somos Americanos [we are all Americans]. And in this country, we rise and fall together.
> —*Barack Obama, 2008 Democratic presidential candidate*

> I am proud to work with Senator [Robert] Menendez on trying to make sure that in the process of doing immigration reform, we don't separate families, we try to have family unification as one of the goals. So in addition to giving people a path to legalization, we want to make sure their families can come along with them. . . . Finally, we have to educate the American people about why immigration is as important today as it was when my family came through into Ellis Island.
> —*Hillary Clinton, 2008 Democratic presidential candidate*

What makes this debate potentially relevant to the vote is that the voices in each camp have a distinctly partisan hue. Most of those calling for more punitive measures come from candidates on the Republican side of the aisle. By contrast, most of the individuals offering a more compassionate perspective toward immigration emerge out of the Democratic camp.[1] We do not claim that the elites within either party are fully unified on the issue of immigration. Indeed they are not. There are prominent Republicans like former president George W. Bush and Senator Marco Rubio who have tried various tactics on immigration to try to garner greater support from Latino voters. Even Romney, after winning the Republican nomination in 2012, shifted

[1] A look at campaigns, public statements, and policy platforms on immigration at lower levels of politics would likely reveal a similar divide between Democrats and Republicans. Merely as an example, you have, on the one hand, Republican state representative John Kavanagh, who asserts, "If a burglar breaks into your home, do you serve him dinner? That is pretty much what they do there with illegals" (quoted in Archibold 2010). On the other hand, Democratic representative Luis Guttierez contends that "we need . . . a generous and rigorous legalization program to get immigrants already living here on the books and in the system" (quoted at http://www.llanj.org/announcements/rep-gutierrez-immigration-president-quarterback /01–25–2013).

noticeably to the middle on immigration during the general campaign. And as we write this book, Republican leaders appear to be engaged in an internal debate about the proper course for their party on immigration. Likewise, many Democrats offer at best lukewarm support for immigrants, and many couple the defense of accommodating policies like amnesty with even more vigorous support for increased border security and deportations as well as other punitive measures. But there seems little doubt that on average, the two major parties present Americans with two different alternatives on immigration.[2] There are obvious partisan choices for voters with real hopes or deep fears on immigration.

Yet do these distinct choices actually matter for the vote? Are they clear and compelling enough to influence the choices that individual white Americans make on the ballot? And in particular, are those concerned about immigration—an increasingly large share of the public—sufficiently motivated to choose Republican over Democratic candidates in substantial numbers? We have already seen in the previous chapter that views on immigration can shape the partisan choices of white Americans. This chapter presents the next logical test: an analysis of the link between immigration attitudes and the vote.

This analysis is an important test of just how far immigration is altering the dynamics of the US electoral arena. Elections are the ultimate arbiter in US democracy. They not only determine who wins office but also help to shape policy direction in the ensuing years. Thus, whether and to what extent immigration influences the vote of the white majority can have real consequences.

Our analyses of the vote will hopefully offer a discerning test of the influence of immigration. In what follows, we not only examine whether there is a link between attitudes on immigration and the vote but also if there is a link that goes beyond party identification and the other mainstream factors that we traditionally think structure the vote. We will assess that link not just in one or two electoral contests. Instead, we will explore it in an array of elections that span different years and different electoral offices. The idea is to see if immigration has a broad influence on the candidates we choose in US politics.

[2] These quotes are not meant to be fully representative of Democratic and Republican elite views on immigration, but as we noted in chapter 1, research clearly shows and interest group ratings confirm that Democratic and Republican elites support increasingly divergent positions on immigration (Wong 2013; Jeong et al. 2011; Miller and Schofield 2008; Gimpel and Edwards 1998).

The Aggregate Picture: A Republican Shift over Time

We begin by looking at aggregate trends over time. If the ever-increasing influence of immigration is affecting the white vote, we should see, as we did in the last chapter, a noticeable shift over time to the Republican Party. That is exactly what we see in figure 3.1. The figure shows the white vote between 1974 and 2008 using data from the previously introduced ANES cumulative file. We start by focusing on the congressional vote because it enables us to look more frequently at the white vote than we could with presidential contests. Moreover, aggregating numerous congressional contests each year partially offsets the vagaries of incumbency and candidate qualities that play a prominent a role in presidential elections.

Figure 3.1 indicates clearly that white voters have become increasingly attracted to Republican candidates. Through the 1970s and 1980s, white Americans were largely Democratic supporters. Roughly 45 percent of the non-Hispanic white electorate supported Republican congressional candidates during that time period. But white support for Republicans grows quickly after 1990. The majority of white Americans are now plainly on the Republican side, with roughly 55 percent of white voters favoring Republicans. In 2010—data not reflected in the cumulative file—that figure rose even higher. Fully 60 percent of white Americans voted for Republicans in this congressional election cycle—an unprecedented number in the post–World War II era. White congressional voters have shifted in large numbers to the Republican Party.

And it is not just the congressional vote. The same pattern is evident at the senatorial, and gubernatorial levels. Electoral outcomes for these two types of contests are much more variable from year to year for a variety of reasons, but decade-by-decade analysis reveals a stark increase in the Republican vote among whites for the US Senate.[3] White support for Republican senatorial candidates grows from an average of 47.2 percent in the 1970s, to 50.8 percent in the 1980s, 51.9 percent in the 1990s, and 53.7 percent in the 2000s. In 2008, a whopping 59.3 percent of non-Hispanic whites voted Republican for

---

[3] The high variability in senate and gubernatorial offices is due in large part to the fact that only a handful of these office are contested in any given election year. That means that the peculiarities of the states involved, candidate qualities, and other nonrandom factors can shift the vote considerably. With only two candidates vying for office every four years, the problem is even more severe at the presidential level.

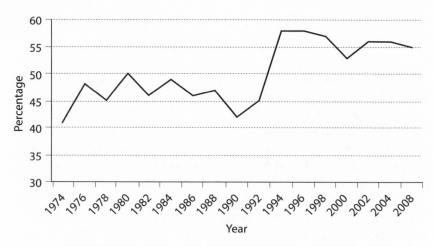

Figure 3.1 White Republican Vote Share in Congressional Races
Source: ANES 2010.

the senate. Gubernatorial contests show a similar though more muted trend.[4] For some reason, large numbers of white Americans have shifted from the Democratic to Republican Party in the last four decades.

The presidency is more complicated. Since 1990, a similar trend appears.[5] The share of the white electorate favoring the Republican candidate has grown in every election but one. As a result, average white support for Republican presidential candidates has also increased over the last two decades. In the 1990s, white Republican support in presidential contests averaged 48.3 percent. That figure rose substantially in the 2000s to 55 percent. Many other factors, of course, shaped the white vote so it is difficult to determine whether this trend is real or just a function of other election-specific factors. It may be that white support for Republican presidential candidates will continue to grow in the next few elections as it has in the last few races,

[4] ANES data on gubernatorial elections are more limited. Most problematically, there are no data on gubernatorial contests after 1998. Nevertheless, the data that are available reveal a clear uptick in Republican voting in gubernatorial contests as well. White support for Republican gubernatorial candidates averaged 48 and 47 percent in the 1970s and 1980s, respectively, but jumped to 56 percent in the 1990s.

[5] If we go back further in time and examine a wider swath of presidential contests, however, the data reveal no obvious trend in the white vote. Instead, there are relatively wide fluctuations in the white vote from election year to election year. We surmise that the limited number of elections along with the powerful effects of incumbency, the economy, candidate characteristics, and other factors unique to presidential contests drown out much of any longer-term trend that might underlie the results.

but it is equally possible that the current trend is just an artifact of the candidates in the five most recent contests.

Ultimately, whether the presidency is included or not, an important shift in the vote is obviously occurring. That change is crucial for our theory and case. If we see no large-scale shift in white partisan choices over time, then the impact of immigration cannot be that extensive. If few white voters are moving their vote choice from the candidates of one party to the candidates of the other party, then the role that immigration plays is likely to be a meager one. Instead, by showing that white support for the Republican Party has increased substantially, we have demonstrated that the pattern of partisan change fits the immigration story that we are telling. Immigration *could* be having widespread electoral consequences.

Having made the claim that our story is feasible, it is now important to note that nothing in figure 3.1 tells us that immigration was the main driving force behind the growing allegiance of whites to the Republicans. We have yet to make a direct connection between immigration and the vote. Furthermore, as was the case with party identification, there are numerous factors that affect vote choice. Immigration is only one of many different potential influences.[6]

Linking Immigration to the Vote: Preliminary Steps

In order to assess the impact of immigration and immigration-related views on the vote, we turn once again to the ANES. We choose the ANES because it includes a long list of questions that get at each of the many different factors known to affect the vote. This is critical, since we cannot conclude that immigration matters unless we can control for all the core aspects of US elections.

We begin with an analysis of the 2008 ANES for two reasons. First, it contains questions on immigration—a requirement that rules out most years of the ANES survey and many other national surveys. Second, 2008 was ostensibly not about immigration. Obama, the first African American nominee for president, was on the ballot. McCain and Obama outlined similar plans on immigration, the nation was in the midst of two wars, and an unprecedented fiscal crisis dominated the election. Immigration was supposedly not a core issue in the cam-

---

[6] Moreover, attitudes on immigration are assuredly correlated with many of the other issues that could be propelling partisan choice along with the shift from Democratic to Republican candidates.

paign. If anything, 2008 was going to be about whites' acceptance of blacks as well as their concerns about the economy, war, and terrorism. As such, 2008 represents a relatively exacting test of our immigration hypothesis.

We realize that if we want to make a more general statement about US politics, though, we need to assess the influence of immigration attitudes across a wider range of data sets, years, elections and contexts. To do this, we repeat our analysis using the ANES cumulative file, 2010 and 2012 CCES, 2000 and 2004 NAES, cumulative file of the GSS, and 2010 Evaluations of Government and Survey. This allows us to test the immigration hypothesis across different years (contests from 1970–2010), different types of elections (presidential, congressional, and gubernatorial), various survey instruments (including a wide variety of questions that vary the wording of the key independent variable—immigration-related feelings—and the key dependent variables—partisanship and vote choice), and distinct survey methodologies and samples. If all these different data points lead to the same story, we can be reasonably confident of our explanation.[7]

We start again with the simplest and often the most telling test: an assessment of the simple correlation between attitudes toward undocumented immigrants and vote choice. Figure 3.2 illustrates the relationship between vote choices in presidential, congressional, and senatorial elections and attitudes toward undocumented immigration. Our measure of views on immigration was developed in the previous chapter and is derived from the four questions in the 2008 ANES that explicitly assess views on undocumented immigrants.[8] If anything, the relationship between immigration and partisan choice is even more pronounced for the vote than it was for party identification. As attitudes toward undocumented immigrants become more positive, the proportion of white voters who support Republican candidates drops 33 percent in the presidential election, 38 percent in congressional contests, and a whopping 44 percent in senate elections.[9] It matters

---

[7] Because our theory focuses on the reaction of white Americans to the United States' changing racial demographics, we include only those individuals who identify themselves as non-Hispanic whites.

[8] Specifically, we create an alpha factor score from these four questions: a standard feeling thermometer that asks how one feels about "illegal immigrants," and ranges from zero (meaning extremely cold or negative feelings) to one hundred (for extremely warm or positive feelings); 2) "Should controlling and reducing illegal immigration be a very important [or] . . . not an important foreign policy goal?"; "Do you favor/oppose the US government making it possible for illegal immigrants to become US citizens?"; and "Do you favor, oppose, or neither favor nor oppose allowing illegal immigrants to work in the United States for up to three years, after which they would have to go back to their home country?"

[9] All these correlations are highly significant (p < 0.001).

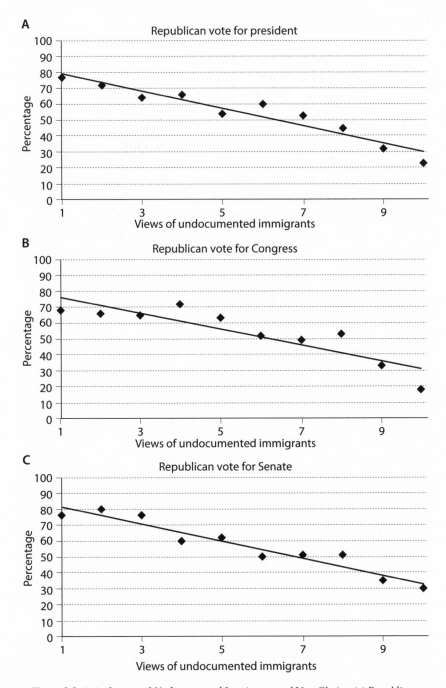

Figure 3.2 Attitudes toward Undocumented Immigrants and Vote Choice: (a) Republican Vote for President, (b) Republican Vote for Congress, and (c) Republican Vote for Senate
Source: ANES 2008.

little how we measure views on immigration. Whether we combine the questions on immigration to create a factor score, use a simpler additive scale, or look at each question separately, the pattern of results is similar. The partisan world of white America seems, at least at first glance, to be fundamentally shaped by perceptions of undocumented immigrants.

But are these relationships spurious—a by-product of a correlation with a third factor that is actually driving vote choice? As in the last chapter, one of the most difficult aspects of this empirical endeavor is ensuring that we include controls for all the different factors that could drive white's electoral decisions and be correlated with white views on immigration.[10] Our empirical models, in short, need to incorporate key elements of US politics. With that in mind, we include measures for: *basic ideology*—the standard seven-point liberal-conservative self-placement scale; *military action*—support for wars in Iraq and Afghanistan, and views on expanding the war on terrorism; *retrospective evaluations*—presidential approval and assessments of the economy; *redistribution*—higher taxes for the rich and welfare spending; *morality and religion*—views on homosexuality and the importance of religion; *other racial attitudes/ethnocentrism*—standard feeling thermometers for "blacks," "Asian Americans," and "whites"; and in alternate tests, *other issues*—universal health care, women's rights, the environment, abortion, crime, schools, science and technology, and so on.[11]

Also, since electoral choices have been linked to class, religion, and other individual demographic characteristics, we control for education (number of years of school completed), household income (divided into twenty-five categories), gender, age in years, whether the respondent is unemployed or not, whether anyone in the household is a union member or not, marital status (married or not), and religious denomination (Jewish, Catholic, Protestant, or other). All told, we have controls for basic ideology, retrospective evaluations, a range of core issues, racial attitudes, and individual socioeconomic characteristics—many, if not all, the factors that are presumed to dominate the vote.[12]

[10] For an overview of the partisan choice literature, see Miller and Shanks 1996.

[11] Since we believe that attitudes toward immigrants and Latinos are closely linked, we do not include a Latino feeling thermometer in the basic model. If we do add a Latino feeling thermometer to table 3.1, however, feelings toward undocumented immigrants remain significant while the Latino feeling thermometer reaches statistical significance at marginal levels. "Other issues" are not included in the main model because they are only asked of half the respondents. For the exact question wording, see the previous chapter.

[12] There are surely other influences on the vote. Evaluations of candidate qualities and questions that ask about the probable future success of candidates (prospective evaluations) are two of

Immigration and the 2008 Presidential Vote

Is immigration important in presidential contests? More specifically, are concerns about immigration associated with a Republican vote? In table 3.1, we begin to answer this question. Table 3.1 presents results for a series of logit analyses on vote choice in the 2008 presidential election. The dependent variable in each case is a dummy variable indicating support for the Republican—McCain (1)—or Democratic candidate—Obama (0).[13]

In the second column, we concentrate on the reported vote of respondents queried after the election. The results in the third column present estimates for intended vote choice for those surveyed prior to Election Day. Later we discuss the fourth and fifth columns, where we include a slightly different, more exogenous measure of party identification. By including party identification in our vote models, we can conclude with some confidence that views on immigration have an independent effect not wholly driven by party identification. In subsequent tests where we examine the vote within partisan primaries, we hope to gain further traction on the independent role of immigration.

The results in the second column of table 3.1 indicate that how white Americans think about immigrants is strongly related to the vote. As we saw before, whites with more positive attitudes toward undocumented immigrants are significantly less likely to opt for the Republican candidate. Moreover, the marginal effects are substantial. All else being equal, more positive views of undocumented immigrants are associated with a 24.3 percent decrease in the probability of voting for McCain, the Republican presidential contender.[14]

The effect for intended vote choice—the results in the third column—is almost identical: a 22.9 percent decrease in the probability of voting for McCain. Impressively, in an election that occurred in the midst of one of the nation's sharpest recessions in history, coinciding with two wars in Afghanistan and Iraq, and that included the nation's first black presidential nominee, views on immigrants still mattered.

---

the most likely contenders. Yet these factors are often viewed as endogenous to the vote. In essence, whoever we vote for, we like. Given their endogeneity and the fact that we are primarily interested in identifying enduring, core elements of US electoral politics, these other factors are omitted from our analysis.

[13] Dropping or including voters who favor third-party or Independent candidates makes little difference to the results.

[14] For this and all other predicted probabilities reported in the book, estimates are calculated using the statistical package Clarify in STATA holding all other independent variables at their mean or modal value, and varying the independent variable of interest plus or minus one standard deviation.

TABLE 3.1
Views on Immigration and the White Presidential Vote

	Support for the Republican candidate in 2008 presidential election			
	(Controlling for party identification)		(With exogenous party identification)	
	Vote choice	Intended vote choice	Vote choice	Intended vote choice
Immigration				
Positive view on undocumented immigrants	−0.66 (0.34)**	−0.62 (0.27)*	−1.17 (0.34)**	−1.08 (0.27)**
Demographics				
Education	0.10 (0.09)	0.07 (0.08)	0.12 (0.10)	0.08 (0.08)
Income	0.01 (0.03)	−0.02 (0.03)	0.04 (0.03)	0.00 (0.03)
Unemployed	−2.75 (0.93)**	−1.5 (0.68)*	−2.6 (0.93)**	−1.30 (0.68)
Age	−0.00 (0.01)	0.02 (0.01)	−0.01 (0.01)	0.01 (0.01)
Female	0.25 (0.38)	−0.22 (0.31)	0.08 (0.38)	−0.37 (0.32)
Married	0.59 (0.36)	0.54 (0.29)	1.06 (0.37)**	0.97 (0.31)**
Union member	−17 (0.49)	−0.80 (0.44)	−0.34 (0.49)	−1.28 (0.45)**
Jewish	1.25 (1.1)	1.3 (0.95)	0.42 (0.46)	0.52 (0.95)
Catholic	0.73 (0.48)	0.37 (0.39)	0.91 (0.48)	0.54 (0.40)
Protestant	−0.26 (0.45)	−0.47 (0.37)	0.42 (0.46)	0.15 (0.37)
Ideology/party identification				
Conservative	1.19 (0.46)**	0.65 (0.33)*	1.19 (0.46)**	0.65 (0.33)*
Republican	0.82 (0.12)**	0.76 (0.09)**	0.82 (0.12)**	0.76 (0.10)**
Issue positions				
War and terrorism				
Expand war on terror	−0.05 (0.11)	−0.02 (0.08)	−0.05 (0.11)	−0.02 (0.08)
Support war in Iraq	−0.18 (0.12)	0.15 (0.10)	−0.17 (0.12)	−0.15 (0.11)
Support war in Afghanistan	−0.18 (0.11)	0.13 (0.10)	−0.18 (0.11)	−0.13 (0.10)
Economy/retrospective				
Economy improving	0.30 (0.29)	0.42 (0.22)	0.30 (0.29)	0.42 (0.22)
Approve president	0.66 (0.16)	0.55 (0.13)**	0.66 (0.17)**	0.55 (0.13)**
Redistribution				
Favor higher taxes on rich	−0.33 (0.18)	−0.26 (0.15)	−0.33 (0.18)	−0.26 (0.15)
Increase welfare spending	−0.03 (0.10)	−0.01 (0.01)	−0.03 (0.10)	−0.06 (0.08)
Morality/religion				
Favor gay rights	−0.39 (0.14)**	−0.03 (0.01)**	−0.39 (0.14)**	−0.09 (0.11)
Religion important	0.10 (0.10)	−0.06 (0.08)	−0.10 (0.10)	−0.08 (0.08)
Other racial considerations				
Warmth toward blacks	0.00 (0.01)	−0.02 (0.01)	0.00 (0.01)	−0.02 (0.01)
Warmth toward Asians	−0.04 (0.02)*	−0.01 (0.01)	−0.04 (0.02)*	−0.01 (0.01)
Warmth toward whites	0.03 (0.01)*	0.01 (0.01)	0.03 (0.01)*	0.01 (0.01)
Constant	−3.04 (2.3)	0.06 (1.8)**	−3.05 (2.22)	2.46 (1.86)
N	556	633633	556	633
Pseudo squared	0.68	0.61	0.68	0.61

*p < 0.05
**p < 0.01

Note: Entries not in parentheses are logit coefficients and entries in parentheses denote the corresponding standard errors.

Source: ANES 2008.

Alternate Tests of the 2008 Presidential Vote

To help convince readers that the relationship between immigration and the vote is real, we proceeded to undertake a range of alternative specifications that use different measures of views on immigration, assess different dependent variables, incorporate different alternate explanations for the vote, and consider the endogeneity of party identification.

We first determined whether our results are robust to various ways of measuring attitudes toward immigration. As we noted earlier, attitudes toward undocumented immigration, legal immigration, and Latinos are highly interrelated, making it difficult to know exactly what aspect of immigration white Americans are responding to. As was the case with party identification, if we substitute questions about legal immigration or general feelings toward Latinos into the analysis, we tend to get similar results as those presented in table 3.1. Attitudes toward undocumented immigration, preferences about legal immigration, and feelings toward Latinos are all statistically significant in predicting vote choice. These findings suggest that white Americans are not making sharp distinctions between these three groups when they think about immigration. Rather, in the minds of many white Americans these three groups are melded together. Race and immigration (regardless of legal status) are closely intertwined.

Our next step was to incorporate alternative measures of candidate preferences. These analyses suggest that it does not much matter how we measure electoral preferences. If we focus on feelings toward Obama and McCain, rather than on the vote itself, we once again find that more negative views of undocumented immigrants are associated with stronger, more positive feelings for the Republican side and less positive views of the Democratic option. Likewise, if we include third-party voters and analyze presidential vote choice using multinomial logit analysis, we arrive at exactly the same conclusion about the centrality of immigrant-related views on vote choice.

We then moved on to consider a range of other issues that we have not yet discussed but that nevertheless are present to one degree or another in the 2008 campaign. Debates about universal health care, women's rights, the environment, abortion, crime, schools, science, and technology were not central facets of the campaign but could still have impacted the vote. Fortunately, the ANES survey queried subsets of respondents on each of these issues areas. Thus, in additional empirical tests, we were able to add these questions to our model in table

3.1.[15] The inclusion of these questions did not appreciably alter the result pattern.

Given the historic nature of the 2008 presidential election, we also considered different aspects of whites' racial sentiments. First, we incorporated the four standard racial resentment questions: "It's really a matter of some people not trying hard enough. If blacks would only try harder they could be just as well off as whites"; "Irish, Italian, Jewish, and many other minorities overcame prejudice and worked their way up. Blacks should do the same without special favors"; "Over the past few years, blacks have gotten less than they deserve"; and "Generations of slavery and discrimination have created conditions that make it difficult for blacks to work their way out of the lower class."[16] According to Kinder and Sanders as well as other scholars, these four questions all revolve around the central element of US race relations: the degree to which blacks face barriers in US society.[17] Our results suggest that racial resentment, like many of the other factors highlighted in table 3.1, did play a significant role in the contest. But the inclusion of these variables did little to affect our main finding.

With Obama as the first African American major party candidate on the ballot, we also incorporated three other variables that specifically asked about black candidates and their abilities. We used the following three measures in alternative tests: Does the idea of a black person being president make you feel uncomfortable?; Do you think most white candidates who run for political office are better suited to be an elected official than most black candidates?; and Do you think most white candidates are better suited in terms of their intelligence than most black candidates? Being uncomfortable with a black person as president and viewing black candidates less favorably was closely associated with the presidential vote in 2008, but controlling for these measures did little to affect the impact of immigration on vote choice. That white political orientations are still shaped by attitudes about blacks is not surprising and indicates that the 2008 contest continued the unfortunate tradition of a racialized pattern in US politics. What is additional here is the element of immigration,

---

[15] For the question wording for universal health care, women's rights, the environment, abortion, crime, schools, science, and technology, see chapter 2.

[16] In each case, respondents were asked whether they agreed or disagreed with the statement, and how strongly.

[17] Kinder and Sanders 1996.

which we contend is a new, independent dimension to the nation's racial politics.

Lastly, we estimated a series of alternate specifications where we added a range of different individual characteristics into our logistic analysis. We specifically delved deeper into religious attachments (the frequency of church attendance and whether the respondent identified as born again), class ties (self-identified class position), and mobility (years in current residence). As well, given that region and race have at times been intricately intertwined at different points in US history, we included controls for region. These additional controls did little to affect the results.

Considering the Endogeneity of Party Identification

We also endeavored to think more closely about the relationship between immigrant-related views and partisanship in our models. In some ways, the results presented in the second and third columns of table 3.1 understate the role that attitudes about immigration play in shaping the vote. Since we have shown in the previous chapter that party identification is at least partly a function of views on immigration, including party identification in our logit model may minimize the role of immigration. Specifically, including party identification as an independent variable eliminates any immigration-related effect that works through changes in party identification. In order to address this concern, we developed and incorporated a measure of party identification that is exogenous to views on immigration. In particular, we estimated the residuals from the party identification model presented in the previous chapter, and used it in our regression analyses presented in the fourth and fifth columns of table 3.1.[18] By using the residuals, we have a variable incorporating aspects of party identification that are not directly explained by immigrant-related views.

When we include this exogenous measure of party identification, the substantive impact of immigration views on vote choice is even larger. The model indicates that all else being equal, a two standard deviation shift toward more negative views on undocumented immigrants is associated with a 39 percent increase in the probability of having voted for McCain and 38 percent increase in the probability of intending to do so.

[handwritten margin note: not table? coming. No.]

[handwritten margin note: ☆ IVI]

---

[18] In practice, the two measures of party identification are nearly identical. The standard party identification scale is correlated with exogenous party identification at 0.93.

The Effect of Immigration within Each Party

Another way to get at the interrelationships between immigration, party identification, and vote choice is to look at vote choice *within* members of each party. By focusing separately on Democrat and Republic identifiers, we gain another perspective on how attitudes toward immigration matter beyond partisanship. [19]

Our results indicate that even among those who claim ties to the Democratic Party, views of undocumented immigrants are moderately related to vote choice. The vast majority of Democrats vote for Obama, but those who have more negative views of undocumented immigrants are 6.5 percent less likely to support him when compared to those with more positive views of undocumented immigrants. This is a small sign that immigration is pushing white Democrats away from their party. By contrast, our analyses indicate that views toward immigrants matter less for Republicans. This is exactly what we would expect to find if immigration is largely pushing whites in one direction—toward the Republican Party. Also as one might anticipate, views toward immigrants and Latinos have the largest impact on nonpartisans. White Independents with more negative views of immigrants are 67.7 percent more likely to vote for McCain than are white Independents with more positive views of immigrants. Immigration attitudes clearly have a distinct, substantively large effect on vote choice that goes well beyond partisan ties.

The Role of Immigration in Other Elections

To make a general statement about the impact of immigration in US politics, we have to look more broadly at a number of different presidential elections as well as across a range of different types of electoral contests. This is exactly what we do in table 3.2. Specifically, we turn to the ANES cumulative file to assess the impact of immigration views on presidential, congressional, and gubernatorial contests. Since the ANES does not generally ask about views on undocumented immigrants, we use a different measure for attitudes toward immigrants and Latinos. The key independent variable here is the standard feeling thermometer toward Latinos, given that feelings toward them and atti-

---

[19] For this test, we ran separate regressions for each of the three partisan groups (Democrats, Independents, and Republicans). For the results, see the online appendix at http://pages.ucsd.edu/~zhajnal/styled/index.html.

tudes toward undocumented immigrants have become synonymous.[20] Also, since policy questions vary from ANES year to year, we include a modified set of policy control variables.[21]

Our results suggest, once again, white Americans' feelings toward Latinos can be a central component in their electoral calculations. Starting with the second and third columns, which display the multinomial logit estimates with presidential vote choice—Democrat, Independent, and Republican—as the dependent variable, we see that those who exude greater warmth toward Latinos are significantly less apt to choose Republican candidates for president.[22] The fourth column, which displays the results for intended presidential vote choice (with a Republican vote as the dichotomous dependent variable), reconfirms the results.[23] Again, more positive views of Latinos are significantly tied to Republican vote choice net party identification and a range of other controls. The magnitude of the relationship is substantial as well. A two standard deviation negative shift in view of Latinos is associated with a 9.8 percent increase in the probability of Republican vote choice in the multinomial model. For intended vote choice, the comparable figure is a 10.9 percent increase in the likelihood of voting for the Republican candidate. And for a recalled vote from the last election (the analysis is not shown), we find an 8.9 percent gain in the probability of supporting the Republican candidate. Across a range of presidential elections—and regardless of how vote choice is measured—we see that attitudes toward Latinos are very much a part of vote choice.

Importantly, the relationship is not isolated to presidential vote choice. As the remaining estimates on vote choice demonstrate, white feelings toward Latinos are linked to gubernatorial vote choice and almost significantly tied to the congressional vote. Moreover, in gubernatorial contests, the magnitude of the relationship is large. All else being equal, those who hold more negative views of Latinos are 35 percent more likely to favor Republican gubernatorial candidates. The one case where there is no apparent relationship is in senatorial con-

---

[20] Pérez 2010. A question that asks about whether legal immigration should be increased, decreased, or kept at the same rate performs similarly, but is not used because it is available for fewer years.

[21] For the policy questions, see the online appendix at http://pages.ucsd.edu/~zhajnal/styled/index.html.

[22] We use multinomial logit here because in several of these presidential elections, there are relatively successful third-party candidates who are difficult to place ideologically along a linear, left-right continuum.

[23] In the model for intended vote choice, we estimate it using a logit model, since the dependent variable is binary in nature.

TABLE 3.2
Views on Latinos and the Vote: Alternate Measures

	Presidential vote (multinomial logit)		Support for the Republican candidate			
	Democrat versus Independent	Republican versus Independent	Intended press vote	Vote for Congress	Vote for governor	Vote for Senate
Immigration						
Warmth toward Hispanics	−0.67 (0.62)	−1.41 (0.61)*	−1.03 (0.45)*	−0.72 (0.47)	−3.80 (1.35)**	0.23 (0.39)
Demographics						
Education	0.36 (0.08)**	0.30 (0.08)**	−0.07 (0.07)	−0.07 (0.07)	−0.03 (0.15)	−0.01 (0.06)
Income	0.01 (0.06)	0.04 (0.06)	0.03 (0.05)	0.02 (0.05)	−0.08 (0.13)	0.02 (0.04)
Unemployed	−0.06 (0.37)	−0.44 (0.40)	0.12 (0.34)	−0.45 (0.38)	−2.0 (1.4)	−0.38 (0.34)
Age	0.02 (0.00)**	0.01 (0.05)	−0.01 (0.01)	−0.01 (0.01)	−0.01 (0.01)	−0.01 (0.00)*
Female	0.32 (0.15)*	0.62 (0.15)**	0.09 (0.12)	0.33 (0.13)**	0.09 (0.28)	0.04 (0.11)
Married	−0.46 (0.16)**	−0.11 (0.16)	0.39 (0.13)**	0.30 (0.13)*	0.32 (0.30)	0.16 (0.11)
Union member	0.35 (0.19)	−0.11 (0.19)	−0.64 (0.15)**	−0.56 (0.15)**	−0.56 (0.36)	−0.40 (0.13)**
Jewish	0.95 (0.58)	0.32 (0.62)	−0.43 (0.39)	−0.83 (0.41)*	−0.51 (0.90)	−0.90 (0.37)**
Catholic	−0.15 (0.23)	0.20 (0.24)	0.37 (0.20)	0.27 (0.22)	0.76 (0.45)	0.07 (0.18)
Protestant	−0.06 (0.21)	0.25 (0.22)	0.26 (0.18)	0.20 (0.20)	−0.45 (0.43)	−0.15 (0.11)
Ideology/PID						
Conservative	−0.25 (0.06)**	0.20 (0.07)**	0.35 (0.05)**	0.44 (0.06)**	0.19 (0.13)	0.24 (0.05)**
Republican	−0.54 (0.05)**	0.31 (0.05)**	0.84 (0.03)**	0.83 (0.04)**	0.65 (0.09)**	0.55 (0.03)**

[handwritten margin notes] Many pres elections? is there an effect over many elections?

[handwritten margin note] coming to which vote a shift in congressional in elections...

Issue positions						
War and terrorism						
More for military	0.09 (0.06)	0.38 (0.06)**	0.28 (0.05)**	0.29 (0.05)**	−0.01 (0.11)	0.14 (0.04)**
Economy/retrospective						
Economy improving	−0.45 (0.08)**	−0.48 (0.08)**	0.10 (0.06)	−0.03 (0.06)	0.22 (0.15)	−0.01 (0.05)
Approve president	0.13 (0.08)	−0.40 (0.07)**	−0.56 (0.06)**	−0.51 (0.06)**	0.24 (0.15)	0.07 (0.05)
Role of government						
More government services	0.25 (0.06)	0.03 (0.05)	−0.22 (0.05)**	−0.27 (0.05)**	−0.01 (0.11)	−0.11 (0.04)**
Favor guaranteed jobs	0.00 (0.05)	−0.11 (0.05)*	−0.15 (0.04)**	−0.13 (0.04)**	−0.17 (0.09)	−0.12 (0.04)**
Social issues						
Favor women's rights	0.00 (0.06)	−0.15 (0.05)**	−0.09 (0.04)*	−0.15 (0.04)**	−0.23 (0.10)*	−0.14 (0.04)**
Racial considerations						
Warmth toward blacks	0.37 (0.63)	0.45 (0.62)	0.34 (0.47)	0.20 (0.49)	2.79 (1.40)*	−0.14 (0.42)
Warmth toward whites	0.92 (0.52)	1.36 (0.51)**	0.39 (0.39)	0.52 (0.42)	0.09 (0.91)	−0.20 (0.34)
Constant	−59 (24)	−27 (24)	49 (18)**	36 (19)	−4.1 (1.5)**	
N	3,674	3,674	3,674	3,406	470	2,672
Adjust R/pseudo squared	0.47	0.47	0.59	0.60	0.42	0.34

*p < 0.05
**p < 0.01

Note: Entries not in parentheses are logit coefficients and entries in parentheses denote the corresponding standard errors.

Source: ANES 2010.

tests. In the next section, we begin to think about why immigration matters in some contests and not in others, but for now it should be apparent that immigration attitudes fill a broad role in the choices that Americans make on Election Day.

Other Elections in Other Surveys

To increase confidence in our findings and further assess the part that immigration plays in US politics, we turned to a number of other data sources including the 2010 and 2012 CCES, 2000 and 2004 NAES, GSS, and 2010 ANES. In all cases, these other surveys confirm the significance of immigration in US politics.

Turning to a range of different surveys not only allows us to assess a wider variety of elections but perhaps equally key, it permits us to test our immigration backlash theory across diverse survey conditions. These different surveys vary not only in their timing but also how they are administered (telephone with the NAES versus face-to-face with the GSS and Internet with the CCES), who they are administered to (adults citizens in the ANES versus English-speaking adults in the GSS), the size of the sample (from ninety-eight thousand in the NAES to one thousand in the GSS), the geographic variation of the sample (forty primary sampling units in the ANES to over twelve hundred zip codes in the NAES), and critically, the specific questions they ask about immigration. All this helps us to test the robustness of our immigrant threat theory and make a general statement about the impact of immigration in US politics.

First, with the 2010 and 2012 CCES, we were able to assess the impact of immigration attitudes using a multistep question that asked whether respondents favor citizenship for those with good employment records, increasing border patrols, and allowing police to question anyone suspected of being undocumented. We found that attitudes on immigration were significantly correlated with vote choice in the 2012 presidential election, and in all but one case in the 2010 and 2012 senatorial, house, and gubernatorial. Effect magnitudes in the CCES are similar to those in the main ANES analysis. A one standard deviation increase in views on immigration in 2010 is, for example, associated with a 12 to 19 percent increase in the probability of voting Republican across the different contests. All this confirms the important, ongoing role that views on immigration play in US politics.[24]

---

[24] Analysis of the 2010 CCES also indicates that immigration influenced the vote for state house, state senate, attorney general, and secretary of state, but the findings do not persist in 2012.

Using the 2000 and 2004 NAES, we were able to examine the link between immigrant-related views (Should the federal government do more to restrict immigration? Is immigration a serious problem?) along with vote choice in the 2000 and 2004 presidential elections as well as intended vote choice in presidential (2000 and 2004), senatorial (2000), and house elections (2000). Once again, immigration matters for the vote. In every case except for senate elections, after controlling for a range of factors that were purported to drive electoral behavior in that year, views on immigration remained robust. More negative views of immigration led to substantially greater support for Republicans in every election.[25]

The GSS cumulative file offers us another opportunity to reexamine the link between immigration and partisan choice. The GSS only includes views on immigration and partisan choice in a select number of years. In any given year, furthermore, it has a much more limited set of political covariates. Nevertheless, in 1996, 2000, and 2004, we were able to assess the impact of immigration on partisanship and presidential vote choice, and in each case found a statistically significant relationship. Whites who feel the government spends too much for immigrants (2004), those who feel that "bilingual education should be abolished" (2000), and those who believe it is "important to be born in America" (1996) were more likely to favor Republican presidential candidates.[26]

The 2010 ANES survey enables us to explore vote choice in 2010 in the gubernatorial, house, and senatorial elections. In both the house and senate contests, after controlling for a similar set of electoral factors, whites who felt "immigration was a burden" were significantly and substantially more apt to support the Republican candidate.[27] Views on immigration, however, had no clear impact on the gubernatorial vote that year.

Finally, we also sought to determine the role that immigration played in partisan primaries. Since few surveys ask about primary vote choice, and fewer respondents actually vote in those contests, our options were limited. Fortunately, the NAES asked a sufficient sample about the primary vote in the 2000 presidential election. In that election, we found that after controlling for a range of factors that were expected to affect vote choice that year, immigrant-related views were statistically significant in predicting vote choice in the Republican pri-

---

[25] For more details, see the online appendix at http://pages.ucsd.edu/~zhajnal/styled/index.html.

[26] These relationships reached statistical significance at conventional levels.

[27] For the regression, see the online appendix at http://pages.ucsd.edu/~zhajnal/styled/index.html.

mary. All else being equal, those who saw immigration as the nation's most important problem were 7.3 percent more likely to support Bush over McCain—a pattern that fits Bush's relatively tough stance on immigration in that contest. One striking feature of the Republican primary vote is that immigration was especially crucial to Democrats and Independents who switched over to vote in the Republican primary. Attitudes on immigration were roughly five times as powerful a predictor of the vote among non-Republicans voting in the Republican primary. This pattern may indicate that Democrats and Independents who are especially concerned about immigration are shifting over to the Republican Party to favor anti-immigrant candidates. Interestingly, immigration did not appear to be a significant issue in the Democratic primary contest between Al Gore and Bill Bradley, who both offered relatively limited proposals on immigration.[28] Overall, the effects of immigration are robust.[29] Across an array of elections and data sources, restrictive views on immigration led to substantially greater support for Republicans.

Where and When Does Immigration Matter?

The results to this point lead to two conclusions. First, attitudes about immigration and the Latino population appear to play a prominent role in a range of US elections. Immigration is often central. Second,

---

[28] We also looked to see if the within-party effects that we demonstrated earlier with the 2008 ANES presidential vote persisted across elections and data sources. Across each of the data sets and every type of election, views on immigration were always much more consequential for Independents than they were for Democrats or Republicans. Immigration also mattered for the vote choices of Democrats, but the size and statistical significance of the interaction effect varied substantially across elections.

[29] Given claims that much of the instability in party identification comes from measurement error (Green, Palmquist, and Schickler 2002; Green and Palmquist 1990; Goren 2005), we looked to see if immigration still predicted partisanship and vote choice after taking into account measurement error in party identification. To do so, we returned to our main 2008 ANES data set as well as the 2010 and 2012 CCES. With the 2008 ANES, we corrected for measurement error by creating a latent party identification alpha factor score that incorporated the same three different indicators employed by Paul Goren (2005)—a standard party identification scale, feeling thermometer toward the Democratic Party, and feeling thermometer toward the Republican Party. Inserting this latent measure of party identification into the 2008 analysis did almost nothing to alter the results. Immigration still significantly predicted partisanship and vote choice net other factors. Likewise, when we turned to the 2010 and 2012 CCES, and utilized a measure of latent party identification that was based on two standard party identification questions spaced several months apart (pre- and postelection), we discovered that all the statistically significant immigration-related results from the 2010 and 2012 CCES remained robust (for the results, see the online appendix at http://pages.ucsd .edu/~zhajnal/styled/index.html).

the effects of immigration do vary to a certain extent from one election to another. Immigration is not always central. We endeavored to see if there was a pattern to this variation. Does immigration matter more where and when we should expect it to matter more? To study this question, we analyze at each individual election for each year in the NES cumulative file as well as at the results for each of the other elections in the other surveys (2000 NAES, 2004 NAES, GSS cumulative file, 2008 ANES, and 2010 Evaluations of Government and Survey).

In all honesty, looking across elections and years, we could not discern a clear pattern. There is some suggestion that immigration mattered more frequently for statewide contests than it did for house elections. That might suggest that state-level dynamics are an important element of the immigration debate—a point we will return to in chapter 6. And there is real variation in the impact of immigration on presidential contests. We found strong effects for all three presidential contests in the twenty-first century, and more inconsistent effects in the 1990s and 1980s. This might hint at a growing role for immigration in US electoral politics. In the one set of presidential primaries that we examined, there was a greater effect in the Republican primary when the two candidates actively engaged and significantly diverged on immigration than there was in the Democratic primary when immigration was largely ignored. That could indicate either that the salience of immigration in the campaign or policy divergence of the two candidates is consequential.

But none of these differences are all that dramatic. Immigration-related views were relevant in some specific congressional elections (e.g., 2010 and 2000) and irrelevant in some statewide contests (e.g., gubernatorial contests in 2010 and 1976 as well as senatorial elections in 2008, 1988, and 1984). Presidential contests in the most recent decade were always at least in part shaped by immigration, but outcomes in presidential elections in 1976, 1984, and 1988 can also be linked to feelings toward Latinos.

Unfortunately, the available data are not particularly well suited for this sort of time series analysis. All the advantages of having different surveys with varying population samples and distinct questions on immigration that were so critical in trying to demonstrate robust effects now become a liability in attempting to assess variation over time and across space. Is the smaller or null effect in one particular election really because immigrant attitudes were less relevant for that election, or because a different set of covariates are available, because the specific question on immigration is less effective at measuring attitudes, or because of some issue with the sample? We generally cannot exactly say why differences emerge from survey to survey, year to year, or contest to contest.

All we can say on this point is that immigration may be increasing in salience over time, yet before we can assert that with any certainty, much more empirical work needs to be done. It will be hard to generate more data on past contests, but we will certainly have more comparable data for 2012 and future races. Only then will we know if the role of immigration is increasing in a systematic and measurable way.

Discussion

In the last two chapters, we have attempted to demonstrate the power immigration exerts in US politics. As immigration has affected almost every corner of US society and life, it has also impacted the political sphere. With growing immigration comes a dramatic reversal in white partisan attachments. A group that was once dominated by Democrats has become overwhelmingly Republican. This pattern began in the 1960s, but white Americans have become more attached to the Republican Party and more supportive of Republican candidates at almost every level of office even since the 1980s. We fully admit that a range of different factors is driving this massive white Democratic defection in the last three decades. Yet our results indicate that immigration performs an important part in this shift.

We have strived in a variety of ways to tie views on immigration to partisanship and the vote. Those empirical tests have been as rigorous as we could make them. They show—we think decisively—that immigration attitudes plays a real role in shaping the partisan identities and votes of many white Americans. Large numbers of white Americans associate themselves with the Republican Party and its candidates because they have concerns about immigration. The immigrant threat narrative is now very much a central player in US politics. When white Americans choose to align with one of the two major parties, decide which candidate to support in presidential contests, and vote in a range of other elections, attitudes about immigration and Latinos help shape the outcome.

Much remains to be explained, however. We have shown that immigration influences the politics of white America. But we have not clearly demonstrated how. Exactly how and in what ways do changes in the demographics of this country translate into fluctuations in electoral behavior? Do white Americans simply respond directly to the growing immigrant and Latino populations that they witness, is the tone of immigration media coverage becoming more critical, or is something else driving these sharp political reactions? In the next chapters, we address these questions to try to better understand how and why immigration has come to so deeply impact US electoral politics.

PART III

Understanding the Roots of the Backlash

Chapter 4

The Geography of the Immigration Backlash

Immigration impacts all of the United States, but it does so un-
evenly. In California, the state with the largest Latino population,
immigration is felt almost everywhere. With fourteen million
Latino residents, representing almost 40 percent of the state's population, it is hard to move around the California without encountering
some evidence of a changing United States. Immigrants dominate employment in restaurants, landscaping, housekeeping, and numerous
other fields. Immigrants walk the streets. Signs and stores advertise to
immigrants. Given California's long-term and large-scale experience
with immigration, it is not surprising that it was one of the first states to
actively target undocumented immigrants. With Proposition 187, the
Save Our State initiative of 1994, California voters overwhelmingly
passed a measure that sought to exclude undocumented immigrants
from access to a range of public services. Many other states followed
suit. But California was the first.

In Vermont, the state with the smallest Latino population, the
demographic, social, and political story is quite different. Overt evidence of immigration is rare. With only 5,284 Latinos in the entire
state, there are no jobs where immigrants eclipse natives and no
neighborhoods with Latino majorities.[1] Days, months, or even years
are likely to pass before a typical citizen in the state will encounter
an undocumented immigrant. Given the limited impact immigration
has had on the state, it may not be startling to learn that Vermont has
been extraordinarily inactive on the legislative front. In the past five
years, Vermont has adopted only one state law addressing immigra-

---

[1] As of 2012, the total population in Vermont was 626,011.

tion—a bill that urged Congress to authorize more visas for agricultural workers.[2]

Finally, in South Carolina, the state with the fastest-growing immigrant population, politicians and pundits regularly debate the merits as well as pitfalls of immigration there. With Latinos representing only 5 percent of the state's population, daily signs of immigration in the streets are rare. But discussions in the media and elsewhere often return to the subject of South Carolina's rapidly growing immigrant population. That debate stirred widespread concern about the state's immigrant population and eventually led to the passage of the omnibus Illegal Immigration Reform Act (H 4400).[3] That 2008 act increased penalties for businesses that hire undocumented immigrants, forced employers to check the immigration status of their workers, denied public assistance and attendance at public colleges to undocumented immigrants, and in a variety of other ways tried to make the state inhospitable for these immigrants.

These three states highlight one of the most inescapable features of the United States' immigrant transformation: its geographically uneven nature. Some Americans live in areas where there is almost no evidence of large-scale immigration, while others reside in neighborhoods, cities, and states that have been dramatically transformed. Still others are experiencing rapid change for the first time. We believe that this demographic variation matters. These starkly different geographic contexts propel individual white Americans in different directions. We contend that those Americans who are more exposed to the changes wrought by immigration will be among those most likely to feel threatened by immigration, and among those most likely to become politically opposed to policies or parties that might support immigrants. We test this assertion in this chapter. In short, are whites reacting to large, growing concentrations of immigrants with a backlash and shift to the right politically?

In assessing context, we have two goals in mind. The first is to once again demonstrate the broad impact of immigration on US politics. We want to know if the most important political decisions Americans make—issue preferences, party affiliation, and vote choice—can be tied to the context of immigration. The second goal is to try to better understand how the large-scale phenomenon of immigration seeps into the consciousness of individual Americans. What is the mecha-

---

[2] National Conference of State Legislatures 2013.

[3] http://www.postandcourier.com/article/20080605/PC1602/306059853 (accessed July 13, 2014).

nism through which this national trend reaches and influences individuals? Or to put it more plainly, what is it that white Americans are reacting to?

In chapter 2, we outlined two different kinds of mechanisms. One local and direct—living in proximity to large numbers of immigrants—and one national and indirect—seeing, reading, and hearing about the negative consequences of immigration in the media. In this chapter, we assess the first mechanism. Is living near heavy concentrations of immigrants and Latinos threatening enough to produce a reaction by members of the white population? In essence, is context driving at least part of white America's response to immigration?

How Context Might Work:
The Racial Threat Perspective

Why would living near or among a large out-group population lead to any sort of negative reaction? Following a long line of scholars from Key to Hubert Blalock and beyond, we suggest that larger out-groups can represent a threat to members of the in-group.[4] The idea here is that an influx of out-group members can lead to greater competition for available jobs, a struggle for local political offices, reductions in housing prices, white flight, and clashes over any number of public services. From this racial group threat perspective, proximity tends to enhance real or perceived competition for scarce resources. The result is that individuals in contexts with larger minority populations should feel more threatened, express greater animosity, and be especially supportive of a host of policies aimed at maintaining the in-group's social, political, and economic privileges.

This racial group view has traditionally been applied to black-white relations in the US case, but for a range of reasons that we have highlighted throughout the book, we suspect it could also be applied to Latino-white or immigrant-white relations. A pervasive immigrant threat narrative in the media and politics, the widespread concerns of immigrants and immigration expressed by individual Americans in surveys, and the negative stereotypes of Latinos held by many Americans all suggest that the immigrant population does represent a real threat to many white Americans—one that is likely

---

[4] Key 1949; Blalock 1967.

to be sharper in contexts where the immigrant population is larger or growing more rapidly.

Existing Evidence on Immigrant Context

We are, by no means, the first to examine immigrant or Latino context. In fact, a wide range of studies has attempted to assess the link between immigrant context and white attitudes. The bulk of these studies have found that an increase in immigrants can represent a threat and drive a white backlash. Analysis in the United States has demonstrated a robust relationship between the size and growth of the local immigrant population and more hostile views of immigrants.[5] Similarly, a variety of comparative research has found that larger immigrant populations at the national level are associated with more negative views of immigrants and more support for restrictionist immigration policy.[6]

Although the bulk of the research points to an immigrant backlash, there are at least a few studies that reach different conclusions about immigrant context. Some researchers have discovered that immigrant or Latino context has few significant implications.[7] And still others have revealed a positive relationship between immigrant context and white views—especially when the out-group in question is composed primarily of Asian Americans.[8]Finally, several more recent studies have suggested that the impact of ethnic or immigrant context is contingent on either the socioeconomic status of the neighborhood, skill level of the immigrants, or national political debate.[9]

The Limits of the Existing Literature

One read of these mixed findings is that immigrant context has a real though limited and contingent impact on white political behavior. There are reasons to hesitate, however, before concluding that immigrant context is not a central feature in the minds of white Americans.

[5] Newman 2013; Hawley 2013; Ha and Oliver 2010; Ayers and Hofstetter 2008; Campbell, Wong, and Citrin 2006; Hood and Morris 1998; Citrin et al. 1997.
[6] Quillian 1995; McLaren 2003; Dustman and Preston 2001.
[7] Fennelly and Federico 2008; Dixon 2006; Taylor 1998; Burns and Gimpel 2000.
[8] Ha and Oliver 2010; Hood and Morris 1998, 2000; Fox 2004.
[9] Hopkins 2010; Scheve and Slaughter 2001; Oliver and Mendelberg 2000; Branton and Jones 2005.

We contend that there is one important omission in the existent literature that helps to mask the central role played by immigrant context.

The biggest concern with these existing studies is their relatively narrow focus. The vast array of scholarship on immigrant or Latino context in the United States has been narrowly focused on how context affects attitudes about, behavior toward, and policy on the immigrant or minority group itself.[10] In the case of immigration, we either study how context affects attitudes toward immigrants or how it affects policies that explicitly deal with immigrants.[11]

Broader Effects?

The growing reach of immigration in the lives of individual citizens and the political debates of the day suggests that this focus may be too narrow. As we have already noted, there are reasons to believe that the effects of immigration and in particular immigrant context could extend much more broadly. Given the increasingly central role that concerns over immigrants and Latinos play in a range of present-day policy debates, it is certainly possible that the threat associated with higher concentrations of Latinos or immigrants could influence basic policy preferences on everything from education to crime. As well, given the divergent images that the Democratic and Republican parties present when talking about immigration, context could even shape our partisan attachments and vote choices. It is, in our view, crucial that we expand the scope of existing research.

Exactly where should we see these effects? If, as we contend, the debate over immigration has been coupled with a range of other policy debates, the first place to look for effects is in the realm of *policy preferences*. And within the arena of policy, the most obvious set of policies to assess relate directly and explicitly to immigration itself. Indeed, existing studies have already demonstrated that demographic context impacts our policy views on immigration. Generally speaking, higher concentrations of immigrants or Latinos are associated with support for more security at the border, greater restrictions on immigrants once they are in the country, and increased efforts to repatriate immigrants to their home countries.[12]

---

[10] But see Hopkins 2010; Hero and Preuhs 2006.

[11] Scheve and Slaughter 2001; Hood and Morris 1998, 2000; Stein, Post, and Rinden 2000; Burns and Gimpel 2000; Branton and Jones 2005. But see Fox 2004; Hero and Preuhs 2006.

[12] Ha and Oliver 2010; Ayers and Hofstetter 2008; Campbell, Wong, and Citrin 2006; Burns and Gimpel 2000; Stein, Post, and Rinden 2000.

Immigration is not, we argue, the only policy arena to be connected to immigration and especially the immigrant threat narrative. The question of whether Mexican immigrants are "deserving" of social services has long been a subject of debate and continues to be a source of it today.[13] Moreover, Latinos now make up almost 30 percent of the population receiving Temporary Aid to Needy Families benefits.[14] And perhaps most important, the immigrant threat narrative has repeatedly highlighted the heavy reliance of immigrants on public assistance and the costs that this raises for the US taxpayer.

An equally plausible connection could be made between crime and immigration. As we will show in the following chapter, a common frame that the media uses in their immigration news stories is one where immigrants are perpetrators of crime. And as with welfare, a disproportionate number of Latinos have been caught up in the criminal justice system. Latinos now, unfortunately, make up a little over one-fifth of all those incarcerated in the United States.[15] The fact that 19 percent of all immigration-related bills introduced by state legislatures address criminal justice indicates that the connection between crime and immigration is firmly entrenched.[16] One might reasonably assume that white Americans are at least partly thinking about the immigrant or Latino populations when they consider criminal justice policy.

There is also plenty of evidence linking immigration and health care policy. The immigrant threat narrative frequently spotlights the costs of immigrants' use of public health services. Anti-immigrant groups like FAIR proclaim that undocumented immigrants cost federal and state governments $10.7 billion annually in health care spending. State legislatures have responded by introducing hundreds of bills related to immigrant health care over the past decade.[17] The result is widespread public concern. Fully 85 percent of Americans believe that providing services like school and health care to undocumented immigrants costs taxpayers too much.[18]

In all these cases, context is likely to shift policy views in the same direction. Public perceptions that immigrants are disproportionately using public services as well as a sense that immigrants and their off-

---

[13] Chavez 2008; Fox 2012.
[14] Office of Family Assistance 2010, http://www.acf.hhs.gov/programs/ofa/resource/character/fy2010/fy2010-chap10-ys-final (accessed July 21, 2014).
[15] US Bureau of Justice 2012.
[16] National Conference of State Legislatures 2013.
[17] Ibid.
[18] NPR/Kaiser 2004 poll, cited in Polling Report 2014.

spring represent a considerable share of the "receiving" population provide a strong motivation for retrenchment. Additional accounts about the criminality of these groups similarly might shift the balance toward more punitive measures. To the degree that individuals think immigrants and other minorities are using social services without paying taxes, then there is a compelling logic to be less generous, reduce services, and pay fewer taxes. If true, all these connections should lead to a conservative policy shift among members of the white population. Furthermore, if immigration is pushing whites to the right on this array of issues, then there is a possibility that immigration is influencing whites' overall ideological identities and increasing the probability of identifying as a conservative.

Beyond policy, in our immigration backlash theory there are, as we have already asserted, clear partisan implications for all this. Whites who fear and resent immigration's impact on the nation will likely be aware of the growing Latino and Asian American population's overwhelming support for the Democratic Party, not to mention the Republican Party's strong stance against benefits for immigrants and its efforts to limit future immigration. In short, if immigrants are becoming more central to the thinking of white Americans, and if immigrants can and do pose a threat, as many previous studies suggest, then there is reason to believe that Latino context could have broader *political* implications. We need to consider the effects of minority context not just on how Americans think about immigrants and minorities but also on how they think about the broader array of policies that are at different times at least implicitly linked to immigration. Only through a broader study can we begin to understand the extent of immigration's impact on US politics.

Wide-Ranging Effects Are Not New

Although existing studies of immigration have generally been limited to a focus on how immigrants affect attitudes toward immigration itself, studies of black-white relations have examined a wider array of outcomes. Moreover, these tests suggest that a far-reaching white backlash has occurred at several points in the past.[19] Proximity to blacks

---

[19] Often, the nation has experienced periods of white backlash when the African American population has been particularly vocal or active at trying to secure greater rights (Klinkner and Smith 1999). During Reconstruction, the expansion of black political representation was countered with massive resistance as white Southerners instituted a program of unprecedented violence, poll taxes, new residency and registration requirements, and at-large elec-

has been linked to greater racial antagonism by whites in a variety of forms including more negative views of blacks themselves, violence against blacks such as riots and lynching, support for racist candidates, and greater opposition to policies designed to aid blacks.[20]

Critically, the confirmed effects of black context are even broader. Larger black populations have also been linked to more conservative views on a range of implicitly racial policies and large-scale defection from the Democratic Party.[21] While several more recent studies have found that the effects of black context are contingent on socioeconomic status, there seems little doubt that black racial context has often been an important force shaping white political choices and actions.[22] We believe that a similar process is at work when large numbers of Latinos and immigrants enter into a specific locale.

Measuring Context

In our examination of context, one of the first tasks we have to undertake is to determine exactly how we measure it. The first main question here is, Precisely who and what are white Americans reacting to? Are their concerns centered on all immigrants, or are particular subsets of this population viewed as especially problematic and threatening? Likewise, is white unease concentrated solely on the foreign born or are the two pan-ethnic groups associated with immigration today viewed with equal suspicion? Finally, are white Americans reacting to

---

tions (Kousser 1999). Over a century later, the civil rights movement was met with a similarly broad array of defensive white actions (Parker 1990).

[20] On negative views of blacks, see Dixon 2006; Taylor 1998; Quillian 1995. But see Oliver and Wong 2003; Kinder and Mendelberg 1995. On violence against blacks, see Corzine, Creech, and Corzine 1983. On support for racist candidates, see Black and Black 1973. But see Voss 1996. On greater opposition to policies designed to aid blacks, see Giles and Evans 1986; Fossett and Kiecolt 1989; Key 1949.

[21] On implicitly racist policies, see Winter 2008; Soss, Langbein, and Metelko 2006; Hero and Preuhs 2006; Fellowes and Rowe 2004; Keiser et al. 2004; Soss et al. 2001; Johnson 2001; Albritton 1990. On Democratic Party defection, see Huckfeldt and Kohfeld 1989. A different line of research has shown a robust relationship between racial diversity and the provision of public goods. In contexts with greater diversity, Americans appear to be less willing to pay for and provide public services (Alesina, Baqir, and Easterly 1999; Hopkins 2010;Hero 1998; Soss et al. 2008; Hero and Preuhs 2006; Fellowes and Rowe 2004; Keiser et al. 2004).

[22] On socioeconomic factors, see Oliver and Mendelberg 2000; Branton and Jones 2005. Other work revolving around individual attitudes toward minorities rather than on geographic context has been equally persuasive about how broadly attitudes toward blacks can impact core policy views. These studies have shown that a range of nonracial policies can and have become racially coded. In particular, there is strong evidence that individual policy preferences on welfare, education, crime, and a host of other core issue arenas have, at least at some points in the past, been shaped by attitudes toward blacks (Gilens 1999; Kinder and Sanders 1996; Kinder and Kam 2010).

the overall size of the immigrant population or changes in the immigrant population? Studies of immigrant context typically focus on some measure of the overall foreign-born population. We suspect, however, that white Americans do make one important distinction when it comes to outsiders. We argue that Latinos and Asian Americans should be examined separately because the two groups are likely to spark different kinds of reactions from white Americans. Reactions should differ, we maintain, because Asian Americans and Latinos hold dissimilar places in US society and the US psyche.

For one, members of the two pan-ethnic groups tend to end up on opposite ends of the socioeconomic spectrum. Asian Americans tend to fall near whites on the top end of the socioeconomic hierarchy, while Latinos are on average considerably less well-off and fall closer to African Americans on the bottom end of the scale. The median household income of Asian Americans, for example, was almost $75,000 in 2009, or roughly $10,000 more than the figure for whites. At the opposite end of the range, median Latino households only earned about $39,000.[23] Asian Americans are also much less likely than Latinos to be unemployed, substantially less likely to be poor, and on average hold much more wealth than Latinos.[24] Second, stereotypes of the two groups tend to differ dramatically.[25] Whereas large numbers of white Americans tend to view Latinos as less intelligent, more prone to welfare, and not especially hard working, the bulk of white Americans tend to view Asian Americans in roughly the opposite fashion.[26]

Third, the immigrant experience of the two groups is frequently radically different. Far fewer Asian immigrants enter the United States without documentation when compared to Latinos. The US Department of Homeland Security estimates that 75 percent of undocumented immigrants in 2011 hail from Latin or Central America, whereas only 10 percent come from Asia.[27] Furthermore, although the clear majority of Latino immigrants in the United States are here legally, most white Americans believe that undocumented immigrants are the majority of Latino immigrant population.[28] If an immigrant's citizenship status matters in the minds of white Americans—as

---

[23] US Census Bureau 2010.
[24] Ibid.
[25] Bobo 2001; Lee 2001.
[26] Bobo 2001.
[27] http://www.dhs.gov/xlibrary/assets/statistics/publications/ois_ill_pe_2011.pdf (accessed July 13, 2014).
[28] Massey and Sanchez 2010.

many polls indicate is the case—then Latinos are likely to hold a different place than Asian Americans in the psyche of individual Americans.

Survey data on intergroup relations are not extensive, but the available evidence does seem to suggest that white Americans tend to be more concerned about Latinos than they are about Asian Americans. For example, in a poll asking whites how well they generally get along with other racial groups, 92 percent say they get along with Asians, while only 67 percent felt the same way about Latinos.[29] In this light, it is also interesting to note that while fully 48 percent of Americans believe there are too many immigrants from Latin American countries, only 31 percent say there are too many immigrants from Asian countries.[30]

Exactly what all these patterns imply in terms of a threat to the white community is not absolutely apparent. Given these differences in socioeconomic standings and stereotypes, it is certainly possible that Latinos will represent more of threat than the Asian American population. At least if concerns about welfare, redistribution, and criminality dominate white views, then reactions to the Latino population could mirror backlashes against the black population. By contrast, Asian Americans, depicted as the model minority by the media and politicians, could represent less of a threat and more of a potential partner.[31] Whatever the exact response is for each pan-ethnic group, it seems unlikely that whites will react to members of the two groups in the same way.

Individual Americans could also make critical distinctions between different groups within the Latino population—undocumented, documented, foreign born, and/or native born—although, as we have argued throughout this book, we suspect that most of these categories are muddled together in the minds of many white Americans—espe-

---

[29] Intergroup Relations Survey, sponsored by the National Conference for Community and Justice, 2005. The results from this survey also found that a larger percentage of whites responded that they felt closer to Asians relative to blacks and Latinos.

[30] Gallup 2008 poll, cited in Polling Report 2014. Experimental research also indicates that whites report much higher levels of anxiety about the costs of immigration when the images are of Latinos (Brader, Valentino, and Suhay 2008).

[31] Wu 2003. One other possibility is that the higher socioeconomic status of Asian Americans represents *more* of a threat to members of the white community. There have obviously been major periods of anti-Asian discrimination in US history (Kim 2003). The internment of Japanese Americans during World War II is perhaps the most famous instance, but controversy surrounding Asian American financing of political campaigns and concerns about the loyalty of an Asian American scientist in the Wen Ho Lee case suggest that concerns about the Asian American population are likely to be ongoing.

cially since the majority of white Americans think that the most Latinos are undocumented. As we have already noted, white attitudes toward undocumented immigrants are highly correlated with their views toward legal immigrants and Latinos. In our earlier analysis of partisanship and the vote in chapters 2 and 3, measures of these three groups were largely interchangeable and led to similar results. Thus, it is possible that regardless of nativity, all Latinos will be lumped together in the eyes of white Americans.[32] For this reason, we concentrate on the percentage of Latinos in a state as our primary measures of context. Since it is not at all clear in advance who white Americans are reacting to, and as such, what the best measure of context is, we repeat our analysis with each of these different measures. Specifically, we assess context by looking first at racial or pan-ethnic groups, but then consider the undocumented, total foreign-born, and foreign-born Latino populations.

Level versus Rate of Growth

In thinking about context and racial threat it is also important to distinguish between the overall size of a minority group and rate at which that minority group is growing. Scholars have typically focused on overall size, yet there has been considerable media speculation and significant empirical research suggesting that white reactions to immigration are especially pronounced in new destination states where the overall number of immigrants may still be small but the rapid growth is causing widespread anxiety.[33] Given this speculation, it is important that we consider both size and the rate of immigrant population growth as we move forward with our analysis.

Alternative Accounts of How Context Works

We believe that heavier concentrations of immigrants and in particular larger Latino populations will heighten white perceptions of threat as well as spark a wide-ranging political backlash. But a racial threat view is far from the only possible understanding of how immigrant context should work in the US case. An alternative perspective contends that proximity should more often than not lead to greater under-

---

[32] Patterns in racial hate crimes as well as past discriminatory actions by the government also indicate that foreign nativity can be irrelevant to white actions (Almageur 1994).

[33] Severson 2011; Sulzberger 2010; Newman 2013; Hopkins 2010.

standing and acceptance.[34] This *contact hypothesis* argues that out-group animosity is more often the result of inaccurate perceptions about the out-group than it is about real competition over resources. From this vantage point, personal interaction with out-groups exposes majority group members to new, more accurate information about out-group members that should disconfirm negative stereotypes and allow for the development of more favorable views. In many versions of this contact hypothesis, the nature of the contact is critical and positive understanding is only likely to grow when individuals of similar status interact in a cooperative setting.[35]

It is crucial to note that in the analysis that follows, we do not directly test the contact hypotheses. Our primary measure of context—state racial demographics—is probably correlated with contact, but only weakly. It is entirely possible for whites living in extremely diverse states to engage in few personal interactions with members of minority out-groups, especially given the high rates of residential segregation in the nation.[36] In part to address this concern, we will incorporate neighborhood-level demographics in alternate analyses. But even there, we will not be measuring interaction or contact with immigrants. These zip-code-level data do not tell us directly about the amount or nature of contact that members of different groups have at the individual level. Hence, our findings will say little about the potential of specific forms of interracial contact to foster cooperation or goodwill. If we were able to measure actual and meaningful contact with members of the Latino population or different types of immigrants, our story—or at least certain aspects of it—might be quite different.

Finally, another possibility is that context has no independent effect on intergroup attitudes or policy views. Either because group views are predicated on a rigid type of prejudice impervious to change, or because other individual characteristics like education or economic status are the primary factors shaping group as well as policy views, geographic context may be largely irrelevant for understanding intergroup conflict and cooperation. If true, attitudes toward immigrants and policies that might benefit immigrants should be unrelated to geographic context once we control for individual characteristics.

[34] Allport 1954; Jackman and Crane 1986; Pettigrew et al. 2007; Dixon and Rosenbaum 2004.
[35] Allport 1954; Jackman and Crane 1986.
[36] Massey 2001.

Why State Context?

We exploit the uneven nature of racial transformation in the United States by looking specifically at the relationship between *state* racial context and white policy preferences along with partisan proclivities. We focus on the state context for several reasons. The first is theoretical. States are one of the primary actors in the race and immigration debate. In 2011, state legislatures put forward 1,607 measures on immigration alone.[37] We also believe that the presence and political power of Latinos is keenly felt at the state level. In states with sizable Latino populations, the political debate has frequently centered on issues related to race and ethnicity. The debate over Proposition 187 in California in the 1990s and tumult over the recent immigration bill in Arizona, SB 1070, are just two of the most dramatic examples of this phenomenon. Moreover, Latino representation, where it exists, can be especially pronounced at the state level.[38] Latinos, for instance, hold 24 percent of the assembly seats in California.

Second, existing research suggests that state context does have important political effects. We believe that a focus on the state is appropriate given that past research has demonstrated a link between state-level context (both racial and cultural) and state-level policy outcomes as well as between state context and state macropartisanship.[39] Similar mechanisms could certainly be at work at the neighborhood, city, or metropolitan level, but it is clear that when it comes to race and immigration, much is happening at the state level.

Third, there is evidence that individual Americans have a reasonable sense of the demographics of their states. An ever-present concern with contextual analysis is that individual residents do not actually know much about the demographic profile of their area.[40] This problem may actually be less severe at the state level, however. Survey data indicate that Americans do tend to overestimate the absolute number of immigrants and minorities in their state.[41] Yet the same data show that Americans tend to know the size of the state immigrant/minority population relative to other states. There is, in fact, a reasonably close correlation between individual perceptions and actual state rankings.[42]

---

[37] National Conference of State Legislatures 2013.
[38] Casellas 2011.
[39] Hero 1998; Hero and Preuhs 2006; Erikson, Wright, and McIver 1993.
[40] Wong 2007.
[41] Enos 2012.
[42] Ibid. To the extent that Americans do not know the racial makeup of their states, our results

Finally, we believe there is a critical distinction to be made between the more intimate, personal contacts, which existing studies show can have beneficial effects on intergroup understanding, and proximity to out-groups, which research indicates can often exacerbate racial tensions.[43] By focusing on a larger geographic unit like the state, we are more likely to be assessing the proximity and associated political threats that we have outlined in our theory. By contrast, the smaller the geographic unit that we examine, the more likely we are to pick up the effects of intimate contact. In addition, at lower levels, proximity and contact are likely to be increasingly correlated. If, for example, we look at a relatively small geographic unit like the neighborhood, the effects of proximity and contact become intricately intertwined, making it difficult to ascertain whether we are ultimately measuring the effects of contact or proximity, or both. By concentrating on a larger geographic unit, we minimize the confusion, and are able to say more about proximity along with its associated political, social, and economic threats.

The final and perhaps most important reason to focus on state context is a practical one. A principal challenge of studying the effects of racial context on public opinion is selection bias. Individuals with a particular set of political views may decide to move to or away from a particular locale. There is, for instance, clear evidence of large-scale white flight from neighborhoods and cities with large black populations.[44] If past patterns are being repeated today, we may be seeing similar movement away from predominantly Latino or Asian American locales. If this kind of selection is occurring, then any simple correlation between immigrant context and white views would likely understate the role of racial threat, and might even produce a spurious positive relationship between immigrant context and white views. Most studies recognize this problem, but few are able to deal with it effectively.[45]

Fortunately, we can considerably reduce concerns about selection and endogeneity by exploring the larger geographic unit of the state. Selective migration across states is much less common than selective migration across neighborhoods and municipal boundaries. Just as we know that one's neighborhood choice can be significantly impacted by one's racial views, we also have fairly strong evidence indicating that

---

should be biased downward. This "noise" in our contextual measure should only serve to reduce significance levels.

[43] On the contact hypotheses, see Ellison, Shin, and Leal 2011.

[44] Massey and Hajnal 1995.

[45] But see Oliver and Wong 2003.

state of residence is largely unrelated to racial views.[46] The first piece of evidence is that few people move across states. According to the US Census, less than 1 percent of all Americans move across state borders in any given five-year period.[47] If few people move from state to state, there cannot be a significant amount of selection occurring at the state level. Among white Americans who do decide to move, the vast majority either moves within the same county or to a different county within a state.[48]

Second, studies of interstate migration—unlike studies of neighborhoods or municipalities—have not found that race plays a major role in migration decisions.[49] Mobility across states is relatively costly, and thus driven almost exclusively by employment and family.[50] Concerns about the race/ethnicity of one's neighbors may be enough to move one out of the neighborhood or even to the next municipality, but they are seldom strong enough to move one out of the state. As such, state context represents a relatively exogenous context. In secondary analysis we will consider neighborhood effects, although our primary focus will be on state context.

Data and Empirical Strategy

To assess the effects of state and neighborhood context on white views, we turn to the 2000 and 2004 NAES. The NAES is an ideal source because it contains a large sample (well over fifty thousand respondents per survey) and extensive geographic variation (large samples in all mainland states and respondents from over fourteen hundred different zip codes).[51] In addition, the surveys contain questions on a range of policy issues, basic ideology, party identification, and vote choice. In subsequent analyses we present results from the 2000 NAES—largely because it has a much wider array of policy questions—but analysis of the 2004 NAES leads to a similar set of conclusions.

Our analysis consists of a series of hierarchical linear models (HLM) that simultaneously incorporate immigrant/racial context, in-

---

[46] Bobo and Zubrinsky 1996; Clark 1992; Oliver and Wong 2003.
[47] US Census Bureau 2003.
[48] US Census Bureau 2008.
[49] Greenwood 1975.
[50] Gimpel 1999.
[51] By contrast, the main data set that we have been using to this point, the ANES, only samples from forty primary sampling units, and therefore is inappropriate for either state- or neighborhood-level analysis.

dividual characteristics, and socioeconomic context to try to explain the individual political orientations of white Americans. This method can take into account the different units of analysis that we will consider (individual, neighborhood, and state) and minimizes the correlation in error terms among respondents in the same geographic unit.[52] The dependent variables in our models revolve around policy areas that have been most clearly and regularly linked to immigrants as well as the issue of immigration. Specifically, we examine views on immigration (How serious of a problem is immigration to the United States?), social welfare (How serious of a problem is poverty? Should the federal government try to reduce income differences between rich and poor Americans? Should the federal government spend more or less money on health care for the poor?), three different questions related to health care, two different questions on criminal justice, and one question each on education and tax policy.[53]

To determine if racial context has influenced more fundamental political identities, we also analyze ideology, party identification, and vote choice. Liberal-conservative ideology is measured with a standard self-identified question (Generally speaking, do you consider your political views very conservative . . . [or] very liberal?). Party identification is measured with a standard self-identified question (Generally speaking, do you usually think of yourself as a Republican, a Democrat, an Independent, or something else?).[54] We examine the vote in the 2000 and 2004 presidential and congressional elections. The analysis is restricted to major party voters.

As we discussed in the previous section, we measure context by focusing on state-level demographics. Specifically, the percentage of both Latinos and Asian Americans in a state serve as our primary measures of context.[55] Given that several existing studies suggest that

---

[52] The model also takes into account both fixed and random effects.

[53] The questions on health care policy are: Do you favor or oppose using government funds to make sure that every child in the United States is covered by health insurance?; Should the federal government spend more or less money on health care for the elderly?; and, Should the federal government spend more or less money for health care to cover the uninsured? The questions on criminal justice are: Do you favor or oppose the death penalty?; and, How serious a problem is the number of criminals who are not punished enough? The education question is: Should the federal government provide more financial assistance to public elementary and secondary schools? For tax policy the question is: Should the federal government increase taxes on the wealthy?

[54] We employ a three-point party identification scale (Democrat-Independent-Republican) in the analysis presented here, but alternate tests using a five- and seven-point scale measure of partisanship as well as logistic regression analysis isolating Democratic or Republican identifiers lead to the same set of conclusions.

[55] Given uncertainty about which group or groups white Americans are reacting to, we perform a series of alternate specifications that we describe in the robustness checks section below.

changes in the size of the immigrant population are more consequential than the absolute size of the out-group, in alternate tests we also consider growth in the immigrant population.[56]

To help ensure that the relationships we see between context and white views are not spurious, we include key individual characteristics and several different measures of state context that have also been tied to political views. At the state level, we also include controls for socioeconomic status (as captured by median household income and the percentage with a college degree) and current economic conditions (measured by the percent unemployed). As additional controls, we distinguish between respondents who live in urban, suburban, and rural areas. Our sample is restricted to those respondents who self-identify as non-Hispanic white. In terms of individual demographic characteristics, we control for education (the last grade of school completed sorted into nine categories), household income (divided into nine categories), gender, age in years, employment status, union membership, and whether or not there are any children in the household. Also, since policy views are often driven by political ideology and party identification, we include both measures in our models of policy choice.

Context and White Political Views

Does context matter? Do those living near larger Latino populations have distinct political views on political issues related to immigration? In answering these questions, we follow a logical pattern. We begin by looking at immigration policy attitudes, since it is the one issue most explicitly tied to immigration. We then we slowly branch out to consider other issues associated with immigration: welfare, crime, and health services. Our test of context continues by exploring other broader political orientations: ideology, party identification, and the vote. For all these tests, we are interested in knowing if white Americans react to significant numbers of Latinos in their states with a backlash as well as a shift to the right politically.

Immigration

If heavy concentrations of Latinos represent a threat, the clearest indication of that would be finding that whites in states with larger Latino

[56] Hopkins 2010; Newman 2013.

TABLE 4.1
The Effect of Latino Context on Immigration and Social Welfare Views

	Immigration a serious problem	Social welfare policy		
		Poverty a serious problem	Reduce income inequality	Less spending on Medicaid
State context				
Percent Latino	0.05 (0.01)**	0.02 (0.01)+	0.02 (0.008)**	0.03 (0.01)**
Percent Asian American	0.03 (0.06)	−0.01 (0.005)*	−0.05 (0.04)	−0.01 (0.01)
Percent African American	0.03 (0.01)**	−0.09 (0.09)	0.08 (0.08)	0.01 (0.01)
Median income	−0.09 (0.03)**	0.02 (0.02)	−0.01 (0.19)	0.03 (0.03)
Percent college educated	−0.05 (0.04)**	−0.01 (0.02)	−0.01 (0.02)	−0.01 (0.003)+
Percent unemployed	−0.02 (0.08)	−0.06 (0.04)	0.05 (0.04)	−0.02 (0.06)
Political orientation				
Republican	0.04 (0.01)**	0.08 (0.01)**	0.08 (0.01)**	0.13 (0.01)**
Conservative	0.06 (0.01)**	0.11 (0.01)**	0.08 (0.01)**	0.13 (0.01)**
Socioeconomic status				
Education	−0.09 (0.00)**	0.01 (0.002)**	0.02 (0.002)**	0.01 (0.004)**
Income	−0.01 (0.01)	0.02 (0.003)**	0.03 (0.003)**	0.02 (0.004)**
Age	0.00 (0.01)	0.01 (0.008)	0.02 (0.009)**	0.01 (0.01)
Female	0.10 (0.02)**	−0.27(0.01)***	−0.06 (0.01)**	0.02 (0.01)
Union member	0.02 (0.03)	−0.04 (0.01)**	−0.01 (0.01)	0.01 (0.02)
Have children	−0.02 (0.02)	−0.03 (0.01)**	−0.05 (0.01)**	0.02 (0.02)
Controls				
Years in home	0.02 (0.00)**	−0.03 (0.01)**	0.02 (0.004)**	0.04 (0.06)
Urban	−0.12 (0.04)**	0.03 (0.01)*	0.01 (0.01)	−0.03 (0.02)*
Suburban	−0.06 (0.03)*	0.03 (0.01*)	0.04** (0.01)	−0.02 (0.02)
Constant	3.45 (0.11)**	1.56 (0.08)**	0.92 (0.06)**	0.70 (0.09)
N	7,700	18,795	7,584	7,708
Log likelihood	−9,527.73	−19,674.34	−4,965.51	−7,612.37

*p < 0.05
**p < 0.01
+p < 0.10

Note: HLM regression estimates. Entries not in parentheses are the HLM regression coefficients, and entries in parentheses are the corresponding standard errors.

Sources: National Annenberg Election Survey 2000; US Census Bureau 2000.

populations are more concerned about immigration. This is exactly what we discover. Looking at the first row of the first model in table 4.1, we see that white Americans who live in states with larger Latino populations are significantly more likely to view immigration as a serious problem. The magnitude of the effect is relatively small, though. All else being equal, a two standard deviation shift in the size of the Latino population is associated with a 7 percent increase in the likelihood of viewing immigration as a "serious problem."[57] There are no other questions on immigration in the 2000 NAES, but the 2004 NAES asked respondents to identify the "most important problem" facing the nation. Here we found a similar pattern. Whites residing in states with larger Latino populations were more likely to believe that immigration was the country's biggest problem relative to whites residing in states with a smaller Latino population.

As we expected, Asian American context does not have the same effect. Whites who live in states with high concentrations of Asian Americans are no more or less likely to view immigration as a serious problem compared to whites residing in states with a minimal Asian population. The divergent effects for Asian Americans mirror the divergent perspectives that white Americans have of this pan-ethnic group.

Social Welfare

In the rest of table 4.1, we depict social welfare policy—the other policy area that has been most closely tied to immigration. The results in the second and fourth columns of the table indicate that the impact of minority context does, in fact, extend beyond the confines of immigration policy.[58] On all three questions related to welfare, there are signs that living in a state with a higher proportion of Latinos is tied to greater concern about welfare. Whether respondents think poverty is a serious problem, how much they think government should do to try to reduce income differences between rich and poor Americans, and to what extent they believe the government spends money on health care for the poor are all negatively as well as significantly or nearly significantly related to the size of the state's Latino population. In other words, in states with higher concentrations of Latinos, whites are less likely to see poverty as an issue, want to redis-

---

[57] Assessing substantive effects is not straightforward with an HLM. To approximate the marginal effects, we use the STATA package developed by Michael Tomz, Jason Wittenberg, and Gary King (2003), known as Clarify, on an identical linear regression model (or when appropriate, a probit or ordered probit model). There will undoubtedly be some error in this approximation, although an eyeball test of the OLS model and HLM suggests that the substantive effects are not dramatically different. All predicted probabilities are calculated by varying the quantity of interest from the tenth to ninetieth percentile while holding all other independent variables constant at their mean or modal value.

[58] At this point, it is also worth noting that the individual control variables included in the model generally perform as expected. Self-identified conservatives and Republicans are, for example, more anti-immigration and significantly more conservative on the host of policy questions we assess.

tribute income to the poor, and want to spend money on medical care for the poor relative to whites living in states with a small concentration of Latinos. The magnitude of the effects, once again, is not dramatic but it is meaningful. Living in a state with a relatively high share of Latinos is linked to a 10 percent decline in whites' willingness to reduce income inequality.

Across the three welfare questions, we see again that Asian American context exerts a different and largely negligible relationship with white views. In two of the three cases, living in a state with a higher concentration of Asian Americans is unrelated to white policy preferences. The only exception is with respect to white attitudes toward poverty. And in this case, Asian American context is associated with more *liberal* rather than more conservative views. One reading of the divergent contextual effects for Latinos and Asian Americans is that whites are threatened by Latinos but sympathetic to Asian Americans. One could also interpret the results as saying that if the poor or those in need are disproportionately Latino, then individual white Americans are less likely to both think help is necessary and want to help. But if the disadvantaged are more likely to come from the Asian American population, then more whites believe support is warranted. To this point, the results essentially reaffirm existing research on Latino and Asian American context.[59] We now turn to policy areas that scholars of immigrant context have largely ignored.

Health Care and Criminal Justice

The estimates from table 4.2 further the same themes by illustrating a range of links between context and a series of other policy issues connected—but perhaps not quite as closely—to the debate on immigration. We begin with health care. Across all three health care questions, a large statewide Latino population is associated with less support for health care benefits. Whites living in states with large Latino populations are more likely to oppose spending money to insure the uninsured, significantly less apt to want to spend on Medicare, and significantly less eager to expand resources to ensure that all children are covered by health care. All these findings are vis-à-vis whites residing in states where the percentage of Latinos is minimal.

In the fifth and sixth columns of table 4.2, we present results for the effects of Latino context on whites' views toward criminal justice

---

[59] Ha and Oliver 2010; Ayers and Hofstetter 2008; Hero and Preuhs 2006; Stein, Post, and Rinden 2000. But see Hood and Morris 2000; Fox 2004.

TABLE 4.2
The Effect of Latino Context on Health Care and Criminal Justice Views

	Health care			Criminal justice	
	No help to cover uninsured	*Less Medicare spending*	*Less spending on children's health care*	*Favor death penalty*	*Punish criminals more*
State context					
Percent Latino	0.03 (0.01)**	0.02 (0.01)+	0.02 (0.007)*	0.03 (0.01)**	0.02 (0.01)
Percent Asian American	-0.06 (0.06)	-0.04 (0.05)	-0.02 (0.04)	-0.01 (0.004)**	-0.03 (0.06)
Percent African American	0.02 (0.01)	-0.02 (0.009)**	-0.09 (0.06)	0.01 (0.007)+	0.05 (0.01)**
Median income	-0.03 (0.02)	0.02 (0.06)**	0.09 (0.04)	-0.06 (0.18)	-0.02 (0.02)**
Percent college educated	-0.02 (0.03)	0.29 (0.06)**	0.04 (0.04)	-0.01 (0.02)	-0.04 (0.03)
Percent unemployed	-0.05 (0.04)	0.03 (0.05)	0.02 (0.04)	-0.02 (0.04)	0.02 (0.04)
Political					
Republican	0.14 (0.01)**	0.08 (0.01)**	0.08 (0.01)**	0.06 (0.01)**	0.07 (0.01)**
Conservative	0.16 (0.01)**	0.09 (0.01)**	0.08 (0.005)**	0.06 (0.01)**	0.12 (0.01)**

TABLE 4.2
(continued)

	Health care			Criminal justice	
	No help to cover uninsured	Less Medicare spending	Less spending on children's health care	Favor death penalty	Punish criminals more
Socioeconomic status					
Education	0.01 (0.003)**	0.02 (0.003)**	0.01 (0.002)**	−0.02 (0.002)**	−0.07 (0.01)**
Income	0.02 (0.003)**	0.01 (0.004)**	0.01 (0.002)**	0.03 (0.02)	−0.01 (0.003)**
Age	0.02 (0.08)+	0.01 (0.01)	0.03 (0.07)	−0.02 (0.02)	−0.01 (0.01)**
Female	−0.09 (0.01)**	−0.07 (0.01)**	−0.06 (0.01)**	−0.05 (0.01)**	0.15 (0.01)**
Union member	−0.02 (0.01)	−0.04 (0.02)**	−0.01 (0.01)*	0.01 (0.01)	0.05 (0.01)**
Have children	−0.03 (0.01)**	−0.002 (0.01)	−0.04 (0.01)**	0.01 (0.01)	0.06 (0.01)**
Controls					
Years in home	0.09 (0.04)+	0.01 (0.005)**	0.01 (0.003)**	−0.01 (0.003)**	0.01 (0.04)
Urban	−0.03 (0.01)	−0.03 (0.02)+	0.01 (0.01)*	−0.06 (0.01)**	−0.06 (0.01)**
Suburban	0.02 (0.01)	−0.02 (0.02)	0.02 (0.01)	−0.01 (0.01)	−0.06 (0.10)
Constant	0.73 (0.08)**	0.80 (0.07)**	0.81 (0.06)**	1.73 (0.06)	2.99 (0.09)**
N	18,509	8,089	7,885	8,177	18,601
Log likelihood	−19,933.71	−5,907.50	−3,182.90	−3,933.99	−19,908.39

*p < 0.05
**p < 0.01
+p < 0.10

Note: HLM regression estimates. Entries not in parentheses are the HLM regression coefficients, and entries in parentheses are the corresponding standard errors

Sources: National Annenberg Election Survey 2000; US Census Bureau 2000.

policies. The results are not as consistent or robust as they are for health care, but at least in terms of the death penalty, whites' preferences for punishment become more severe as the size of the Latino population increases. All else being equal, whites living in states with larger Latino populations are 10 percent more likely to favor the death penalty than whites living in states with few Latinos. There is, however, no apparent Latino contextual effect on the degree to which white respondents feel that "criminals are not being punished enough."[60]

As before, we also see a different effect for Asian American context. Proximity to Asian Americans is either unrelated to white views or associated with greater leniency with respect to the death penalty. The contrast between the punitive nature of the response to Latino context and forgiving character of the response to Asian American context again suggests that white perceptions vary widely about how threatening or deserving the two pan-ethnic groups are.[61]

The other interesting conclusion that emerges from the results presented in tables 4.1–4.2 concerns the relevance of black context. Although the effects are uneven, we see some signs of its relevance. Echoing past research, whites appear to react negatively to large black populations. Whites who live in states with a large black population are especially apt to favor harsher punishments for criminals.[62]

Other Policy Areas

The NAES also asks about education and tax policy—two areas that are less directly tied to immigration, but where the rhetoric over immigrants' use of public services could be relevant. In these two policy areas ties between Latino context and policy views are much more tenuous, although they cannot be ruled out. In terms of tax policy, there are fewer reasons to suspect a link with immigration. The public debate on tax policy is generally not focused on immigrants. Nevertheless, on occasion critics of undocumented immigration will highlight the fact that many of these immigrants do not pay income taxes. Educational reform is likewise an issue not always associated with immigrants, but there are times when immigrant access to educational funding does get widespread attention, as in the case of Ala-

---

[60] There were also no significant effects for Latino context on two questions that asked about gun control laws.

[61] Brader, Valentino, and Suhay 2008.

[62] Gilliam and Iyengar 2000.

bama's latest anti-immigrant law or the US Supreme Court ruling in *Plyler v. Doe*.[63]

Our pattern of results on tax and education policy matches these irregular relationships. Answers to most of the questions included in either the 2000 or 2004 NAES related to taxes were unconnected to Latino context, yet in one instance—a question on tax redistribution from the wealthy to the poor—whites living in states with larger Latino population shares were substantially less likely to favor redistribution from the wealthy to the poor.[64] Similarly, on the one question in the 2000 NAES that asked respondents about funding for education, there was no apparent connection to Latino context. But on one question in the 2004 NAES that addressed school vouchers, whites living in states with larger Latino populations were almost significantly more likely to support school choice. The overall pattern suggests that the effects of Latino context fade as we move away from polices that are closely associated with the Latino or immigrant population to policies and debates that have less direct ties to either population.

Beyond Policy

Does context have even broader effects? Are whites living in states with more Latinos more apt to identify as conservative and Republican as well as favor Republican candidates? We address these questions in table 4.3. All the dependent variables in our model are coded so that higher values are more conservative or Republican, and lower values are more liberal or Democratic. The broader goal is to see how far reaching the effects of newcomers to the United States have become.

Latino Context and Ideology

An important test of how far Latino context is reshaping white views is to determine whether or not proximity to Latinos affects how Americans identify ideologically. Are the rightward shifts that we see on immigration, health, welfare, and criminal justice accompanied by a broader shift to the right on the core liberal-conservative ideology scale that underlies much of this nation's politics? In the first column of

---

[63] For a more in-depth discussion of the relationship between education policy and immigrants, see chapter 6.

[64] The tax policy measures unrelated to Latino context were a question about a flat tax (2000) and another about reducing taxes (2004).

TABLE 4.3
The Effect of Latino Context on White Ideology, Party Identification, and Vote Choice

	Conservative ideology	Party identification: Republican	Vote for Republican in . . .	
			House election	Presidential election
State context				
Percent Latino	0.04 (0.01)**	0.03 (0.01)**	0.04 (0.01)**	0.02 (0.008)**
Percent Asian American	−0.02 (0.01)*	−0.02 (0.008)**	−0.02 (0.006)**	−0.01 (0.003)**
Percent African American	0.03 (0.01)*	0.02 (0.01)	0.03 (0.01)*	0.03 (0.01)
Median income	−0.09 (0.03)**	0.01 (0.01)	0.06 (0.03)+	−0.04 (0.02)*
Percent college educated	−0.05 (0.04)	0.21 (0.11)	−0.02 (0.04)	0.02 (0.02)
Percent unemployed	−0.13 (0.05)*	−0.29 (0.37)	−0.19 (0.09)*	0.04 (0.05)
Political orientation				
Republican	—	—	0.41 (0.01)**	0.34 (0.01)**
Conservative	—	—	0.05 (0.01)**	0.11 (0.01)**
Socioeconomic status				
Education	−0.03 (0.003)**	0.01 (0.002)**	−0.04 (0.05)	−0.03 (0.03)
Income	0.03 (0.003)**	0.03 (0.003)**	0.02 (0.05)	0.01 (0.03)
Age	0.05 (0.001)**	−0.07 (0.08)	−0.03 (0.02)	−0.05 (0.10)
Female	−0.15 (0.01)**	−0.09 (0.01)**	−0.02 (0.02)	−0.02 (0.01)*
Union member	−0.10 (0.02)**	−0.18 (0.01)**	−0.03 (0.03)	−0.05 (0.01)**
Have children	0.06 (0.01)**	0.06 (0.01)**	0.01 (0.02)	0.01 (0.01)
Controls				
Years in home	0.07 (0.005)**	−0.03 (0.004)**	0.02 (0.08)	−0.04 (0.05)
Urban	−0.19 (0.02)**	−0.02 (0.02)	0.05 (0.03)+	−0.04 (0.02)**
Suburban	−0.05 (0.02)**	0.04 (0.01)**	−0.05 (0.02)*	−0.02 (0.01)
Constant	3.85 (0.11)**	0.88 (0.09)**	1.58 (0.11)**	−0.39 (0.07)**
N	22,933	20,582	967	3,310
Log likelihood	−30,543.24	−22,826.59	−221.47	−943.43

*p < 0.05
**p < 0.01
+p < 0.10

Note: Entries not in parentheses are the HLM regression coefficients, and entries in parentheses are the corresponding standard errors.

Sources: National Annenberg Election Survey 2000; US Census Bureau 2000.

table 4.3, we attempt to answer this question. Self-described ideology is coded with the standard five-point scale, with higher values representing a more conservative identity.

The results are striking. Minority context does play a role in the core political identities of white Americans. The effects mirror the patterns we have already seen. A large Latino population in a state is associated with an increase in the probability of identifying as a conservative among whites. The marginal effects are once again small but statistically significant. Whites living in states with many Latinos are, all else being equal, approximately 5 percent more likely to identify as conservative or strongly conservative than whites in states with few Latinos.

Latino Context and Partisanship

The public's views on policy and ideology are an integral part of US democracy, but nothing in US politics is more central than party identification. If Latino context can influence this core political identity, than it is apparent that immigration's impact on US politics is being broadly felt. In second column of table 4.3, we test this connection. The results are telling. State racial context and partisanship are clearly intertwined with one another. Similar to the pattern that we saw for policies and ideology, larger numbers of Latinos in a state appears to increase the chances that white Americans see themselves as Republicans as opposed to viewing themselves as Democrats. All else being equal, white Americans who live in states with a sizable Latino population are 5 percent more likely to identify as Republican than those residing in states with few Latinos.

To test the robustness of the relationship between Latino context and partisanship, we repeated the analysis with the 2004 NAES data. The results were nearly identical. Living in a state with a higher proportion of Latinos was linked to a 6 percent higher probability of identifying as Republican.[65] The effects are by no means massive, yet any effect on party identification is important. How white Americans identify themselves politically is at least in part connected to where they live and the size of the Latino population. Immigration is leading to small though highly visible alterations in the foundations of US politics.

It is also worth noting that the effects of Latino context on white party identification are evident after controlling for a range of individual- and state-level characteristics. Not only are we controlling for the normal range of individual socioeconomic characteristics, but we are also accounting for political ideology. In essence, whites in states with

[65] We also obtained similar results in both years if we used a dichotomous measure of partisanship (Democratic, Independent, and Republican identifiers) rather than a scaled measure of party identification. In 2004, for example, all else being equal, whites in states with larger Latino populations were 6 percent less likely to identify as Democratic and 8 percent more likely to identify as Republican.

larger Latino populations are identifying as more Republican than their conservative ideology, age, gender, and class status would imply. In the analysis, we also control for current economic conditions and the overall socioeconomic status of the state so it is hard to imagine that features of these states not included in the analysis are driving our results. It cannot be that whites in states with more Latinos are more Republican because those states are somehow distinct economically or educationally.

Alternate specifications also indicate that controlling for region or the political culture of each state does little to alter the effects we see here. These racial context effects are also robust to the inclusion of the mean ideology of state residents as measured by state public opinion or average state public opinion on specific issues, including racial policy, tolerance, the death penalty, and welfare.[66] As such, whites in states with more Latinos are not more Republican simply because the residents of those states are more conservative. The connection between Latino context and partisanship is a robust one.

Latino Context and the Vote

In the end democracy rests on the vote. No candidate is elected and no policy enacted without this fundamental act. Thus, we present one last critical test of Latino context. Do we see the same sort of rightward backlash in the vote that we have seen for policy, ideology, and partisanship? In the last two columns of table 4.3, we assess the effects of Latino context on the presidential and congressional vote in 2000. The results indicate that the impact of Latino context does, in fact, extend to the vote. As we saw before, whites living in states with more Latinos were, all else being equal, significantly more likely to opt for the political right. In this case, that means substantially greater support for the Republican candidate in presidential and congressional contests. The effects are relatively small in the presidential contest and relatively large for congressional elections. Controlling for a range of other factors, living in states with a large share of Latinos is associated with a 7 percent increase in the probability of voting for Bush, the Republican presidential candidate. In congressional contests, moving from a large to a small Latino population is linked to a 32 percent increase in the likelihood of a Republican vote.

Moreover, when we repeat the analysis on the 2004 elections in the NAES, we see an identical pattern of results. In 2004, whites living

---

[66] Erikson, Wright, and McIver 1993; Lax and Philips 2009.

in states with larger shares of Latinos were once again more likely to favor Republican candidates in both types of contests. And at least in congressional elections, the Latino population had the power to shift partisan preferences in a dramatic fashion. In congressional contests in 2004, the white Republican vote was, all else being equal, 20 percent higher in states with large Latino populations than in those with small Latino populations. When white Americans decide who to support in the key national contests, one of the factors that impacts that decision is the racial context that they live in.[67]

Finally, if we assess whites' opinions of the candidates rather than who they voted for, we arrive at a similar pattern. Whites who live in states with a high concentration of Latinos are more apt to view Bush favorably in terms of honesty, knowledge, and other character traits, and less apt to view Gore and John Kerry favorably on these dimensions. Latino context in each of the estimates reach statistical significance at conventional levels after controlling for ideology and party identification. Whites are not voting Republican simply because they are conservative leaning or consider themselves Republican identifiers. Beyond these two factors, Latino context plays an important role. These results are also not caused by state economic conditions, mean state ideology, or region—all factors that we control for in the models in table 4.3 or alternate analyses (not presented here).[68]

There are also signs of the ongoing importance of black context in the partisan choices of whites. As past studies have found, proximity to a large African American population is generally associated with a shift to the right politically. Looking across table 4.3, we see that in every case black context was positively related to the conservative or Republican option. In two instances—ideology and the presidential vote—that relationship reached statistical significance. Moreover, when we repeated the analysis with the 2004 NAES, black context was positively and significantly related to white views and behavior across all four measures. Once again, the effects were not large. Living in a state with a higher concentration of African Americans was associated with a 5 to 10 percent increase in the likelihood of identifying as conservative, aligning with the Republican Party, and voting Republican.

[67] If we focus on intended vote choice for respondents interviewed prior to the elections in 2000 and 2004, we find the same effects for the size of the Latino population. These estimates are available, on request, from the authors.

[68] It is also worth noting that the results we see in table 4.3 could be understating the influence of Latino context. By controlling for both ideology and party identification—two factors that we have already demonstrated are linked to Latino context—we are essentially controlling away the indirect effects of Latino context on the vote.

If we couple this with our earlier results on policy, there is a clear, albeit not always significant, relationship between black context and white politics. All this echoes existing accounts, which suggests that some white Americans do view the black community with antagonism, are threatened when the black population is large enough, and mobilize to support the Republican Party along with more conservative policies to try to counteract that threat.[69]

The other important finding depicted in table 4.3 concerns Asian American context. If we look across the different regressions in the table 4.3, we see that Asian American context is relevant for all three political choices: ideology, party identification, and the vote. And in each case, the results are statistically significant and in the opposite direction as those for Latino context. Proximity to Asian Americans has a liberalizing effect on white politics. Whites who live in states with higher concentrations of Asian Americans are more likely to identify as liberal, feel attached to the Democratic Party, and support Democratic candidates than whites residing in states with few Asians—at least as assessed in the 2000 NAES. The magnitude of the effects in each area is similar to what we see with Latino context: a 5 to 10 percent shift on ideology, partisanship, and the presidential vote, and a slightly larger effect for the congressional vote.

If we shift to the 2004 data, though, we discover that the effects of Asian American context are not as robust. On all three measures—ideology, party identification, and the vote—there is no discernible link between Asian American context and white preferences in 2004. Why Asian American context is not as robust is not immediately apparent. Perhaps the link between Asian Americans and the left-right divide in US politics is less ingrained, and thus more dependent on the context of the campaign and particular election.

Nevertheless, it is clear that how white Americans react to Asian Americans differs from how they react to Latinos. As we earlier noted, the liberalizing effects of the Asian American population may be surprising to some readers, but these results do echo past research. In a number of existing studies, there is at least a hint that the impact of the Asian American population is different from the effect of the black and Latino population. M. V. Hood III and Irwin Morris, Hero and Preuhs, and Caroline Tolbert and her colleagues in different ways all find that proximity to larger Asian Americans communities breeds more positive views about Asian Americans or policies related to Asian Ameri-

---

[69] Carmines and Stimson 1989; Edsall and Edsall 1991; Gilens 1999.

cans.[70] Hood and Morris, for example, note that whites living in counties with larger Asian American populations were less willing to support Proposition 187—the California measure designed to cut a range of public services to undocumented immigrants.[71] Whether the effect of the Asian American population is negligible (as it is in half our tests) or liberalizing, the contrast between Asian American context, on the one hand, and black and Latino context, on the other, indicates that the Asian American community represents different threats and possibilities to members of the white population.

Robustness Checks

To help ensure that the results in tables 4.1–4.3 measure underlying relationships between context and white political views, we performed a serious of additional tests and alternate specifications. First, we sought to verify our explanation by examining Latino contextual effects in areas where we should not find them: on views of groups that are orthogonal to discussions of Latinos and Latino immigration. Accordingly, we found no statistically significant relationship between Latino context and attitudes toward feminist groups, gay and lesbian groups, and Muslims.[72] As such, we are not observing effects for Latino context merely because Latinos move into areas where whites are especially intolerant or conservative. Instead, Latino context tends only to be associated with white views on those issues where the policy debate frequently focuses on immigrants or Latinos. We also saw no associations between Latino context and a wide variety of political interest and political participation measures—everything from discussing politics to contributing to campaigns. Whites who live in states with more Latinos appear to be different in only one sense from whites residing in sparsely populated Latino states: they are, on average, more opposed to pro-Latino policies and political outcomes.

Second, as we have already alluded to, we repeated as much of the analysis as possible on the 2004 NAES. The 2004 survey has fewer policy questions, but does have the same large sample and wide geographic sampling, and includes questions on the same set of individual characteristics that we incorporated into the regression models in

---

[70] Hood and Morris 1998, 2000; Hero and Preuhs 2006; Tolbert, Lowenstein, and Donovan 1998.

[71] Hood and Morris 2000.

[72] Views of Muslims nevertheless were tied to black context. Whites who lived in areas with larger black populations had significantly less favorable views of Muslims.

this chapter's analyses. Thus, for at least a few of the policy areas as well as the liberal-conservative ideology question we can replicate our earlier tests. This replication largely corroborates the results from the 2000 survey. In 2004, as in 2000, proximity to large concentrations of Latinos is associated with some significant shifts to the political right. The effects in 2004 were not as consistent as those in 2000, but in 2004 whites living near large numbers of Latinos were once again more conservative on some aspects of social welfare and crime, and tended to be more likely to self-identify as Republican and vote Republican. The effects of Asian American context were, as we see here, either insignificant or led in some cases to more left-leaning policy choices. Black context once again had an uneven though at least partially conservative impact.

Third, we sought to update some of our results using the 2012 CCES.[73] The CCES has fewer policy questions, but we did find similar patterns on questions that we could examine. Specifically, all else being equal, living in states with heavier concentrations of Latinos was associated with more restrictive or conservative views on immigration and spending, a higher chance of identifying as Republican, and greater support for Republican candidates at the presidential, house, senatorial, and gubernatorial levels.[74]

One potential issue is multicollinearity between the key contextual variables. Fortunately, at the state level, the proportions of residents who are Latino, Asian American, and African American are not closely correlated with each other ($r < 0.15$). Nonetheless, to help ensure that correlation between different contexts was not affecting our results, we repeated the analysis while including only one of the three racial contexts and dropping the other two. This did nothing to alter the basic conclusions that we present.

Another possibility is that the relationship between immigrant context and white views is nonlinear. That is, white reactions to Latino context may be a function of their rate of change as opposed to their overall levels. We therefore estimated an alternative statistical model where we controlled for both the rate of change in the Latino state population as well as its overall size. The results indicate that no clear signs of nonlinearity in whites' responses. It may also be the case that our results are driven by a particular state. To be sure that one state did not account for the pattern of results, we repeated the analysis dropping each large state one by one. Basic conclusions about the impact

---

[73] Ansolobahere and Schaffner 2012.
[74] This analysis is available, on request, from the authors.

of Latino, Asian American, and African American context remained the same whether states like California, Texas, or New York are included or dropped. Also, to help ensure that our analysis is not picking up regional effects or the distinct political cultures of a state, in alternate analyses we include dummy variables for region along with updated measures of Daniel Elazar's state political culture.[75] The regional variables were occasionally significant (the South was often more conservative), but their inclusion did little to alter the basic pattern of results.

In addition, we also performed a series of tests in which we added a range of different individual characteristics into our model. We specifically accounted for one's religious denomination (Catholic, Protestant, Jewish, and Muslim), and included a measure for whether the respondent was born again or not, another for households with a member in the armed forces, and a variable that gauged occupational status. As well, to help discount the role of whites selecting into and out of areas with more or fewer minorities, we controlled for mobility by adding a variable that measures the number of years the respondent has lived in their current address. Again, these additional controls did little to affect our main results.

Latino Population Growth

The analysis to this point in the chapter has implied a somewhat-static process. Rather than looking at changes in the racial makeup of different states over time, we have simply compared states with higher and lower proportions of minorities. It may well be that size is, in fact, the critical variable and white Americans are most affected by the share of the state population that is Latino. But as we have already noted, there is at least some evidence that reactions to the Latino population are dynamic and whites become concerned more than anything else by rapid expansion of the Latino population.[76] To test this possibility, we added various measures of Latino population growth to the statistical models presented in tables 4.1–4.3.[77] The results are far from consistent, but there are weak signs that growth in the immigrant population does matter. In particular, recent growth in the proportion of a state that is foreign born appeared to play some role in shaping white views.

[75] Sharansky and Hofferbert 1969.
[76] Newman 2013; Hopkins 2010.
[77] We captured growth by controlling for change in the total number and proportion of Latinos in the state, change in the number and proportion of foreign born in the state, and percent growth in the Latino and foreign-born populations either measured as five- or ten-year change.

Whites in states with faster immigrant growth were significantly more apt to want to spend less on health care and significantly more punitive on some criminal policy questions.[78] On most of the other political views we explored—including the vote—we could find no link between any measure of population change and white political behavior. Overall, at least one of our different measures of population growth was significantly linked with rightward leaning in politics in about one-third of the outcomes we examined.

Similar patterns emerged when we repeated the analysis with the 2004 NAES. Change, especially when it was measured by change in the proportion of the state that is foreign born, mattered, but it did so inconsistently. More rapid growth in 2004 was associated with a desire to restrict immigration, less interest in reducing inequality, and more conservative positions on crime. The one real difference between 2000 and 2004 was that immigrant growth was also associated with a Republican vote in the 2004 presidential election.

Overall the results on immigrant growth are not impressive but they are suggestive. The pattern of findings does suggest that white Americans can and do react to rapid changes in the immigrant population. Importantly, when we add these new population growth measures, the original effect for the Latino population proportion remains robust. White Americans may be somewhat responsive to the growth of the immigrant population, yet they are clearly influenced by the overall size of the Latino population.

As we discussed earlier in this chapter, one other key consideration is the question of exactly which group white Americans are reacting to. Our analysis to this point suggests that white Americans are more threatened by the Latino population and less concerned by the Asian American population. But there is a range of other ways that white Americans could make distinctions between different elements of the United States' immigrant population. Perhaps white Americans are not all that concerned about the Latino population as a whole but instead are more troubled by particular subsets of the immigrant population. Surveys and some existing research seem to indicate that white Americans are especially anxious about undocumented immigration.[79] Likewise, the immigrant threat narrative seems particularly focused on Mexican immigration, and less concerned about other Latino national origin groups like Puerto Ricans or Cubans.[80]

[78] On views that immigration is a problem and the propensity of identifying as a Republican, the effect of Latino context was not statistically significant at conventional levels.

[79] Hood and Morris 1998.

[80] Huntington 2005.

Empirically, it is often difficult to distinguish between these different groups. At least at the state level, measures gauging the size of many of the different groups are highly correlated. The percentage of Latinos in a state is, for example, correlated at $r = 0.91$ with the size of the Mexican population and at $r = 0.89$ with the percentage of undocumented immigrants. We performed a series of additional tests, however, to try to see if we could determine exactly who white Americans are reacting to. Specifically, we repeated our analysis with a range of different measures of immigrant context at the state level: the percentages of foreign born, undocumented immigrants, Mexicans, Cubans, and Puerto Ricans.[81]

These alternate tests indicate that the percentage of foreign-born residents statewide is rarely related to white American political behavior. We believe that the relative insignificance of the percent foreign born follows directly and logically from the divergent reactions whites have to Latinos and Asian Americans. Since white Americans tend to react to Latinos (or immigrants from Latin America) by shifting to the right politically, and to Asian Americans (or immigrants from Asia) either not at all or by shifting to the left politically, the two effects tend to offset each other. The null findings for the foreign-born population suggest that we cannot accurately assess the white backlash by looking at the immigrant population as a whole. If scholars want to uncover how immigrant context is shaping white views, they need to consider and incorporate the contrasting effects of the Asian American and Latino populations in their analysis.

Are white Americans, as much of the political rhetoric implies, really only concerned about undocumented immigrants? Or are they worried about immigrants specifically from Mexico? Here our tests are much more inconclusive. When we substituted in the state undocumented population or state Mexican-origin population into our regression models, both measures generally reached statistical significance, and in both cases the size and direction of effects was similar to what we saw with our measure of the Latino population. A large percentage of undocumented/Mexican immigrants is associated with more conservative policy views, greater identification with the Republican Party, and increased support for Republican candidates.[82] All this helps to

---

[81] All these measures are from the US Census except estimates of the undocumented population, which are derived from the work of Jeffrey Passell and D'Vera Cohn (2009). We recognize that the controls for the various Latino subgroups are less relevant for some states.

[82] Interestingly, the size of the Puerto Rican and Cuban populations were generally not significantly related to white policy preferences or partisan choices. This could be because white Americans are not threatened by either of these groups. But we believe it is more likely that

demonstrate the robustness of our story, but given the high degree of correlation between each of these different measures of the immigrant population, it unfortunately does not help to tell us which group whites view as most problematic.

We also looked to see if the socioeconomic standing of the local Latino population affected white reactions. Perhaps Americans aren't concerned about change in general but instead are worried about the influx of poor, unskilled, and uneducated immigrants? When we reran the analyses adding a measure for the state Latino poverty rate along with an interaction between the Latino poverty rate and Latino population size, however, we uncovered no new significant results. White Americans tended to be more regressive when they live in states with large Latino populations whether the Latino population was largely poor or not. The overall picture at this point appears to be one of a less than discerning white public. As far as we can tell, white Americans tend to react negatively regardless of who comprises the Latino population.

Neighborhood Context

A reasonable concern with the analysis to this point is that we may be focusing on the wrong geographic context. One could argue that individual white Americans are more apt to concentrate on their neighborhoods, where they live, work, and interact with minorities, than on their states, where interaction is likely to be much more limited and contact with minorities is more likely to be filtered through the media. Moreover, the fact that state racial context tends to be correlated with neighborhood racial context means that the state-level effects we see could actually be picking up neighborhood dynamics.[83] We therefore reestimated our basic models where we included neighborhood context. Specifically, we added the percentages of blacks, Latinos, and Asian Americans at the zip code level.[84] Each regression thus incor-

there is not enough variation in the size of these two groups at the state level. Cuban Americans represent more than 1 percent of the population in only one state and Puerto Ricans represent more than 2 percent of the population in only five states. We just cannot accurately assess effects for groups that are this small.

[83] For the NAES respondents, the three state racial contexts that we look at—the percentages of Latinos, Asian Americans, and African Americans—are correlated between 0.43 and 0.59 with the same variables at the zip code level.

[84] Since zip codes are relatively small, there is more likely to be a correspondence between the demographics of the zip code and experiences of any given respondent in that zip code. Although zip codes are the smallest-available geographic level, we readily admit that they represent an imperfect measure of local context in that they are not always drawn around well-defined neighborhoods in which individuals from the neighborhood regularly interact. It is

porated three distinct contextual levels: the state, neighborhood, and individual.

Two points about this analysis are worth highlighting. First, the inclusion of neighborhood-level context failed to alter our results for state racial context. Even after controlling for neighborhood racial context, whites who lived in states with higher concentrations of Latinos were more likely to favor conservative and punitive policies, identify with the Republican Party, and support Republican candidates. As such, these additional tests alleviate concerns that state racial context is picking up the effects of zip code or neighborhood context.

Second, the effects of zip code racial context on policy views and partisanship generally failed to reach statistical significance. In the few cases where local context was significant, the direction of the effects was highly inconsistent. Residing in areas with a sizable Latino community was linked to more liberal views on one health care question, but more conservative views on one question related to crime. Given the problem of whites moving into or out of different neighborhoods with different concentrations of minorities, it is hard to offer any firm conclusions about neighborhood effects. We doubt that state context is the only level at which racial context operates in a meaningful way. But any further conclusions about neighborhood context will have to wait until more rigorous testing can incorporate selection issues at lower levels of aggregation.

Heterogeneity in White Attitudes

Finally, our analysis has assumed that all white Americans react to minority context in the same way. Yet there is little reason to expect a uniform reaction across the entire white population. Logically, how white Americans react to immigration and the racial transformation that has accompanied it should depend critically on how they feel about minorities in the first place. In two key studies—one by Regina Branton and Bradford Jones, and the other by Eric Oliver and Tali Mendelberg—reactions to minority context did vary across the white population.[85] We unfortunately do not have a measure of white racial tolerance in either the 2000 or 2004 NAES. We do have a measure of education, though—a variable frequently correlated with racial tolerance. Given that those with lower levels of education tend to be more resentful of minorities and more racially intolerant, we might expect

also not clear how aware individual whites are about the racial makeup of their neighborhoods (Wong 2007).
[85] Branton and Jones 2005; Oliver and Mendelberg 2000.

less educated Americans to react more viscerally to large Latino populations.[86]

We consider the mediating role of education by adding an interaction term between education and state Latino context to each of the HLMs in tables 4.1–4.3. The analysis suggests that reactions to Latino context do depend on white education levels. The results are not consistent across all the policy and partisanship measures, but in half the cases the interaction is statistically significant, and it indicates that as education increases, the effects of Latino context decreases substantially. The marginal effect of context is about three times greater for less educated whites. For example, the probability among the less well educated of supporting government efforts to reduce income inequality drops by 13 percent in states with large Latino populations. For the well educated, the probability of supporting efforts to reduce inequality increases by only 4 percent as one shifts from a state with a small proportion of Latinos to one with a large share of Latinos. The same is true for the presidential vote. Among the less educated, changes in Latino context account for a 12 percent increase in the probability of supporting George W. Bush, yet among the well-educated, the marginal impact is only 3 percent.[87]

Although we view these interactions with education as telling, we also believe that this is far from the last word on how white reactions differ across the population. There are numerous factors that could influence how one responds to minority context. Kenneth Scheve and Matthew Slaughter, for example, have predicted that the consequences of immigrant context will be more severe when natives and immigrants possess similar skills levels and are in direct economic competition.[88] Others might contend that minorities and immigrants are more likely to be viewed as scapegoats when there are tough eco-

---

[86] Hurwitz and Peffley 1998; McClosky and Brill 1983. But see Federico and Sidanius 2002.

[87] A slightly different way of testing this same hypothesis is to see if reactions to minority context are more pronounced among conservatives. Given that conservatives tend to be less racially tolerant than liberals, one could expect conservatives to react more harshly to the new Latino population (Sniderman and Carmines 1997; Kinder and Sanders 1996). This is exactly what we find. Although the effects are not entirely consistent, on most of the questions we look at in tables 4.1–4.3, we see that the reaction to Latino context is significantly heightened among conservatives. We err on the side of caution and have more confidence in our education interactions because education is clearly exogenous to Latino context while conservatism is not. But the general story in both cases is that those who have more negative views of minorities in the first place tend to react more severely to proximity to large Latino populations.

[88] Scheve and Slaughter 2001. In light of Scheve and Slaughter's predictions, in alternate tests we included interactions between Latino context and the size of the educational and income gap between the state Latino population and state white population. Neither set of interactions revealed a clear relationship with white policy views or partisan preferences.

nomic times.[89] Still others maintain that white responses will be more negative when there are large numbers of immigrants and a highly permissive welfare system.[90] Some scholars also point to the interaction of local minority context and the national framing of immigration.[91] Our tests on education are merely an initial foray into this line of inquiry. It is apparent that more work needs to be done before the full contours of white reactions are known.

Discussion

The patterns illustrated in this chapter suggest that the nation's increasingly diverse population is having a profound impact on the politics of white America. This may not be particularly astonishing to many observers. Indeed, numerous individuals have suspected this sort of effect. Few have been able to clearly demonstrate it, however.

What is novel here is the wide-ranging consequences of Latino context. In a political era in which many claim that the significance of race has faded, we find that larger concentrations of Latinos appear to be leading to a fundamentally distinct political orientation among many white Americans. On several of the major policy debates that we face and the core liberal-conservative ideological line that delineates much of US politics, Latino context is a key contributor. Party identification—the most influential variable in US politics—is at least in part a function of the racial context that white Americans live in. So too is the vote in national contests for the presidency, senate, and house. The degree to which white Americans live in areas with large numbers of Latinos seems to shape who they are politically.

Our findings also suggest that all minorities are not equal in the minds of white Americans. Whites react extremely differently to Latino context than they do to Asian American context. Asian Americans, it appears, may be more of a model minority and ally, whereas Latinos seem to be a real threat that whites counter with more restrictive and more punitive policy making.

All this is an important step in understanding the dynamic role that immigration plays in US politics. It is, of course, not the last one. As with most contextual analysis, the results we have presented here are somewhat of a black box. We can demonstrate that different sets of

[89] Fetzer 2000.
[90] Hanson 2005.
[91] Hopkins 2010.

demographic numbers translate into distinct sets of views, but we have not come close to showing how proximity actually "operates" to change individual white perspectives and actions. Any number of different factors could explain this relationship. Are whites responding to personal interactions with Latinos, immigrant political activism in the state, political campaigns, portrayals of immigrants in media outlets, or something else altogether? We are doubtful that individual interactions have a big role—partly because state context is such a poor proxy for interracial contact. We are also doubtful that personal interactions drive negative white reactions to Latinos because studies that are able to measure and test the effects of personal interactions find that they generally lead to more rather than less tolerant views.[92]

The other explanations seem more plausible. A higher concentration of Latinos frequently means that they are more visible in the local political sphere, and therefore more of a potential threat to white power and resources. We know, for example, that the election of Latinos to statewide and congressional office is closely correlated with Latino population size.[93] Similarly, in places where Latinos live in larger numbers, political campaigns appear to be more apt to focus on immigrant-related issues. We know that the degree to which state and local governments raise as well as deal with immigration and other Latino-related issues is correlated with the size of the Latino population.[94] Studies have also shown that a larger Latino population means greater attention to Latino-related issues in the local media.[95]

Our goal at this point is not to rule out any of these different mechanisms. But we are especially attentive to the role that the media could play in shaping white reactions to immigrant transformation in the United States. To that end, our next chapter examines the way the news media has framed and portrayed the issue of immigration over the past three decades. We contend that news organizations have a tendency to view immigrants through the prism of the Latino threat narrative. That narrative, we argue, intensifies existing fears about immigration—a development that helps to explain the dramatic movement of so many whites into the Republican Party. Chapter 5 presents a detailed content analysis of immigrations news stories from 1980–2011 and then assesses the impact of those stories on aggregate trends in partisanship during the same time period.

[92] Dixon and Rosenbaum 2004.
[93] Casellas 2011; Hajnal and Trounstine 2010.
[94] Rivera 2013; Ramakrishnan and Wong 2010; Varsanyi 2010.
[95] Branton and Dunaway 2009.

Chapter 5

Media Coverage of Immigration and White Partisanship

with Hans Hassell

GUERILLA WAR ON IMMIGRATION.
—New York Times, *editorial headline, August 27, 1982*

T-SHIRT COMPANY IS CHARGED IN PLOT
TO SMUGGLE MEXICANS.
—New York Times, *headline, December 23, 1997*

DEPORTATIONS FROM U.S.
HIT A RECORD HIGH.
—New York Times, *headline, October 7, 2010*

These headlines from the *New York Times* are suggestive of the ways in which immigrants and the issue of immigration are discussed by the news media. The first headline uses the metaphor of a war to describe the state of immigration in the United States, whereas the latter two focus on unlawful activities associated with immigration—human smuggling and residing in the country without legal documentation. All three represent negative frames that have the potential to spur anxiety about immigrants and immigration.

These headlines are not fully representative of media portrayals of immigration. The media can and does present immigration in a more positive light. But we contend that these headlines are emblematic of much of the overall discourse in the media's coverage of immigration. The news media, we argue, has tended to adopt a particular narrative that centers on Latinos and other negative aspects of immigration. By more regularly adopting this immigrant threat narrative versus alternate frames with more positive messages, we maintain that the news media is helping to generate fear and anxiety among the public regarding the presence of immigrants, and specifically Latinos, in society.

There are, we believe, clear partisan implications to all this. By concentrating on immigration and highlighting its negative aspects, the media not only generates fears and concerns but also increases the motivation for many Americans to side with the Republican Party. For those whose fears are sparked or amplified by the media, the Republican Party's increasingly tough stance on the immigration becomes ever more attractive. One of the main goals in this chapter, then, is to demonstrate that the media is one of the main mechanisms helping to shape partisan identities.

The notion of the media influencing political attitudes is not new, of course. Yet there is real debate about the extent of this influence. Are media effects ephemeral and fleeting, subject to rapid decay and counterframes?[1] Or are media effects deeply felt and enduring?[2] We add to this literature in two ways. First, we assess media effects on a core political predisposition. When studies assess framing or agenda setting, they tend to focus on relatively unstable issue opinions. For these largely off-the-cuff issue responses, it may be fairly easy to sway respondents one way or another. But party identification is another story altogether. As one of the most stable identities in US politics, it represents a particularly tough test of media effects. Second, we assess the impact of the media not in the quiet confines of the lab but instead in the real world, where multiple frames and multiple voices are always present, and where individual Americans can choose to listen to or tune out these messages. If we see framing and agenda-setting effects here, we will have gone a long way to demonstrating the full potential of the media.

In order to assess the role of the media in framing immigration, we first have to determine what the media actually reports on news

[1] Druckman 2004; Druckman and Nelson 2003.
[2] Lecheler and de Vreese 2011; Mendelberg 1997; Bartels 1988.

155

stories that revolve around immigration. Are the frames used to discuss immigration indeed disproportionately negative? Are they overwhelmingly centered on Latinos? And are they focused on more problematic policy issues like crime and terrorism than on more positive topics such as families and assimilation? While anecdotal evidence suggests this is the case, there has been relatively little systematic study of media content of immigration.[3] To fill this gap in the existing research, we rely on a national newspaper with one of the largest circulations, the *New York Times*, to determine the content of news stories that mention the issue of immigration from 1980–2011. Specifically, we analyzed the issue frames used in the articles (e.g., the particular policy linked to immigration), types of group-centric frames used (e.g., Latino or Asian immigrant), and overall tone (negative, positive, or neutral) of each article.

The findings from our content analysis indicate that news coverage is largely negative, largely focused on Latinos, and largely attentive to the negative policy issues associated with immigration. Such patterns in the content and frames used in immigration news articles validate our claim regarding the predominance of the immigrant threat narrative. We then go on to show how the immigrant threat narrative effects the partisan beliefs of the US public. Using macropartisanship data from the CBS/*New York Times* poll series, we find that the framing of media coverage predicts subsequent shifts in macropartinaship. Indeed, the immigrant threat narrative is just as predictive of aggregate shifts in partisanship as standard measures such as presidential approval and the state of the economy.[4] In particular, when the coverage is framed to emphasize one specific immigrant group, Latinos, it negatively impacts the percentage of Democratic identifiers, and results in greater independence and more support for the Republican Party.

These findings help to establish the importance of the mass media as a primary mechanism driving the public's reaction to immigration. It also greatly expands our sense of the strength of framing by showing that media coverage can lead to measurable shifts on one of the most immovable political identities. Finally, it reinforces our larger goal in this book by again demonstrating the centrality of immigration in shaping US politics.

---

[3] On metaphors and media message, see Chavez 2008; Santa Ana 2004; Brader, Valentino, and Suhay 2008. For a more systematic approach, see Valentino, Brader, and Jardina 2013; Pérez, forthcoming.

[4] MacKuen, Erikson, and Stimson 1989.

How the Media Influences Public Opinion: Agenda Setting and Issue Framing

Accessibility, many argue, is at the heart of much of the media's effects.[5] Because we are cognitively limited, we organize concepts thematically, and we can only retain a finite number of important considerations in the forefront of our minds. When queried about issues or opinions, it is from these immediate sets of considerations that one's response is generated. Thus, the media or other actors can influence our opinions by privileging some considerations over others. We concentrate on two mechanisms, agenda setting and framing, that can affect these considerations and that the existing research has identified as having an effect on public opinion.

Agenda setting, the process through which news organizations look at certain issues more than others, can affect what issues individuals think about and how much weight they place on them.[6] Shanto Iyengar and Donald Kinder find that problems that receive prominent attention on the national news become the problems that the public also views to be important.[7] A little extra coverage of a military conflict, for example, can in an experimental setting lead the public to consider that conflict as more crucial in evaluating the president. Therefore, even when an issue is not of daily or immediate concern to us, regular media attention to that issue raises our awareness and weight of the issue by making it more accessible in our mind as well as increasing the significance we attach it.[8] There is already some evidence that coverage of immigration can influence public perceptions about its salience.[9]

How issues are framed and presented in a news story can also influence voters' evaluations of political leaders and issues.[10] Dennis Chong and Jamie Druckman define framing as "the process by which people develop a particular conceptualization of an issue or reorient their thinking about an issue."[11] The literature has demonstrated framing effects across a wide range of issues and contexts. We highlight three different types of framing here. First, framing can alter the way we see an issue by privileging one aspect of a problem over anoth-

[5] Zaller 1992.
[6] Baumgartner and Talbert 1995; Zaller 1992; Mutz 1995.
[7] Iyengar and Kinder 1987.
[8] Nelson, Clawson, and Oxley 1997; Lau and Redlawsk 2001.
[9] Dunaway, Branton, and Abrajano 2010.
[10] Iyengar and Kinder 1987; Iyengar 1987.
[11] Chong and Druckman 2007b.

er.[12] By bringing forward different aspects of a problem, the media can forefront different considerations that ultimately alter our conclusions about that issue. For example, experimental studies have shown that our support for welfare can change depending on whether coverage highlights work requirements or need.[13]

Second, media frames can alter the group imagery associated with an issue. By focusing repeatedly on a particular group, news coverage can lead to evaluations of an issue based on attitudes toward the group in question rather than on the issue at hand.[14] If that particular group has negative associations or stereotypes—as is often the case with racial/ethnic minorities—news coverage can lead to more limited public support for certain policies.[15] Disproportionate coverage of African Americans in welfare stories has led to welfare being closely associated with blacks, which has in turn reduced public support for welfare.[16]

The third category of framing is more direct. The media can affect our evaluation of an issue simply by altering the tone of coverage.[17] Coverage that is more negative in tone and highlights undesirable features of a phenomenon instead of positive attributes can sway our opinions as well as limit support for that phenomenon.

The Minimal Effects View

There are, however, those who question the impact of agenda setting and framing.[18] Most of our understanding about the influence of framing has emanated from research conducted in experimental settings where individuals receive only a single frame in a single exposure. Critics have emphasized several problems with this format. First, subjects typically do not receive a counterframe as they would in most political debates. If only one side speaks, it is likely to be powerful and effective. Critically, recent experimental studies that present a counterframe show little to no overall effects.[19] Second, in the laboratory subjects tend to receive limited stimuli, all the "noise" of daily life is blocked out, and there is little to focus on other than the frame. Yet

[12] Nelson and Kinder 1996.
[13] Shen and Edwards 2005.
[14] Nelson and Kinder 1996; Gilens 1999.
[15] Gilliam 1999; Gilliam and Iyengar 2000.
[16] Gilliam 1999; Gilens 1999.
[17] Hester and Gibson 2003.
[18] Druckman 2004.
[19] Chong and Druckman 2013; Druckman 2004.

studies indicate that more information reduces the impact of any one piece of information.[20] Subjects in these experiments also had no control over which frames or media outlets they are exposed to. Studies suggest that framing effects in the real world are more limited because citizens selectively screen out certain frames, and ignore frames or sources they do not trust.[21]

Another real concern is that the effects of framing tend to be ephemeral or fleeting. When tested immediately after being exposed to a particular frame, subjects display distinct views. But the effects of framing tend to erode quickly over time. When the subjects are queried a day, week, or month later, few significant results emerge.[22]

When studies of framing switch to natural-world settings, evidence of framing becomes more limited in its impact and scope.[23] Broader studies have found few clear instances of framing altering the outcomes of prominent political battles or frames changing the overall balance of power in an election of partisan battle.[24] It is uncertain just how much framing matters in the real world.

Last and most important, research about framing effects has centered almost exclusively on the opinions individuals have about specific issues. As many scholars have demonstrated, though, individual positions on most issues are not well thought out and are often highly volatile.[25] If issue positions are not deeply held and change regularly over time, it may be easy for framing or agenda setting to have an effect. Issue positions in this sense represent an easy case for media effects. To this point, researchers have not been able to demonstrate media effects for more core political predispositions like party identification. Party identification is one of the most stable political identities, and for many, is the unmoved mover that alters a range of other political considerations and is rarely altered by these other factors.[26] If we find media effects here, we will have greatly expanded our sense of what the media can do to shape politics. In short, by addressing some of the limitations of the literature, we hope to provide evidence of a much broader impact of framing than scholars have previously demonstrated.

[20] Druckman and Nelson 2003.
[21] Druckman 2004; Lupia and McCubins 1998.
[22] Chong and Druckman 2007a. But see Lecheler and de Vreese 2011.
[23] Sides and Vavreck 2013; Hill et al. 2013; Gerber and Hopkins 2011; Druckman 2004; Druckman and Nelson 2003.
[24] Gelman and King 1993; Sides and Vavreck 2013; Lazarsfeld and Merton 1948. But see Mendelberg 2001; Stoker 1997; Bartels 1988.
[25] Converse 1964.
[26] Goren 2005; Green, Palmquist, and Schickler 2002; Campbell et al. 1960.

The Immigrant Threat Narrative

How does all this apply to the issue of immigration? How might media coverage of immigration sway opinions and partisanship? As we have discussed throughout the book, the issue of immigration is a highly complex and multifaceted one. News outlets therefore have a wide array of immigration frames to choose from. When covering immigration, the news media can opt to cover anything from the economic and social benefits of hardworking immigrants to criminal activity at the border. They can draw our attention to more successful members of the Asian American immigrant population or highlight the difficulties faced by members of the undocumented Latino immigrant population.

We expect, however, that the media is likely to put greater emphasis on an immigrant threat narrative that underscores the costs and disadvantages of immigration, and that frequently frames the issue around Latino immigrants. The reason for this stress can be attributed to the profit-based incentives of the news media. As James Hamilton contends, the news is an information commodity fueled by market forces.[27] Given this, the content of the news needs to be crafted in such a way that is appealing to a sizable audience.[28] Stories and headlines focusing on the negative aspects of immigration have all the components that make them compelling to the public: they are emotional and attention getting, and in turn, such stories have the power to activate fears and anxieties about immigration. Given the Republican Party's strong stand against immigration, these frames should ultimately lead to movement toward the Republican Party.

We explore <u>four different elements of this narrative</u> that previous research suggests could be effective in spurring anxiety and ultimately generating a political response. Perhaps the easiest way for news stories to do this is to employ <u>negative group imagery</u>.[29] In the US immigration case that means honing in on Latino immigrants. Stories that focus on Latino immigrants rather than Asian or European ones, according to the existing literature, should cause individuals to think about immigration policy in terms of their attitudes and opinions toward Latinos. <u>This would shift the emphasis away from evaluating the policy proposal itself and transfer it to opinions on Latinos.</u> Since whites tend to hold negative stereotypes of Latinos, viewing them as particularly prone to

---

[27] Hamilton 2004.
[28] McManus 1994; Hamilton 2004; Berry and Sobieraj 2014.
[29] Nelson and Kinder 1996; Gilliam 1999; Gilliam and Iyengar 2000.

welfare, especially violent, and less intelligent than whites on average, this group imagery should lead to less favorable views of immigration.[30] Indeed, existing research by Perez as well as Brader and his colleagues suggests that fear of immigration may really be a fear of a specific group of immigrants—Latinos.[31] Most relevant to our study, there is strong evidence that priming respondents with images of Latinos can elicit more negative assessments of immigration.[32]

Another alternative is for the media to center on immigration-related policy issues that may be especially problematic in the minds of Americans. Crime is perhaps the most likely case here. Crime stories have been effective in associating African Americans with crime.[33] Also, there is already somewhat of an association between immigrants and crime, particularly when it comes to unauthorized immigration.[34] Most Americans think the majority of immigrants are unauthorized.[35] Polling data also indicate that this segment of the immigrant population sparks the strongest, most negative reactions among the public. Whether it is in the form of clandestine border crossings, deportations, immigration raids/busts, or immigrants as perpetrators of crime, almost all crime frames portray immigrants in an unfavorable light. Even brief uses of terms such as illegal alien, illegal, and illegal immigrant could ignite readily available criminal scenarios that in turn increase opposition to immigration.[36]

But crime is not the only policy issue that could frame immigration in a negative light. The economic costs of immigration could be another important policy frame. Past scholarly research has shown that attitudes toward immigration are shaped by economic concerns and in particular the perceived economic costs of immigration.[37] As such, when immigration is mentioned in the context of the economy and employment, there is a possibility that this will spark economic considerations that lead to more negative views of immigration and potentially greater support for the Republican Party.

In the end, the most effective way to generate fear may be the most direct: offer negative appraisals of immigration. The more that news stories supply pessimistic or downbeat conclusions about immigration, and the more that these stories present immigration in a negative light,

---

[30] Bobo 2001.
[31] Pérez, forthcoming; Brader et al. 2008.   Δ TV news media
[32] Brader, Valentino, and Suhay 2008.
[33] Gilliam 1999.
[34] Cisneros 2008; Lakoff and Ferguson 2006; Chavez 2008.
[35] Enos 2012; Citrin and Sides 2008; Kaiser 2004.
[36] Ngai 2004.
[37] Scheve and Slaughter 2001. But see Hainmueller and Hiscox 2010.

the more Americans are likely to oppose immigration and potentially support a party that opposes it too.

News outlets also have another important choice. They can opt to cover immigration or ignore it. This kind of agenda setting may also have consequences.[38] In our specific case, heightened coverage could cause immigration to be more salient to the public. It nonetheless is not immediately clear how increased salience should impact partisanship choices. For those who harbor negative views of immigration, the increased salience of immigration could well play into the Republican Party's anti-immigration stance. But for others who have more sympathetic views of immigration, increased salience might favor the Democrats. Given that the public holds an array of different perspectives on immigration, a greater volume of media coverage may or may not lead to a pronounced partisan shift in one direction or the other.

In our empirical analysis, we investigate these two mechanisms, framing and agenda setting, by looking at the volume of immigration news coverage as well as its specific content.

Analyzing the Frames Used in Immigration News Coverage

To assess the effects of news media coverage on immigration, we studied the volume and content of all articles from the *New York Times* between 1980 and 2011 that mentioned the immigration issue—almost 7,000 in total.[39] We selected the *New York Times* for two reasons. For one, we were interested in an outlet that would provide national coverage and readership. The *New York Times* has the second-largest circulation in the United States, at approximately 1.86 million, and reaches a nationwide audience.[40] Second, as a more liberal news outlet, the *New York Times* makes for an especially difficult test of our immigrant threat hypothesis. The *New York Times* is one of the news outlets that would be least likely to propagate the immigrant threat narrative.[41]

[38] Dunaway, Branton, and Abrajano 2010.

[39] Using the LexisNexis database of newspapers, we employed the following search terms: immigration, immigrant, immigrants, migration, and so on. We searched only the newspaper headline or lead, since we wanted to ensure that the main focus of the story was on immigration. If such a criterion was satisfied, the content analysis was performed on the entire article. News stories were restricted to those focusing on the United States. Along with news stories, editorials were also included in our universe of cases.

[40] Had we conducted our analysis on the newspaper with the greatest circulation, the *Wall Street Journal*, we would have run into a selection bias since the *Wall Street Journal* primarily covers stories dealing with the US economy and international business.

[41] We readily admit that over time, individual Americans have become more selective in their

Our choice to concentrate on newspaper articles, as opposed to television news programs, was motivated by the amount of information that can be gained from newspapers versus televisions news. A typical television segment about immigration may be, at best, twenty to thirty seconds in length. As our theory and hypotheses focus specifically on the frames used by the media, newspapers offer much more content to assess these frames than does broadcast news. It is worth noting, however, that our results are not likely to differ dramatically from analysis of television news coverage. Studies indicate that the volume and content of national political news coverage on television is remarkably similar to coverage in the *New York Times*.[42] We look at the time frame from 1980 to 2011 since this is roughly the period where immigration has been on the nation's agenda. As a robustness check, we will also examine coverage in *Time* magazine and *US News and World Report*.

To test agenda setting, we measured the volume of coverage on immigration by simply tabulating the total number of articles that mentioned immigration for each time period. Following a long line of research in the area of framing effects, we also assessed various aspects of the content of these articles.[43] Specifically, we coded stories across three dimensions of framing: tone, issue content, and immigrant group mentioned.

The most subjective of these frames is the tone of the news story. We grouped stories by whether the article provided a positive, negative, or neutral account of immigration. Our coders judged an article to be negative if the primary focus was the problems associated with immigration; for example, an article about an arrested immigrant is coded as negative. Likewise, an article looking at the benefits of labor migrants to the national economy would have been coded as positive. Negative and positive tone was also derived from the overall conclusions presented in the article. If, for instance, the story appeared to be critical of politicians or organizations that supported immigrants' rights, it was coded as negative. The coders identified neutral tone when no preference was given for either side of a policy.

Issue content coding was more straightforward. In terms of the specific frames that were coded for, we examined whether the newspa-

---

media consumption and are increasingly likely to be exposed to political views similar to their own. Still, since we believe that the vast majority of all mainstream media outlets are likely to be even more negative on immigration than the *New York Times*, few Americans will escape the immigrant threat narrative.

[42] Hassell 2011; Durr, Gilmour, and Wolbrecht 1997.

[43] See, for example, Gamson and Modigliani 1987; Chong and Druckman 2007b; Dimitrova et al. 2005; Nisbet, Brossard, and Kroepsch 2003.

per article focused on crime, economic issues, homeland security, and/or immigration policy. We expect that crime, economy, and security to frame immigration in a negative light, and immigration policy to frame it in a neutral or positive light. For this particular coding, a news story could be coded to contain up to three types of frames.

Finally, we coded for the particular immigrant group featured in the article. We noted stories that mentioned Latinos, Hispanics, or immigrants from Latin America, those stories that referred to Asian Americans or Asia, and those that highlighted immigration from Europe or other regions. More than one immigrant group could be mentioned in the article. It is also important to mention that these three types of frames (tone, issue content, and immigrant group) are not mutually exclusive from one another; that is, an article that features a Latino immigrant could discuss crime and the economy, and also adopt a negative tone.

We then aggregate these various frames by month and quarter, or year depending on the analysis. Thus, we assess the proportion of articles over a given time period that mention Latinos. For tone, we take the proportion of articles that are negative versus those that are positive in nature.

Due to concerns about the subjective nature of some of this coding, we performed the coding using two distinct methods. Newspaper articles were coded both by research assistants as well as using a machine coding procedure. The automated content analysis used machine learning techniques and the text classification package, RText-Tools, and incorporated information from the hand-coded classification for the articles before 2000.[44] Several tests of intercoder reliability between the automated and hand-coded data sets reveal a high degree of agreement. Moreover, the results of the following analysis are largely consistent across the two different coding methods. How we code the articles makes little difference.[45]

This data collection effort significantly improves on existing studies that focus on media coverage of immigration since it offers comprehensive yet detailed information about the content and frames used in the stories.[46] Existing work has detailed a range of powerful images and frames, but has been largely anecdotal in nature.[47] Nota-

---

[44] Jurka et al. 2012.
[45] Details on each method and a comparison of the two are included in the online appendix at http://pages.ucsd.edu/~zhajnal/styled/index.html.
[46] See Dunaway, Branton, and Abrajano 2010; Hopkins 2010; Chavez 2001, 2008; Simon and Alexander 1993.
[47] Chavez 2008; Santa Ana 2004; Brader, Valentino, and Suhay 2008.

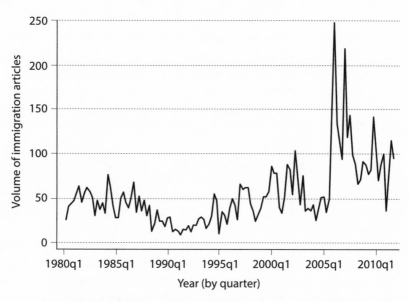

Figure 5.1 Volume of Immigration News Coverage, by Year and Quarter
Source: Authors' coding of *New York Times.*

ble exceptions are Nicholas Valentino and his colleagues, who assess the group imagery in immigration coverage, and Perez, who notes whether coverage of immigration explores legal or undocumented immigrants.[48] Our data set is the first that we are aware of that examines the content of immigrations news articles for such an extended period of time. This sort of detailed information makes it possible to determine how exactly the immigrant threat narrative and other frames have been depicted over the last three decades as well as assess the mechanisms of agenda setting and framing.

Is Immigration on the Agenda?

Does the *New York Times* devote time and space to immigration? The short answer is yes. Altogether, we identified 6,778 articles that discussed the issue of immigration for the time period of interest (1980–2011). That is roughly 227 articles per year—arguably enough coverage to make the issue salient and potentially sway opinions.[49] Moreover, as figure 5.1 shows, there is considerable variation in the

[48] Valentino, Brader, and Jardina 2013; Pérez, forthcoming.
[49] As a point of comparison, there were 1,463 articles that focused on the economy in 1986, 1,234 articles in 1996, and 990 articles in 2006.

volume of immigration news coverage across this thirty-one-year time span, making it possible to rigorously assess the effects of salience on white macropartisanship.

The most obvious pattern is the increasing attention that immigration has garnered over time.[50] If the volume of coverage matters, that pattern of expanded reporting could help to explain the shift of so many white Americans from the Democratic to Republican Party.

How Is Immigration Framed?

We now turn to our analysis of the various frames used by the media to cover the issue of immigration. Again, we expect that news coverage will generally follow the immigrant threat narrative and that most of the frames used to describe immigrants will be negative ones. This is generally what we find. Judging by the overall tone of stories, there are, in fact, four times as many negative news stories on immigration as there are positive ones. All told, 48.9 percent of immigration news articles adopt a negative tone. By contrast, only 12.1 percent of immigration news stories frame immigrants in a positive manner. The remaining news reports, 39 percent, take on a neutral tone.

What makes these patterns all the more telling is the fact that we are focusing on stories in the *New York Times*. If a mainstream, liberal news outlet has fallen prey to using the immigrant threat narrative, then it is likely that other media outlets, especially those with a conservative bent, would see a much larger share of their immigration news stories adopting this narrative.

When the public reads pieces that deal with immigration, a scant few do so in such a way that portrays immigrants in a positive light. The immigrant threat narrative, as previous accounts have argued, is indeed prevalent.[51] This skewed coverage makes it difficult for the majority of Americans to consider the full spectrum of immigrants' contributions to society, particularly with respect to the positive contributions that they can impart. This predominantly negative coverage certainly has the potential to fuel fears among the public—fears that could well shift the white public toward the Republican Party.

The immigrant group depicted in news coverage of immigration is equally lopsided. Fully 65.5 of all articles mention immigrants from

---

[50] There is also a clear spike in coverage in 2006. That increased volume is likely related to the introduction of the Sensenbrenner Bill (HR 4437), which increased penalties for being an undocumented immigrant, and sparked protests from millions of immigrants' rights supporters across more than 140 cities and 39 states.

[51] Valentino, Brader, and Jardina 2013; Chavez 2008; Santa Ana 2004.

Latin America. By contrast, only 26.3 percent of stories reference immigrants from Asian countries, and fewer still concentrate on immigrants hailing from Europe, Russia, eastern Europe, or the Middle East. All this is consistent with the composition of the immigrant population in the United States, but it nevertheless highlights just how prevalent the Latino immigrant frame is in these news stories.[52] If, as we suspect, images of Latinos spur negative associations among the bulk of the public, this coverage could have real consequences for partisan ties.

We now move on to examine the issue content of these immigration articles. Among all the different issues that could be associated with immigration, the *New York Times* most frequently used the economy as a frame. Approximately 25 percent of all immigration news articles adopted this theme. The next most commonly used frame discussed immigration in the context of some aspect of immigration policy. About 20 percent of the news stories featured these frames. Crime was associated with only 9 percent of all immigration news articles; this percentage is perhaps less than the immigrant threat narrative would suggest. Finally, national security frames were used rarely—only about 1.84 percent of the time.[53] Given the predominantly negative view of immigrants' contributions to the economy, crime, and national security, we expect these three frames to have negative consequences, while focusing on policy solutions might be neutral or even have positive effects.[54]

Given that we will be analyzing changes over time, the other important pattern to note about these different immigration frames pertains to temporal variation. Figures 5.2–5.3 illustrate wide temporal differences to the extent that they center on Latinos and employ a negative or positive tone. Coverage generally highlights negative over positive aspects of immigration, but it does so to varying degrees over time. Critically, figure 5.3 shows a gradual increase in the proportion of coverage focusing on Latinos over this thirty-one-year period. Again, if an emphasis on Latinos drives negative views of immigration and shifts whites to the political right, this increase in coverage over time could account for some of the movement of whites to the Republican Party.

---

[52] These results closely mirror those of Valentino and his colleagues (2013).

[53] Somewhat surprisingly, welfare was mentioned in only 1.1 percent of all stories. Other issues that received limited attention were health (0.7 percent) and family reunification (0.4 percent). In contrast, national culture or the social fabric of the nation frame was present in 3.8 percent of news stories.

[54] There is no increase in the volume of coverage on crime over time, but there is a slight buildup in attention to the economy and immigration policy over time.

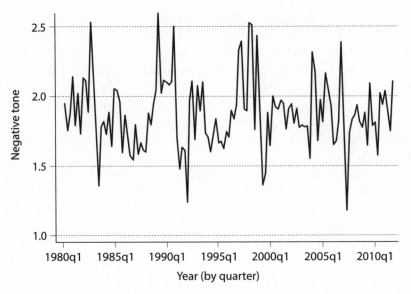

Figure 5.2 Proportion of Negative versus Positive Frames, by Year and Quarter
Source: Authors' coding of *New York Times*.

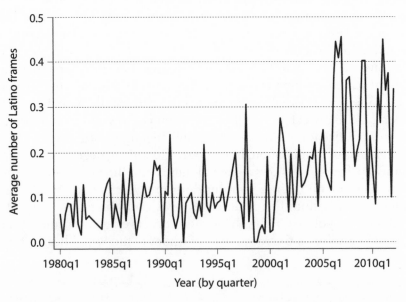

Figure 5.3 Average Number of Latino Immigrant Frames, by Year and Quarter
Source: Authors' coding of *New York Times*.

How Immigration Frames Affect
White Macropartisanship

[handwritten margin notes:]
☆ NB
But when
is the media
(rousing a[?]fecting
immigration
attitudes?

The patterns presented so far highlight the prevalence of the immigrant threat narrative and hint at the role that media coverage could have played in the widespread movement of white Americans to the Republican Party. But they by no means prove the causal link. In this next section, we assess the relationship between media coverage of immigration and white macropartisanship.

Such an analysis requires us to collect data on partisan preferences from the same period as our media data (1980–2011). For our party identification data, we turn to the CBS/*New York Times* poll series.[55] This poll series is unique in that it contains a considerable amount of data over regular intervals of time. Altogether, 488 surveys contain the party identification variable during our period of interest. There are 934 non-Hispanic white respondents on average in each survey.[56] The breadth of these data allows us to assess white partisanship systematically and perform a rigorous test of the effects of immigration coverage on partisanship. Importantly, the CBS/*New York Times* series asks respondents about their standard party identification: "Generally speaking, do you usually consider yourself a Democrat, Republican, or what?"[57]

In our main analysis, we look at the percentage of white respondents who identify as Democrats, Independents, or other in response to the first party identification prompt, and the percentage who identify as weak Republicans.[58] Mirroring the work of Michael MacKuen and his colleagues on macropartisanship, we calculate the mean re-

---

[55] Our data is from the iPoll data bank housed at the Roper Center's Public Opinion archives, http://www.ropercenter.uconn.edu/data_access/ipoll/ipoll.html (accessed July 13, 2014).

[56] The average number of surveys per year is 18. White samples range from a minimum of 405 to a maximum of 3,909 respondents.

[57] The only other series that we could have used—the Gallup poll—asks respondents to indicate their partisanship "as of today." That small difference in wording can, according to some research, artificially inflate changes in partisanship in the Gallup poll (Green, Palmquist, and Schickler 2002). We therefore opt for the more conservative measure.

[58] We focus on weak Republicans or those who "lean" toward the Republican Party, as opposed to those who already self-identify as Republican in their partisan affiliation, since this is the group of individuals where we would expect immigration to exert its greatest affect. Such individuals are at the "cusp" of identifying with the Republican Party. In contrast, those who already self-identify as Republican are unlikely to become "more" Republican as a result of immigration news coverage. Alternate tests also incorporate the proportion of respondents who "strongly favor" the Democratic/Republican Party and those who lean toward either party.

[handwritten margin note:]
↳ what about Network
effects?

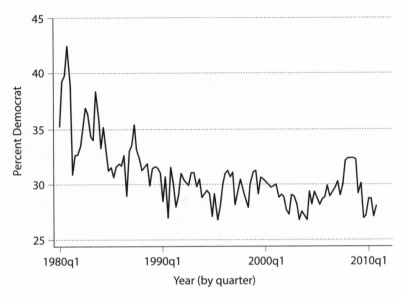

Figure 5.4 Percentage of Democratic Identifiers, 1980–2011
Source: CBS/New York Times poll series, cited in Roper 2014.

sponses from each survey and aggregate them by year/quarter.[59] Given that the time period we concentrate on contains thirty-one years, we have a total of 124 data points.

Figure 5.4, which plots mean support for the Democrats spanning from 1980 to 2011, makes it clear that white support for the Democratic Party has been declining dramatically. White attachment to the Democratic Party falls from a high of 43 percent in 1980 all the way down to about 28 percent in 2010.[60] These gains accrue both to Independents and the Republican Party. The other important trend to remark in figure 5.4 is that despite the widespread view that party identification is stable, there is actually quite a bit of variation in white macropartisanship from quarter to quarter. As MacKuen and his colleagues as well as Erickson and his colleagues have shown, substantial shifts in aggregate partisanship can and do occur regularly.[61]

But do immigration and its framing in the media have anything to do with all of this? Can the immigrant threat narrative help explain movement in white partisanship? To test that connection, we estimate a model of macropartisanship that assesses four different aspects of

[59] MacKuen, Erikson, and Stimson 1989.
[60] If we add those who lean Democratic to figure 5.5, we see the same sharp decline.
[61] MacKuen, Erikson, and Stimson 1989; Erikson, MacKuen, and Stimson 2002.

media coverage of immigration. Specifically, in terms of framing we evaluate the tone of the coverage (as measured by the ratio of negative to positive news stories), immigrant group featured in the story (as measured by the proportion of stories mentioning Latin American immigrants), and proportion of stories that use the crime and economy issue frame. To gauge the impact of agenda setting, we also account for the total number of stories on immigration. In addition, our model controls for the state of the economy, as measured by national unemployment rates as well as the political climate of the time (captured via presidential approval ratings)—the two factors that have been found to exert a strong influence on macropartisanship.[62] Based on a series of test diagnostics, we estimate our time series data using the Prais-Winsten AR(1) regression. As such, the independent variables are each lagged by one-quarter. We are in essence looking to see if immigration coverage predicts changes in aggregate partisanship after controlling for other factors.[63] The estimates are presented in table 5.1.

As expected, the immigrant threat narrative can and does influence white macropartisanship. The more that stories focus on Latino immigrants, the more likely whites are to subsequently shift away from the Democratic Party, and the more likely they are to favor independence or the Republican Party. Latino immigrant frames exert its strongest impact on the tendency to identify as Republican. The model predicts a 7 percent increase in white Republican identity in the quarter after *New York Times* coverage centers exclusively on Latino immigration as compared to the quarter after coverage focuses on non-Latino immigration. Similarly, the Latino frames reduce the proportion of whites identifying as Democratic in the next quarter by about 3 percent. In fact, the marginal impact of this specific frame is greater than standard predictors of macropartisanship such as presidential performance and the state of the economy.[64]

---

[62] MacKuen, Erikson, and Stimson 1989; Green, Palmquist, and Schickler 2002. Presidential approval is coded as the percentage in support for the president in office, and has been rescaled in accordance with the party of the president in office so that higher values indicate support for Republicans in office.

[63] To determine whether serial correlation exists in our data, we calculated the Durbon-Watson test statistic. We were unable to reject the null of no serial correlation. As such, we estimate our time series data using the Prais-Winsten AR(1) regression, which assumes that the errors follow a first-order autoregressive process.

[64] More fine-grained analysis of each of the different seven-point party identification categories indicate that the bulk of the movement caused by immigration coverage is from stronger to weaker identification with the Democratic Party, from weak Democratic identifiers to Independents who lean Democratic, and from pure Independents to those who lean Republican.

In what way how ever (or other way controlled media effects?

Chapter 5

TABLE 5.1
The Effect of Immigration Frames on the White Macropartisanship

	Percent Democratic identifiers	Percent Independent identifiers	Percent Republican identifiers
Immigration frames			
Tone			
Negative tone	−0.85 (0.61)	0.61 (0.69)	−0.13 (1.02)
Immigrant group			
Latino	−3.32 (1.61)**	5.01 (1.90)**	7.28 (3.00)**
Issue content			
Crime	−1.86 (1.89)	1.76 (2.01)	−1.13 (2.94)
Economy	1.62 (3.20)	−5.61 (3.17)	−.38 (4.58)
Agenda setting			
Volume of coverage	0.001 (0.006)	−0.004 (0.006)	−0.002 (0.01)
National indicators			
Presidential approval	−0.05 (0.02)**	−0.01 (0.01)	0.05 (0.02)**
Unemployment rate	0.34 (0.30)	0.51 (0.14)***	−0.36 (0.28)
Constant	32.24 (2.51)***	28.12(1.27)***	43.6 (2.40)***
N	115	115	94
R^2	0.74	0.44	0.84

*$p < 0.05$
**$p < 0.01$
***$p < 0.01$

Note: Coefficients are Prais-Winsten AR(1) regression estimates. Standard errors in parentheses.

Sources: CBS/New York Times poll series, cited in Roper 2014; authors' coding of New York Times.

These findings point to two conclusions. First, framing effects may be more powerful than many have suggested. Real shifts in party identification—the unmoved mover of US politics—appear to be linked to how the media covers immigration. If the framing of news stories can affect the national balance of power between Democrats and Republicans, it must be a formidable shaper of political behavior. Second, the immigrant threat narrative is a potent one. These results indicate that stories that highlight Latino immigrants can activate the fears of large segments of the public and generate enough anxiety to sway long-held partisan attachments.

We also considered the possibility that group-centric frames that focus on the second-largest immigrant group in the United States, Asians, may provoke the same reaction among white Americans. As such, we also performed an analysis that includes Asian immigrant frames. Our findings indicate that such frames do not exert the same effect on macropartisanship as Latino immigrant frames do. That is, the coefficient capturing Asian immigrant frames fails to achieve statistical significance at conventional levels.[65] As the existing research suggests, Asian immigrants do not elicit the same the kinds of anxiety and fears that Latino immigrants generate, either due to the way Latinos are covered by the media and/or the differential stereotypes associated with each group.[66]

The remaining estimates presented in table 5.1 also indicate that not everything the media puts forward resonates with the public enough to alter partisan identities in a measurable way. Existing research on the media framing of African Americans suggests that the crime frame can be an extraordinarily effective tool in shaping white views.[67] It is not, however, statistically significant here. The proportion of immigration-related stories framed from a crime perspective is unrelated to subsequent white partisanship. Moreover, when we controlled for other issue frames in the statistical model, the primary results remain largely unchanged. More coverage that featured border security or terrorism had no appreciable effect on aggregate white partisanship. Likewise, greater media attention to the impact of immigration on the economy did not push white partisanship one way or the other. There were signs, albeit weak ones, that when the *New York Times* focused specifically on immigration policy frames, white Democratic identity increased. But we could find no link between immigration policy coverage and Republican Party attachment or independence.[68] All told, issue specific frames seemed to matter little.

There was also no evidence on the effects of agenda setting on aggregate partisanship. An increase in the number of immigration-related news stories may increase the perceived salience of this issue to the public, but as table 5.1 reveals, there is no sign that it leads to systematic shifts to one party or another. Alternate tests that assessed the proportion of *New York Times* stories on immigration (rather than the total volume), evaluated volume without other controls, or interacted volume with the tone and/or group images of coverage all suggested that the volume of news coverage does not matter. In many circumstances, agenda setting is one of the most powerful tools in a democracy, yet it was relatively unimportant for this study of partisanship.

[65] For the results, see the online appendix at http://pages.ucsd.edu/~zhajnal/styled/index.html.

[66] Chavez 2001, 2008; Masuoka and Junn 2013; Kim 2003; Lee 2001.

[67] Gilliam 1999; Gilliam and Iyengar 2000.

[68] For the results, see the online appendix at http://pages.ucsd.edu/~zhajnal/styled/index.html.

Robustness Checks

To help increase confidence in our conclusions, we conducted a series of robustness checks that altered the analysis in various, hopefully informative, ways. First, rather than focusing separately on the number of Democrats, Independents, and Republicans in the population, we created a series of different measures of overall partisanship that either measured the ratio of Democratic identifiers and leaners to Republican identifiers and leaners, or stressed the absolute difference in the proportion of Democratic and Republican identifiers. The general pattern of results was the same. As table 5.2 shows, regardless of how we measure macropartisanship, news coverage on Latinos is associated with statistically significant and substantial shifts to the partisan right.

We also looked to see if altering how we measure the key independent variables makes any difference. Specifically, rather than measure the proportion of stories that focus on each immigration frame, in alternative tests we concentrated on the total number of stories that employed each frame. Once again, our general story was unchanged. Group-centric images continued to be central while tone and issue context were still not relevant to white partisan choices.

Yet we arrive at several more interesting and novel findings if we interact the tone of coverage with the total amount of immigration coverage. Essentially, we find that tone matters more when immigration gets lots of coverage. In other words, the greater the overall coverage, the more negative coverage leads to declines in Democratic Party identity. This suggests that at least when the immigration issue is particularly salient, the tone of the coverage can matter. This is a tentative finding, though, as the interaction between tone and total coverage is only marginally statistically significant when added to one of the models in table 5.1 (the proportion Democratic), and is statistically insignificant in the other two cases.[69]

One might also wonder whether the partisan effects of immigration framing have increased in recent decades when the Republican and Democratic parties have been more polarized on immigration policy. It is hard to pinpoint an exact date for the divide since partisan divisions on immigration appear to evolve differently at different levels. One could argue that there was no major partisan gap on immigration at the presidential level until the 2012 election, but also note that partisan divisions on immigration were well entrenched in California in the early 1990s (e.g., Proposition 187). We choose to disaggregate

---

[69] The analysis is available, on request, from the authors.

TABLE 5.2

The Effect of Immigration Frames on White
Macropartisanship (Dependent Variable: Democrats
Relative to Republicans)

	Democrats relative to Republicans
Immigration frames	
Tone	
Negative	−1.36 (1.84)
Immigrant group	
Latino	−12.03 (5.39)**
Issue content	
Crime	−2.72 (5.27)
Economy	0.87 (8.41)
Controls	
Presidential approval	−0.12 (0.05)**
Unemployment rate	0.81 (0.62)
Volume of coverage	−0.02 (0.03)
Constant	−0.55 (5.13)
N	94
R^2	0.13

*p < 0.10
**p < 0.05
***p < 0.01

Note: Coefficients are Prais-Winsten AR(1) regression estimates. Standard errors in parentheses.

Sources: CBS/New York Times poll series, cited in Roper 2014; authors' coding of *New York Times*.

our analysis into periods before and after the 1986 Immigration Reform and Control Act (IRCA). This law, which was signed by President Ronald Reagan, is a seminal moment in that it generated the nation's largest-scale legalization effort. Specifically, we look to see if immigration framing has more partisan consequences when the parties diverge after 1986. That is exactly what we find. As table 5.3 illustrates, we see no effect of framing prior to this law.

In more recent years, however, the Latino immigrant frame depicted by the media exerts a statistically significant and substantial effect on partisanship. This suggests that the real-world political effects of framing depend critically on context.

The test in table 5.3 is important for a second reason. The increase in Republican identity over time and increased attention to immigration over time raise the possibility of a spurious correlation. Both could be moving in the same direction with little causal relationship. Still,

TABLE 5.3
The Effect of Immigration Frames on White Macropartisanship
(before and after ICRA)

	Democrats relative to Republicans	
	Before ICRA	After ICRA
Immigration frames		
Tone		
Negative	–0.85 (0.61)	–2.18 (1.42)
Immigrant group		
Latino	–0.19 (15.3)	–9.88 (3.61)***
Issue content		
Crime	–8.29 (7.80)	–0.53 (4.85)
Economy	3.72 (12.50)	3.12 (7.92)
Controls		
Presidential approval	–0.07 (0.09)	–0.10 (0.03)***
Unemployment rate	1.99 (1.37)	–0.40 (0.36)
Volume of coverage	0.02 (0.07)	–0.003 (0.02)
Constant	–19.49 (13.24)	–8.12 (2.81)***
N	34	60
R^2	0.0	0.51

*$p < 0.10$
**$p < 0.05$
***$p < 0.01$
Note: Coefficients are Prais-Winsten AR(1) regression estimates. Standard errors in parentheses.
Sources: CBS/New York Times poll series, cited in Roper 2014; authors' coding of New York Times.

since the bulk of the movement toward the Republican Party came before 1986, we can assuage this concern by dropping this time period and reestimating our analysis. This alternate analysis actually strengthens our results by showing that immigration frames matter in the latter period though not in the earlier one.

Three Concerns

One legitimate issue that skeptics might raise is whether immigration coverage by the New York Times can, in and of itself, really have this sort of impact on partisanship. After all, the vast majority of Americans never even read the newspaper.[70] We, in fact, have no doubt that the New York Times cannot do all this alone. But we have reason to expect

[70] Delli Carpini and Keeter 1996.

so how is extrapolation safe at all?

that its coverage over this period will mirror that of other news outlets.[71] There is already persuasive if somewhat-anecdotal evidence that the media generally chooses an immigrant threat narrative when it covers immigration.[72] We also have compelling evidence that *New York Times* coverage tends to closely match the coverage of not only other print outlets but also television coverage.[73] Therefore, we believe that the evident effects on macropartisanship here are the cumulated ones of the entire range of media coverage at different points in time. The *New York Times* may not be powerful enough to influence the partisan balance of power on its own, but the media as a whole appears to be capable of doing just that.

extrapolation

One could question a different aspect of the causal story. Cynics about media framing might argue that the media is simply reporting real-world events, and the events rather than the media itself are driving changes in white partisanship. We offer two rejoinders. For one, we know that all media outlets have some sort of bias in the news-making process, and hence no coverage of news is ever purely objective.[74] Second, the media coverage of immigration is overwhelmingly negative, yet academic studies of immigration tend to show that immigrants today are assimilating just as rapidly as those in the past, and the actual economic consequences of immigration are either positive or inconsequential for the vast majority of Americans.[75] The media, as we have repeatedly mentioned, has the choice of covering a complex, multifaceted issue like immigration in any number of different ways. If the underlying story is a relatively positive one, why is the coverage so regularly negative? As we discussed earlier, because the news media outlets are primarily driven by profit, they are apt to favor stories that feature border violence and clandestine border crossings, because they are attention getting and emotionally riveting; such sto-

---

[71] We also analyzed *Time* and *US News and World Report* magazines' immigration coverage. We applied the same coding scheme as the one used to analyze the content of the *New York Times*. Overall, we find a similar trend in terms of the volume and tone of coverage; that is, we see an increase in the number of immigration articles from 2006 to 2011, and most of these news stories adopt a negative tone. For instance, 72 percent of all immigration articles from *US News and World Report* are negatively framed, and for *Time* magazine, this percentage is even greater at 88.7 percent. The patterns in immigration coverage we observe from the *New York Times* thus are fairly conservative when compared to other news sources. Finally, the policy content of these ads followed the same general pattern as those we uncovered in the *New York Times*. This particular robustness check provides us with assurance that the news outlet used in our analysis is not a major outlier when compared to other sources.

[72] Chavez 2008; Santa Ana 2004.

[73] Hassell 2011; Durr, Gilmour, and Wolbrecht 1997.

[74] Graber 2009.

[75] Alba and Nee 2005; Bean and Stevens 2003.

ξries drive up readership and in turn increase profit.[76] As such, even though the vast majority of Americans does not see or experience these events firsthand, the media plays a critical role in deciding what the public is exposed to. By choosing what to cover or not cover, and then by choosing how to cover it, the media can sway opinions and be consequential.

Other skeptics might ask why we see such powerful media effects here when numerous recent studies have shown that framing has relatively little, long-term impact in the real world.[77] We think the answer is that immigration may in some senses be a unique issue in US politics.[78] For most issues, there are vocal champions in the media on both sides of the concern. But as we have seen here, positive stories on immigration are relatively rare. Even in the liberal bastion of the *New York Times*, negative stories on immigration outnumber positive articles by three to one. More than likely that ratio of negative to positive is even more severe elsewhere. If the public is only exposed to one dominant frame and no counternarrative, the research tells us that this frame can be powerful. If, on the other hand, the respondent is exposed to a counterframe, then the effects generally wash out. Immigration coverage may have real, widespread effects because it is so lopsided, and immigration may be shifting white America to the right because that one-sided coverage is so negative.

Conclusion

The primary goal of this chapter was to explore one of the main mechanisms that we believe helps to shape attitudes toward immigration and subsequently impacts the core political identities of white Americans. Our detailed content analysis spanning three decades of a prominent national newspaper reveals that much of the news coverage does, in fact, put forward what amounts to a Latino threat narrative. Coverage of immigration in the *New York Times* is lopsided—with an emphasis on the negative consequences of immigration and heavy reliance on Latino images in its coverage. All this appears to fuel fears tion and leads to real shifts in the core partisan attachments America. After white Americans read about Latino immigrants read with greater support for the Republican Party.

why not start with this vr "immigrant threat narrative"?

These patterns have important implications for our understanding of framing and media effects. They suggest that the media and framing may be much more powerful than recent minimalist critics have argued.[79] Our test of the link between media framing and individual views differs fundamentally from existing studies in several compelling ways that, we believe, make it highly informative. In our analysis, we have left the isolated world of the lab to examine media and framing effects in the real world, where individuals are exposed to a plethora of different messages across various formats—messages that they can choose to hear or ignore. We have conducted time series analyses that assess the effect of news coverage on changes in white partisanship. And we have controlled for other factors that could influence these views. After conducting these tests, the relationship between news coverage and party identification seems to be evident.

Our analysis differs profoundly from existing studies of framing effects in two other important ways. First, unlike previous studies that look for relatively short-term, individual-level shifts on specific issue positions, we focus on party identification—one of the most stable, deep-seated psychological attachments in the realm of politics. Partisan attachments are not fleeting, often-altered, off-the-cuff responses. Party identification is, for some Americans, something that arrives in early adulthood and rarely, if ever, changes. The fact that the group frames presented by the media predict changes in white partisanship is evidence of the powerful, wide-ranging effects that framing can have. Second, the fact that these framing effects work at the aggregate level to lead to real shifts in the balance of national partisan power only serves to reinforce the notion that media framing can change politics at its core.

These changes in partisanship also serve to alter our view of what partisanship is and how malleable it can be. The sharp quarterly shifts in white macropartisanship that we see here indicate that party identification is less rigid than some claim.[80] Furthermore, the fact that these shifts in partisanship can be logically tied to variation in media coverage suggests that party identification can be more responsive and more rational than the authors of *The American Voter* and its followers frequently maintain.

---

[79] Druckman 2004.
[80] Campbell et al. 1960; Green, Palmquist, and Schickler 2002.

PART IV

The Consequences

Chapter 6

The Policy Backlash

The results thus far suggest that immigration has wide-ranging effects on how white Americans think and act politically. But to what extent do these opinions actually affect what government does? The ultimate test of this backlash is to determine whether it leads to the adoption of policies that would result in an unfavorable environment for immigrants and Latinos. Does this backlash ultimately hurt immigrants, racial/ethnic minorities, and other disadvantaged segments of the US population? In this chapter, we provide an answer to that question. Specifically, we look to see if states with large or rapidly increasing Latino populations enact more punitive and restrictive policies.

There are already growing signs that this kind of policy backlash is occurring at the state level. A number of contextual studies have shown that proximity to larger Latino populations is associated with the passage of more anti-immigrant measures.[1] Moreover, this kind of anti-immigrant policy pattern is not limited to policies that explicitly deal with immigrants. Hero and Preuhs along with other scholars have shown that the backlash extends at least to the arena of welfare policy.[2]

Our main goal in this chapter is to look at a broader set of policies to see if the influence of immigration and impact of the Latino threat extend to other policy areas implicitly tied to immigration. In the previous chapters, we suggested that three other policy areas—health,

---

[1] Rivera 2013; Campbell, Wong, and Citrin 2006; Hood and Morris 1998; Citrin et al. 1997.

[2] Hero and Preuhs 2006; Soss et al. 2008; Fellowes and Rowe 2004. In different contexts, greater racial/ethnic diversity has been found to also exert a negative effect on the overall provision of public goods (Alesina, Baqir, and Easterly 1999; Habyarima et al. 2007; Miguel and Gugerty 2005). Most relevant to our analysis here, Daniel Hopkins (2010) finds that US municipalities tend to respond to rapid increases in the immigrant population with a reduced tax effort.

criminal justice, and education—as well as larger taxing and spending decisions had all become intertwined with the immigrant debate and threat narrative. We now attempt to see if state policies in each of these areas can be directly linked to immigration and immigrant context in particular. Does the Latino population represent a threat that pushes the white majority to the right and leads to a policy backlash along with the passage of more punitive and regressive policies?

This immigration backlash story is only part of the policy story that we seek to tell, though. Our second aim in this chapter is to incorporate the role that *Latinos* themselves perform in this process. Up to this point in the book, the only part that the Latino population has played is in sparking a white reaction. Our immigration threat theory details how the presence of Latinos changes the attitudes and actions of white America. That is an important piece of the story—especially considering that white Americans make up the vast majority of the voting population. But it is far from the entire one. In the rest of the book, we begin to consider the other side of the equation: the role that racial and ethnic minorities play in US politics, and how it differs dramatically from that of whites.

One of the implications of our argument so far is that Latinos can do little on their own to affect change. In this chapter, we wish to dispel the notion that Latinos are powerless. While we have contended that the immigrant backlash is a powerful force, we believe that given sufficient numbers, Latinos and others can begin to overcome it. Once the size of the Latino population passes a certain threshold, Latinos should be able to mobilize to influence policy outcomes, and policy should begin to shift back to the left.

Finally, our analysis seeks to disentangle exactly what whites are reacting to. Is it the overall size of the Latino population, as a range of contextual studies have suggested?[3] Or as other studies have implied, is it the rapid growth of the Latino population that most threatens and mobilizes the white population?[4]

Theorizing Latino Context: White Threat and Latino Countermobilization

We have already detailed our immigration backlash theory and therefore will not go into great detail here. The logic is fairly straightfor-

[3] Campbell, Wong, and Citrin 2006; Hood and Morris 1998; Citrin et al. 1997.
[4] Hopkins 2010.

ward. To the degree that whites are threatened by Latinos and concerned about immigration, they will be opposed to policies that might benefit these newcomers. Critically, as we saw in chapter 4, that threat tends to be more pronounced as the Latino population grows in size. Indeed, we saw across a range of issues that white attitudes hardened when the Latino population grew larger. Given that whites form the overwhelming majority of voters in most states, changes in white views should fairly directly translate into policy outcomes.[5] The end result is that larger Latino populations should be associated with more punitive and regressive policy.

But as we have just noted, we believe that Latinos do have some agency in the policy process. It is already abundantly clear that large numbers of the Latino community can and do mobilize to try to influence policy. The protests in 2006 that drew millions of Americans together to fight for immigrants' rights are just one of the more prominent examples.[6] Scholars also point to the decisive role of Latino votes in electoral contests.[7] The growing influence of the Latino giant is also evident in the halls of US democracy. In states like California and Texas, Latinos now make up about one-fifth of the legislature. With Latinos representing almost 40 percent of the population in those two states and sizable shares in many others, it would be surprising for state legislators to totally ignore their concerns and preferences.

Thus, we believe that the pattern of immigration backlash should only hold until the Latino population becomes large enough to mobilize to effect policy change on its own. Once Latinos pass this threshold, a larger Latino population should be associated with more pro-Latino outcomes. The end result, we maintain, is that the relationship between Latino context and policy should be a curvilinear one.[8]

---

[5] Our story largely ignores the intermediate role of state legislators in this process. We simply assume that lawmakers will abide by the preferences of their constituents and pass policies that mirror those public views. There is, of course, a long-standing literature demonstrating responsiveness to public opinion at the state level (Lax and Phillips 2009; Burnstein 2003; Erikson, Wright, and McIver 1993). But at the same time, there is evidence of important distortions (Gilens 2012; Bartels 2008; Griffin and Newman 2008; Leighley and Nagler 2013). To the extent we are wrong and state legislators are not responsive to public opinion, then our tests should reveal few significant relationships between Latino population size and policy.

[6] Pantoja, Menjivar, and Magana 2008.

[7] Abrajano and Alvarez 2010.

[8] The actual relationship is likely to be an even more complicated one that will also depend on the size and interests of other minority groups as well as the liberal white population. We cannot, unfortunately, effectively model such a complex demographic process and so choose to model a simpler curvilinear relationship that sets aside the role of these other groups. In our analysis, however, we control for the size of the black and Asian American populations, and incorporate the political leaning of the entire state population.

Yet we readily admit that there are real questions as to just how much influence the Latino population has in US politics at the national level. A range of factors limits Latino participation in the electoral arena (e.g., a large foreign-born population) to the point where Latinos often participate at half the rate of whites.[9] Latinos are also hampered by the fact that they have more limited economic resources relative to whites. If money is a factor in US politics, Latinos simply have less of it to give.[10] Politicians, in turn, may merely be less receptive to Latinos. Indeed, John Griffin and Brian Newman find that legislators are less responsive to the views of Latino constituents than they are to those of white constituents.[11]

As such, it is critical that we do more to assess and understand the role that Latinos play in the policy arena. Existing studies of racial threat have largely ignored the potential influence and agency of the Latino population, and instead assumed that the relationship between minority context and outcomes is linear. More minorities typically meant more antiminority policy.[12] If we can show that a more complex relationship exists and Latinos can—if their numbers are large enough—sway policy in a more pro-Latino direction, then our expectations about the future change radically. The backlash will persist to a certain point, but over the long term as the immigrant population grows ever larger, a coalition of Latinos, other ethnic/racial minorities, and liberal whites may win out.

Why Health, Education, Criminal Justice, and Taxes?

There are, as we have already detailed, several reasons to expect a link between immigration and the policy areas of education, health, criminal justice, and taxation.[13] All four of these policies arenas are linked to the immigrant threat narrative. According to that narrative, immigrants' use of public services like education and health care create a substantial fiscal drain on the nation. The narrative also regularly highlights the supposed criminality of the immigrant population as well as the idea that the undocumented do not pay taxes. Importantly, immigration has also begun to permeate larger public policy debates.

[9] Verba et al. 1995; Hajnal and Trounstine 2010.
[10] Verba et al. 1995.
[11] Griffin and Newman 2008.
[12] But see Rivera 2013; Cameron et al. 1996.
[13] Martinez-Ebers et al. 2000.

Discussions over reforms in education, health, and criminal justice along with disputes over taxes have all become at times closely inter-twined with debates about immigration. When white Americans think about these policies, in our view, they often have images of immigrants and/or Latinos in their heads. Finally and most critically as chapter 4 illustrated, white policy views in each area are tied to the immigrant population's size. In each case, a larger Latino population was associated with more regressive or punitive policy preferences. All this suggests that state policy in these areas should be at least partly a function of immigrant context.

These are only logical deductions, however. We do not yet know if state policy in any of these areas really is a function of immigrant context. No study that we know of has even tried to make this empirical connection.[14] Daniel Hopkins's study of local tax policy is the closest. He finds that municipalities with rapidly expanding immigrant populations tend to tax themselves less.[15] Others have similarly illustrated a negative relationship between overall ethnic diversity and overall public goods provision at the local level in the United States and elsewhere.[16] Hero, Key, and others have demonstrated a close connection, too, between other aspects of racial diversity—often measured by the size of the black population—and a range of different state policies.[17] These studies are important and certainly suggestive, but if we want to know whether immigrant context influences state policy across these three broader arenas of policy, we have to offer a direct test.

Why States?

We focus on the state level largely because states have become the primary actor legislating on the welfare of immigrants in this nation. The inability of the federal government to enact comprehensive immigration reform has in recent decades encouraged states to act. Over the last eight years, states passed over seventeen hundred bills that explicitly deal with immigration or immigrants.[18] These new laws have done everything from expanding welfare eligibility to preventing

[14] As we have noted, Hero and Preuhs (2006), Matthew Fellowes and Gretchen Rowe (2004), and Joe Soss and his colleagues (2008) have all demonstrated ties between ethnic diversity and state welfare policy.
[15] Hopkins 2010.
[16] Alesina, Baqir, and Easterly 1999.
[17] Hero 1998; Key 1949.
[18] Rivera 2013.

undocumented immigrants from accessing public schools. There is little doubt that what states do or do not do can have a dramatic impact on the well-being of the immigrant population living within their borders.

There is also, as we have already shown, a crucial state-level dimension to white policy preferences. Given that whites' views on policy are closely linked to their state's immigrant context, there is every reason to believe that state policy will be intimately tied to state immigrant context as well.

Measuring State Spending and Latino Context

We now turn to a discussion of our empirical strategy. To make the connection between immigrant threat, Latino agency, and each of these different policy areas, we need measures of both policy outcomes and Latino population size. Although there are a variety of different ways to measure policy, we choose to emphasize one of the most basic: the amount of money that states devote to each these different policy areas.[19] The extent to which a government does or does not invest significant resources into a particular policy area is arguably one of the most revealing measures of a government's priorities. More money for education, for instance, suggests that the state cares about education and is willing to invest its limited resources to try to improve educational outcomes.

We examine the proportion of the state budget that goes to each of the three policy areas of health, education, and corrections. By focusing on the proportion, we get a measure of the government's priorities *relative* to other functions, and avoid some of the variation caused by the fact that some states are richer than others and thus able to spend more money. Yet in a series of robustness tests, we also look at per capita spending in each area.

Information on budget expenditures for all fifty states is available from annual reports provided by the National Association of State Budget Officers.[20] A nice feature of these data is their availability for more than a decade, spanning 1995–2011. For education, we only in-

---

[19] Alternatives might include tests that assess specific, concrete policies in each area. For example, we could have looked at sentencing for drug violations or violent crimes in each state. It is difficult, however, to come up with a single policy that accurately encompasses the state's overall policy record in any given area.

[20] National Association of State Budget Officers.

clude K–12 and exclude higher education spending, since postsecondary education tends to be much less clearly associated with the immigrant or Latino population. On average, 20.5 percent of state expenditures go to K–12, but that figure varies widely from a high of 32.2 percent to a low of 3.8 percent. Our measure of corrections funding incorporates spending to build and operate prison systems.[21] Corrections expenditures are considerably lower, comprising only 4.1 percent of state spending on average. Our measure of health care spending is admittedly less encompassing and therefore may be a less accurate portrayal of state efforts. Specifically, we look at the proportion of all state funds that go to Medicaid—a means-tested program that provides medical care for low-income individuals. About 2.5 percent of all state funds go to Medicaid.

How governments spend their money is only half the fiscal story. State governments also have to make weighty decisions about how they raise their revenues. Here taxes come into play. States can choose to raise revenue through more progressive tax measures like property taxes or more regressive means like sales taxes. Thus, we also examine the proportion of all taxes generated through each method (sales versus property tax).

To assess the Latino threat hypothesis, we need to measure Latino context in a state. As we discussed previously, it is not apparent whether the *size* or *growth* of the Latino population is driving overall state and public service spending. The public and its policy makers may be responding to rapid, sudden surges in the Latino population, particularly in areas that were once largely ethnically/racially homogeneous, but they could also be responding to the overall size and increased visibility of this group. The existing research on this subject matter is mixed; it has found effects both with respect to changes in the Latino population and its overall size.[22] In order to determine more precisely what sort of Latino context is driving state policy decisions, our analysis will consider both possibilities. Latino population growth is measured as the change in the percentage of the Latino population each year while the size of the Latino population is measured as the percentage of the state population that is Latino.

Lawmakers may not only be responding to Latino context. That the racial/ethnic composition in a state has exerted such a pronounced effect in previous studies of state policy making makes it necessary to also control for both the percentage of Asian Americans and blacks in

---

[21] A minority of states also reports funding of juvenile and/or drug rehabilitation, but this represents a small fraction of corrections spending.

[22] Hopkins 2010; Hero 1998; Hero and Preuhs 2006; Soss et al. 2008.

a state. Along with a state's racial/ethnic context, socioeconomic and political conditions as well as regional variations across states could certainly affect policy decisions. Our socioeconomic indicators include a measure for the unemployment rate along with the average individual income and education levels for a given state.[23] Higher levels of unemployment could be associated with a decrease in public goods spending, especially those that could benefit immigrants. Our other socioeconomic indicator, education, is measured as the percentage of individuals in a state with bachelor's degree. Educational attainment tends to have a liberalizing influence on overall attitudes.[24] As such, more educated individuals may be supportive of state spending on public services.

The political climate could play an important role in determining the amount of spending allocated to public goods as well—particularly since distinct partisan differences exists over the role of government in society.[25] Hence, we incorporate a measure that captures the partisan composition of the state legislature, with the expectation that Republicans will be less favorable to increases in public goods spending relative to Democrats.[26] We also include a measure developed by Peverill Squire that assesses a legislature's level of professionalization, since the research on state politics has firmly established variations in legislator behavior based on this institutional setup.[27] Another political indicator that could be relevant in determining the level of public goods spending is the ideological leanings of a state's citizenry. Our measure of state ideology is drawn from Erikson and his colleagues, who use public opinion survey data to estimate the percentage of a state population that is liberal, conservative, or moderate.[28]

Finally, in alternate tests we build on the research by Hero and Preuhs by controlling for regional variations across states that might

---

[23] For the unemployment data, see US Bureau of Labor Statistics, http://www.bls.gov/lau/home .htm (accessed July 13, 2014). For the average individual income, see US Bureau of Labor Statistics, "Employment and Wages Online Annual Averages, 2009," http://www.bls.gov/cew /cewbultn09.htm (accessed July 13, 2014).

[24] Erikson and Tedin 2007.

[25] Erikson, Wright, and McIver 1993.

[26] For state legislature partisanship data, see US Statistical Abstract, 1990–2012, in US Census Bureau 2012.

[27] Squire 2007; Kousser 2005.

[28] Erickson, Wright, and McIver 1993. For the state ideology data, see http://php.indiana .edu/~wright1/cbs7603_pct.zip (accessed July 13, 2014). William Berry and his colleagues (1998) also have a measure of citizen ideology based on interest group ratings of congressional members, however due to limited scope of their data (2002–8), we opted to use the Erikson and his colleagues' measure. For how their measure compares to Berry's, see Erikson, Wright, and McIver 1993.

affect their support for public goods spending on immigrants.[29] Specifically, these two scholars argue that states along the US–Mexico border as well as those with an international port may have distinct policy regimes and be especially sensitive to the amount of state funds allocated to immigrants.[30]

To account for the nonindependent nature of the measure within states as well as the time-varying nature of our data, our model of state spending on immigrant-eligible public services is estimated using a cross-sectional time series regression model that includes all years from 1993 to 2011.[31] Each of the time-varying independent variables is lagged by one year in order to address potential concerns about the direction of causality.

The Impact of Latino Context
on State Spending

Does Latino context play a role in shaping state policy? Is there a white backlash? And finally, can Latinos begin to assert themselves when they grow sufficiently large in number? In table 6.1, we attempt to answer these questions by presenting the results of three time series cross-sectional regressions that focus in turn on education, corrections, and health.

The results show that state policy is strongly linked to the Latino population size. At least in two of the three policy areas, our expectations are confirmed. States with larger Latino populations are significantly less likely to spend money on education, and significantly more likely to devote money to prisons and criminal justice. This pattern fits closely with other work assessing the impact of Latino population size on immigrant-specific policies.[32] It also strongly suggests that the United States' increasingly diverse population is generating a real and wide-ranging backlash. As the Latino population increases, whites become less willing to invest in public services like education that might benefit immigrants and more eager to punish criminals—a group tied to the immigrant population.

---

[29] Hero and Preuhs 2006.

[30] We employ the same coding scheme as Hero and Preuhs (2006) in defining which states are along the US-Mexico border and those states with an international port. We generate a dummy variable that is coded as one if a state shares a border with Mexico, and zero otherwise. The same coding scheme is used to denote those states with an international port.

[31] Specifically, we use a random effects model to account for variation across years.

[32] Rivera 2013; Campbell, Wong, and Citrin 2006; Hood and Morris 1998; Citrin et al. 1997.

TABLE 6.1
The Effect of Latino Context on State Spending

	Proportion of state spending going to:		
	Education	Corrections	Health
Latino context			
Percent Latino	−0.65 (0.23)**	0.09 (0.04)*	0.10 (0.07)
Percent Latino squared	0.02 (0.005)**	−0.002 (0.001)*	−0.002 (0.001)
Other racial context			
Percent black	0.00 (0.09)	0.02 (0.02)	0.05 (0.03)
Percent Asian	0.87 (0.51)	−0.08 (0.09)	−0.72 (0.16)**
Political			
Republican to Democratic legislature ratio	−4.1 (3.3)	0.10 (0.54)	−0.07 (0.88)
Liberal citizen ideology	0.08 (0.06)	−0.01 (0.01)	−0.01 (0.02)
Professional legislature	−18.5 (6.1)**	−2.6 (1.0)**	−0.69 (1.66)
Socioeconomic status			
Percent college degree	0.09 (0.15)	0.05 (0.02)*	0.11 (0.04)**
Household income	−0.01 (0.00)*	−0.02 (0.01)*	−0.00 (0.01)
Unemployment rate	0.26 (0.13)	−0.00 (0.02)	0.22 (0.03)**
Total population	0.03 (0.02)	0.06 (0.04)	0.02 (0.01)*
N	745	742	745
R^2	0.06	0.22	0.14

*$p < 0.05$
**$p < 0.01$
Note: Entries not in parentheses are OLS coefficients and entries in parentheses denote the corresponding standard errors.
Source: US Census of Government Finances 2012; US Census Bureau 2010.

At the same time, the results in table 6.1 also indicate that the size of the Latino population serves as more than just a threat to the white community. Latinos themselves appear to have an impact on policy. As evidenced by the statistically significant coefficients for *percent Latino squared*, there is a robust curvilinear effect to the Latino population size. Once Latinos pass a particular threshold, Latino population growth starts to be associated with increasingly liberal policy outcomes for education and corrections.[33]

To help illustrate this curvilinear effect, figure 6.1 graphs the relationship between Latino context and state corrections spending. The

[33] The importance of the Latino population in shifting policy outcomes in a more pro-Latino direction somewhat contradicts the work of Griffin and Newman (2008), Larry Bartels (2008), and Gilens (2012), which all suggests that ethnic/racial minorities and the poor have limited influence over government policy. The truth may be that the Latino population has a real say in US politics, but only when it passes a certain threshold in size—a situation that has not yet happened at the national level.

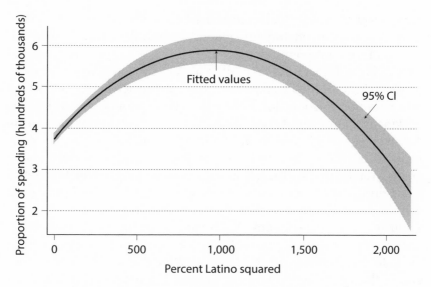

Figure 6.1 The Effect of Latino Context on Corrections Spending

figure clearly shows that growth in the Latino population first leads to a rise in the proportion of state funds that go to corrections, but as Latinos become a larger and larger share of the state, the amount of corrections spending declines substantially.[34]

California's history with immigration and its policy response aptly capture this complex relationship. As one of the first states to face large-scale Latino immigration, California was one of the first to try to actively impose restrictions on services to undocumented immigrants, as evidenced by the now-infamous Proposition 187. Over time, whites in the state became more conservative, with more and more moving to the Republican Party, and policy on immigration, education, and corrections shifted decidedly to the right. California fell from among the top half of all states in per pupil education funding in 1980, when whites represented the overwhelming majority of schoolchildren, to near the bottom (forty-fourth place) in 2009, when Latinos were the single-largest racial/ethnic group among school-age children.[35] Likewise, corrections funding more than tripled as a proportion of the budget from only about 2.9 percent in 1980 to well over 10 percent in 2005.[36] Driving this growth in prison spending was a series of stricter

[34] Although the effect of Latino context on corrections spending is no longer statistically significant at larger values.

[35] Anand 2012.

[36] Ibid.

sentencing laws like California's famous 1994 "three-strikes law," which imposed mandatory life sentences for all three-time felons.

As the Latino population has grown and amassed enough influence to be an important part of the state's Democratic majority, policy has once again shifted back to the left. With the active support of Latinos, who now account for 38 percent of the population, and strong backing of Latino legislators, who now hold 19 percent of the seats in the state legislature, a series of proimmigrant measures has passed the legislature.[37] This includes measures offering undocumented immigrants in-state tuition, drivers' licenses, and the opportunity to practice law. Education and corrections funding are also now slowly following suit. In the last few years, state education funding has already seen a slight but noticeable uptick. With voters passing Proposition 30 in 2012, a tax measure expected to raise billions for K–12, the state is likely to see even more growth in education spending. On the other end of the spectrum, corrections funding has dropped markedly and the state has initiated a number of steps to gain early release of prisoners. As well, it has shifted efforts from imprisonment toward greater rehabilitation. A range of different factors has contributed to these policy changes in California, but Latino context and the immigrant threat narrative appear to be a critical part of the story.

Still, the reach of Latino context does not extend to all three of the policy areas we focus on in table 6.1. We found no statistically significant link between the size of the Latino or immigrant populations and the proportion of the budget devoted to health care spending. It is quite possible that immigration and the Latino population are less closely associated with health care than they are with the other two policy areas. But it is also possible that our measure of health care — the proportion of all spending that goes to Medicaid — is a poor proxy for health care efforts. Federal mandates could, more than anything else, be driving funding in this area.

State Taxation

All our efforts to this point have been concentrated on understanding state *spending* decisions. But states face equally critical decisions about how they *raise* their money. And the key element of that state fundraising equation is taxation. Do states choose to raise revenue through more regressive taxes that might place an exceptional burden on Lati-

---

[37] Medina 2013.

TABLE 6.2
The Effect of Latino Context on State Taxation

	Percent of state taxes coming from:	
	Sales taxes	Property taxes
Latino context		
Percent Latino	0.46 (0.13)**	−0.46 (0.13)**
Percent Latino squared	−0.01 (0.00)**	0.01 (0.00)*
Other racial context		
Percent black	−0.11 (0.15)	−0.09 (0.06)
Percent Asian	−1.22 (0.31)**	0.43 (0.31)
Political		
Republican/Democratic ratio legislature	−0.03 (0.01)*	0.02 (0.02)
Liberal citizen ideology	0.03 (0.02)	0.11 (0.02)**
Professional legislature	−0.07 (0.03)**	0.05 (0.03)
Socioeconomic status		
Percent college degree	0.07 (0.06)	0.28 (0.08)**
Household income	−0.02 (0.00)**	0.03 (0.03)
Unemployment rate	0.11 (0.04)**	0.09 (0.07)
Total population	0.08 (0.01)*	−0.03 (0.01)*
N	751	751
R^2	0.08	0.13

*$p < 0.05$
**$p < 0.01$
Note: Entries not in parentheses are OLS coefficients and entries in parentheses denote the corresponding standard errors.
Source: US Census of Government Finances 2012; US Census Bureau 2010.

nos and other disadvantaged groups, or do they favor more progressive taxes that rely more heavily on whites and the wealthy? Our results, displayed in table 6.2, suggest that the backlash extends to revenue-raising decisions as well. This analysis assesses the links between Latino context and one regressive tax (sales tax) as well as one progressive tax (property tax). Each is measured as a percent of the state's total tax effort.[38] Our control variables remain the same as the ones used in our main model.

The results very much mirror our earlier findings on spending. We once again see an important curvilinear effect between Latino context and policy. States with larger Latino populations are statistically significantly more likely to favor regressive measures like sales tax to raise revenue and less likely to increase more progressive tax structures like

[38] Sales tax accounts for 31 percent of the total state tax revenue on average while property tax amounts to 2.6 percent. The remainder is largely income tax, which can range from regressive to progressive and thus is hard to characterize overall.

property taxes. All this fits all too neatly with a group conflict model where whites, as the majority, are increasingly likely to shift the costs of government onto less advantaged segments of the population as those less advantaged segments are increasingly comprised of Latinos. This effect is attenuated, however, after the Latino population reaches a certain threshold. Once that threshold is reached and Latinos are large enough to influence policy on their own, larger Latino populations are associated with more progressive tax policy.

Finally, in alternate tests, we sought to confirm and expand on existing work on the connection between welfare policy and immigration. Hero and Preuhs as well as Joe Soss and his colleagues have demonstrated crucial ties between state immigrant context, on the one hand, and welfare benefit levels and state efforts to devolve control of welfare from the federal government, on the other. In both cases, the relationship was linear.[39] A larger Latino population meant less state welfare effort. Do those effects extend to overall state welfare spending? Is the relationship between Latino context and policy as simple as existing accounts suggest, or is there a more complex, curvilinear effect on welfare spending as well? Our results, displayed in the online appendix, are mixed. In line with these two existing studies, we find that states with larger Latino populations spend significantly less on welfare. At the same time, we see no evidence of curvilinear effects for the percentage of Latinos in a state. For whatever reason, the positive influence of Latino voters does not yet appear to have extended to the arena of welfare policy.

The findings regarding black and Asian American context, as tables 6.1–6.2 demonstrate, are far less clear and consistent. With one exception, the black population plays no evident role. Yet that exception is an important, well-documented one. States with larger African American populations devote significantly smaller portions of their budgets to welfare. This is consistent with the findings of Soss and his colleagues about the central role that the black population plays in driving welfare devolution, and follows from Gilens' research, which shows that white attitudes toward welfare are in large part shaped by their stereotypes of blacks.[40] The size of the Asian American population also fails to reach statistical significance in our models. When it is statistically significant, the pattern largely matches our earlier results on state context and white views. Here we discover that a larger Asian American population is associated with greater support for welfare and

[39] Hero and Preuhs 2006; Soss et al. 2008.
[40] Soss et al. 2008; Gilens 1999.

less regressive taxes. As we noted earlier, one interpretation is that white Americans are more generous when Asian Americans make up a larger share of the population, and less generous when Latinos or blacks are present in large numbers. This pattern for Asian Americans also seems to confirm earlier work that has at least on occasion found that proximity to large Asian American communities is associated with more positive views about Asian Americans or policies related to them.[41]

Assessing the Rate of Change within the Latino Population

All the analysis to this point ignores a potentially critical aspect of Latino context: the rate of change within the Latino population, as opposed to its size, is what influences policy decisions. Looking across the nation, some of the toughest anti-immigrant omnibus bills have been passed in states like Alabama and South Carolina, which have small (e.g., less than 2 percent of the state population) though gradually expanding immigrant populations. Thus, it may be the growth or change in the Latino population rather than the overall population size that most affects policy outcomes.

To test this possibility, we included a set of measures that capture Latino population grown to our models presented in tables 6.1–6.2. Since it is not apparent exactly which aspect of growth for a given time period most stirs white reactions, we introduced a range of different measures that assessed Latino population growth over one year, the past two years, or the past five years. We also measured growth in two ways. One simply counted the percentage of newcomers for a given state, and the other revolved around the percentage increase in the overall Latino population.

In the end, most of these measures of population growth failed to reach statistical significance.[42] Moreover, in some cases where a statis-

---

[41] Hood and Morris 2000; Hero and Preuhs 2006; Tolbert, Lowenstein, and Donovan 1998. In terms of the other controls that we include in our models of state spending, we find that the socioeconomic characteristics of the state exert a more consistent impact than do political indicators. For socioeconomic status, the story appears to be one of funding going to areas where it is most needed. So, for example, states with lower socioeconomic status tend to spend more on corrections, Medicaid, and welfare. As for our political controls, the results are somewhat inconsistent when we focus on the proportion of the budget going to each policy area. Yet if we shift to emphasize per capita spending—as we do in alternate tests—we see somewhat more of a conventional political story. Republican and conservative states, for example, spend significantly less on education.

[42] Adding these different measures of growth did little to influence our main results on the effects of Latino population size on state policy expenditures.

tically significant effect could be observed on state policy spending, its impact was mixed. As such, the association between Latino population change and state policy spending remains unclear at least for the specific models that we estimated. Our overall conclusion is that recent changes in the size of the state Latino population do not appear to trigger a sharp policy reaction. Conflict can and does occur in new immigrant destinations, but it may be more prevalent in states with more long-standing immigrant populations. In the end, politicians and the public appear to be responding more to the overall size of the Latino population than to its growth.

Race versus Immigration and Race versus Citizenship Status

Are the views of Americans and the policies they pass really a function of the racial environment along with the size of the Latino population, as we have suggested here? Or could the reaction be more closely related to immigration-specific population changes? Our immigrant backlash theory is after all ostensibly focused on immigration and not race. Furthermore, there are reasons to suspect that the policy backlash we see is less a response to the Latino population and more a reaction to the undocumented population. Recall that unauthorized immigrants were the ones specifically targeted in Proposition 187 back in the 1990s in California as well as in more recent laws in Arizona, Georgia, and South Carolina. Recall also that when Americans are asked about immigration in surveys, they reserve their most negative assessments for the undocumented population. Given that so much of the immigration debate over the last three decades has centered on the undocumented population, it is important that we also examine this specific group. To assess this possibility, we substituted a measure of the state's undocumented population into the models in tables 6.1–6.2. No official records exist for the actual size of the unauthorized population by state so we rely on the estimates provided from Jeffrey Passel and D'Vera Cohn of the Pew Hispanic Center.[43]

We could find no obvious link between the size of the undocumented population and policy at the state level. The undocumented proportion of a state is signed in the expected direction in almost every

[43] Passel and Cohn 2009.

case, but the relationship is usually not quite significant. These results indicate that policy changes are driven more by the larger Latino population than they are by the smaller undocumented population.

Likewise, we could find no robust relationship between the foreign-born population of a state and that state's policies. Given that whites tend to react differently to Asian Americans and Latinos—the two main immigrant groups—this is perhaps not surprising. But it does reinforce the view that the overall patterns are driven more by race than by nativity. Immigration is changing the United States, yet those changes appear often to be noticed and filtered through the lens of race. In the end, the group that is targeted more than any other seems to be Latinos.

Robustness Checks

To help increase confidence in our findings, we repeated our basic tests with several alternate specifications in a number of important ways. First, rather than look at the proportion of government spending in each policy area, we shifted to per capita spending. Employing this new set of dependent variables, the story remained largely the same. Although the levels of statistical significance dropped marginally in several cases, the size of the Latino population continued to be a robust factor shaping a broad set of state policies. Second, to see if our results might be driven by one or two exceptional states with particularly large or small Latino populations, we reran our analysis, dropping each state one at a time.[44] The overall findings remained robust and only one difference emerged.[45] To further test the robustness of our results, we incorporated a range of different measures of politics (dummy variables for which party controls the senate, house, and governor's office) and geography (controls for border states and various regional dummies). None of these alternative specifications affected the basic results.

[44] Including a large number of states with a negligible Latino population could also be skewing our results. In alternate tests, we therefore excluded from our analysis those states where Latinos comprise less than 3 percent of the total population. These states include Maine, Mississippi, New Hampshire, North and South Dakota, Vermont, and West Virginia. Even when these seven states are dropped from our sample, it leads to no substantive change in our main findings.

[45] Dropping Texas reduces the significance of our results for corrections spending, suggesting that it is an influential outlier and the greater corrections spending in high high-density Latino states is in large part a function of the heavy corrections spending in Texas.

Discussion

All told, these findings indicate just how far reaching the effects of immigration are. Latino population size in a state impacts a wide range of policies. Unfortunately, that relationship is often a negative one. States with more Latinos generally spend and raise money in a way that produces an unfavorable environment for members of the group—decreased funds to education that could potentially be of great use to this community, a larger criminal justice apparatus, and more regressive taxation. All this could have real and negative consequences. Latinos already lag far behind whites and Asian Americans in nearly every indicator of educational performance (graduate rates, standardized test scores, etc.), and are already greatly overrepresented in the criminal justice system, so the decision to reduce education funding and increase corrections funding in states with a large Latino community may exacerbate the problem even further. This rightward policy shift also runs counter to the preferences of the bulk of the Latino population.[46]

But the story is not a purely negative one. Latinos, despite all the barriers they face, also have some agency and are able to shift policy in a pro-Latino direction if their numbers are large enough. If the population projections of the US Census hold, so that whites lose their majority status in a few decades, then this emerging pattern bodes well for Latinos over the long term. Latinos' influence should only grow more pronounced and policy should become more aligned with Latino preferences. Given that at least some studies show that policy makers often ignore Latinos, this potentially represents a major step forward.[47]

All this further underscores the increasingly central role that immigration and Latinos play in modern-day US politics. While our results indicate that blacks continue to represent a threat to some white Americans and their presence does affect state welfare spending, we find that Latinos are becoming much more central in the policy-making process. Hence, the black-white paradigm that has guided most of the work on racial politics in the United States must now also take into account the nation's largest ethnic/racial group. When states make a range of policy decisions, many of those decisions are affected in important and complex ways by the size of the Latino population.

[46] Fraga et al. 2012.
[47] Griffin and Newman 2008.

Conclusion

Implications for a Deeply Divided United States

The arrival of tens of millions of immigrants to US shores raises both hope and fear. The hope is that the actions and efforts of immigrants in the economic, cultural, and social spheres will win over the hearts and minds of native white Americans, and ultimately lead to a nation where racial divisions are muted and intergroup conflicts are rare. The fear is that concerns about immigrants, lost jobs, diminishing wages, increased crime, and the demise of culture will heighten intergroup tensions, and lead to a widespread white backlash. In this book, we assess the reality.

What are the consequences of large-scale immigration for US politics? One part of the answer is already clear. Scholars have taught us a fair amount about the growing strength and electoral preferences of immigrants themselves.[1] But those immigrants represent only 13 percent of the population. Native-born whites, by contrast, represent 63 percent of the population, and perhaps more important, some 75 percent of its voters. Thus, assessing how the majority of the US population responds to immigration is central to understanding the impact of immigration on this nation. Here our knowledge is much more limited. We have some real understanding of the factors that drive our attitudes on immigration, but much less analysis of whether those attitudes have broader political consequences.

The pages in this book tell a largely negative tale about those consequences. Although there may still be reason for optimism about the future, and hope that immigration will breed understanding and coop-

---

[1] Fraga et al. 2012; Wong et al. 2011.

eration, the patterns to date have been more about fear, anxiety, and ultimately backlash.

At the onset of this book we proposed an immigration backlash theory that, we argue, is leading to a significant shift in the political preferences and orientations of a considerable segment of the US public. Specifically, we contend that the growth of the immigrant population over the last thirty years, combined with the news media's reliance on the Latino threat narrative, work together to fuel concerns over immigration. In the current political environment, where Republican politicians have been much more vocal and adamant in their opposition to immigration, the millions of white Americans who feel real anxiety about immigration are drawn to the political party that has promised to ease such concerns. The end result, we hope to have convincingly demonstrated, is greater support for the Republican Party and its candidates, a preference for more conservative policies, and a shift in heavily Latino states toward policies that target and often punish the disadvantaged segments of the population. Large-scale immigration has generated a less generous, more indignant politics that seeks to punish immigrants as well as limit the social services and public goods available to them.

In the ensuing pages we have carefully attempted to illuminate just how widespread the effects of immigration are on the political behavior of whites. We began by revealing a largely overlooked but nevertheless dramatic and ongoing shift in aggregate white partisanship. In 1980, white Democrats dominated white Republicans numerically. Today the reverse is true. We then link this shift in white partisanship to immigration. Chapters 2 and 3 show that white Americans who harbor anti-immigrant sentiments are much more likely than others to identify as Republican and favor Republican candidates across a host of different elections from the presidential to gubernatorial level. These relationships held true even when taking into consideration other factors known to influence partisanship and the vote. Critically, we also illustrated that attitudes toward immigrants predict shifts in partisanship—a key test in demonstrating causality.

Next we turned our attention to the casual mechanisms that can help us to understand *how* immigration affects the partisan and political choices of white Americans. That is, in what ways are public fears and anxieties over immigration triggered? We focused on two mechanisms that we believe are particularly significant: racial/ethnic demographics and media coverage. In chapter 4, our analysis reveals a relationship between the size of a state's Latino population and whites' policy views, partisanship, and electoral choices. Whites faced with a larger Latino population were more apt to favor less generous policies that in different ways reduced the commitment that the United States makes to its immigrants. Whites in more heavily Latino states were also substantially more likely to favor the Republican Party and Republican candidates. In short, how whites react to immigration depends a lot on how much immigration has transformed their demographic environment. In chapter 5, we analyzed *New York Times* coverage of immigration over the last thirty years to show that changes in media coverage of Latinos and immigration closely map onto aggregate changes in white partisanship. When media coverage focus on more negative aspects of immigration as well as Latinos, the proportion of whites who identify as Republican markedly increases.

In our final empirical test, we examine the consequences of this rightward shift for policy in US states. We demonstrate that the public's fears and concerns over immigration have been powerful enough to shift the core spending priorities at the state level. In states with larger Latino populations, less spending goes to education and welfare, whereas increased spending goes to criminal punishment; a greater use of regressive tax measures also occurs. In other words, when Latinos make up a larger share of the disadvantaged population, states are less generous and more punitive.

What Is Missing?

Our account of immigration backlash politics has, we think, helped to portray the many ways immigration and the United States' changing demographics are reshaping US politics. Nevertheless, in writing this book we had to make difficult choices about what to focus on and what to ignore. We readily admit that the patterns detailed here fail to present the entire story of immigration, race, and US politics.

One area that we believe could use greater attention is identifying and assessing a wider range of the mechanisms that could drive white reactions to immigration. The two mechanisms we have highlighted here—demographic change and media coverage—appear to be critical factors shaping the political actions of white America. But as we have briefly noted, there are likely to be other equally important influences on white behavior. Perhaps the biggest omission here is our lack of attention to the role that strategic politicians play in motivating a white backlash. Political elites can choose to ignore or engage immigration. And what they choose will often have considerable consequences. Governor Wilson arguably ignited the backlash by putting

Proposition 187 on the California ballot. Today, countless Republican political entrepreneurs actively use immigration to garner votes and mobilize supporters. The strategic choices that political elites make on immigration certainly deserve more attention.[2]

Another potential trigger is the political activity of the Latino population.[3] While we have incorporated the Latino population in our models, we have not directly considered the effect of Latino mobilization. It is possible that Latinos, by being more forceful, active, and successful in the political arena, can intensify white fears. After all, history is replete with episodes of white countermobilization in the face of active demands from the African American community for expanded rights and privileges.[4] Thus, we might expect that white reactions will be more pronounced and more negative where Latinos turn out to vote in higher numbers, where protest activity is greater, and where Latino representation in state and local office is higher.[5]

Finally, there is also one institutional arrangement that might help to foster a white backlash. Since direct democracy gives the majority the ability to directly target minorities, one might expect the success of the white backlash to be more marked in areas with direct democracy.[6] If legislators are reluctant to act on the fears and concerns of their white constituents, whites in direct democracy states can always turn to the ballot to put forward initiatives restricting Latino or immigrant interests. Efforts in California and other states to mandate English as the official language, curb bilingual education, and prevent certain immigrants from obtaining social services all seem to fit this story.[7] All these different mechanisms represent critical avenues for future research.

There is also more to do in the arena of policy outcomes.[8] How much do the public's views of immigration impact policy decisions

---

[2] We have not honed in on strategic political actors largely because problems with endogeneity make it difficult to empirically assess their influence. Researchers will have to determine if elite actors are generating a backlash, or are in fact responding to a backlash already growing in size and scope.

[3] Dancygier 2010; Pantoja, Menjivar, and Magana 2008.

[4] Parker 1990; Kousser 1974.

[5] One could also add interest groups, social movements, and party activists to the list of potentially influential actors in the dynamics of the immigration backlash.

[6] Gamble 1997; Hajnal, Gerber, and Louch 2002.

[7] We conducted a preliminary test of this direct democracy theory. Specifically, we expanded on the analysis in chapter 6, and sought to determine if state spending was markedly less favorable to minority and immigrant interests in states with direct democracy. We did find that the effect of the size of the Latino population on education spending was significantly greater in direct democracy states than in other states. But there was no clear sign of a direct democracy interaction effect for any of the other spending policies or tax measures we looked at.

[8] Hero 1998.

beyond spending and taxation? Have concerns about immigrants helped to generate an ever-increasing number of voter identification laws, as some suggest?[9] Does immigration play a role in shaping criminal sentencing laws, education policy, or any number of other areas at the state level? And further still, how much does unease over immigration alter local policy outcomes?[10] All these questions should be answered.

One other obvious omission in our analysis is a failure to incorporate the reactions of racial and ethnic minorities to immigration. We have—we think for good reason—concentrated exclusively on the political behavior of non-Hispanic whites. But an assessment of the reactions of African Americans, Asian Americans, and Latinos to immigration would help to offer a fuller, more complete picture of immigration's impact on the United States. In fact, we have performed a range of tests with our various data sets to see if attitudes on immigration shape the policy preferences, partisanship, and electoral choices of these three minority groups.

Our preliminary results using the 2012 ANES and other surveys suggest that African Americans experience the strongest reaction to immigration of the three minority groups. Not only are their views about immigration more negative than those of Latinos and Asian Americans (and relatively close to those of whites), but we also find that concerns about immigration are significantly associated with support for the Republican Party among blacks. This accords well with existing studies that find a reasonably robust sense of threat from the Latino population and fairly widespread resentment toward immigrants among African Americans.[11] Much more work certainly needs to be done, but it appears that immigration can push African Americans to the right politically. The story for Latinos and Asian Americans is much less clear. As others have discovered, our surveys indicate that Latinos and Asian Americans generally have much more positive opinions of immigration.[12] Yet there are at least some weak signs in our data that for the few Latinos and Asian Americans who do hold more negative views on immigration, those perspectives are associated with greater support for the Republican Party. With smaller sample sizes for Latinos and Asian Americans along with highly variable samples (e.g., voters versus citizens versus adults) across the different surveys, the results are far from consistent and the substantive effects are never large.

---

[9] Bentele and O'Brien 2013.
[10] Hopkins 2010.
[11] Bobo et al. 2000; Lee 2001. But see Citrin et al. 1997.
[12] Masuoka and Junn 2013.

We cannot rule out the possibility that ongoing large-scale immigration could begin to divide the Latino and Asian American communities politically. Whether that will actually happen remains to be seen.

Finally, in offering our account we have generally tried to illustrate the overarching effect of immigration on white Americans. This basic story will miss important variation across individuals and contexts. Some people as well as some particular states and locales simply will not fit here. We could, for example, pick out respondents in our surveys who strongly oppose immigration yet continue to be staunch Democratic Party supporters. There are also extraordinarily interesting cases like New Mexico, a state that has a Latina Republican governor who is relatively popular among both whites and Latinos. New Mexico is also a state that despite having the highest concentration of Latinos, has experienced relatively limited conflict over immigration. Why are race, immigration and partisan politics so different in New Mexico than they are in neighboring Texas, which has a similar racial profile? These kinds of questions are not easily answered, and are likely traced to their distinct histories and political contexts.[13] Yet they are critical. By identifying and understanding these anomalies, we may be able to uncover ways of alleviating tension over immigration or at least mitigating its impact on the political arena. Exceptions do not disprove the rule but they can illuminate ways of altering a current reality in which immigration appears to breed conflict and divide the nation.

Implications of Our Research

Despite these omissions, we believe this book makes several significant statements about race, immigration, and US politics. The most obvious one is just how important immigration politics is in the United States today. Few would doubt that immigration is relevant for at least some aspects of US politics. But what is remarkable here is how robust and wide-ranging the effects of immigration are. Who white Americans are politically at the core is in large part a function of their attitudes on immigration. Immigration is a central factor helping to determine how they vote, a crucial determinant of their partisanship, and sharply influences their policy preferences on everything from criminal justice to education. The role of immigration in structuring partisan identify is especially notable. Party identification is often viewed as the bedrock political identity on which everything else political rests.

[13] Garcia and Sierra 2004.

Yet we have shown here that party identification responds in rational and meaningful ways to the immigration issue. How one thinks about immigration is a strong predictor of individual changes in partisanship. How the media presents immigration is an equally strong predictor of mass partisanship. We are by no means claiming that immigration is the main driving force behind US partisanship, but it is clearly an important one. On this point it is also worth highlighting the salience of immigration in shaping policy outcomes, and in particular how and on whom states spend their money. It should now be apparent that immigration plays a considerable role in shaping US politics.

This book is about race just as much as it is about immigration. Immigration is changing the United States, but those changes are frequently noticed and filtered through the lens of race. When white Americans consider immigration, the images in their heads are likely to be of Latino immigrants. Moreover, those images are likely to evoke strong reactions and important political change. Whites' views of Latinos are intimately linked with their partisanship and votes. The size of the Latino population, more than any other demographic measure, influences individual policy positions and ultimately shapes core state policy decisions. Stories of Latinos in the media rival the economy as a predictor of changes in mass partisanship.

All this suggests that the dynamics underlying race relations in the United States have shifted. In the past, when race mattered, it was typically driven by a black-white dynamic. That is less the case today. The increasing visibility of Latinos in the economic, social, cultural, and political spheres of this nation appear to have fundamentally restructured the dynamics of race. Blacks still matter, but when scholars discuss the role of race in US politics, they have to talk about the fears and concerns that the Latino population provokes. Attitudes toward Latinos are certainly related to views of blacks, but the former represents a new and growing dimension to racial politics. Race plays an enduring though shifting role in the politics of the nation.

As a core variable in US politics, party identification has been a central subject in this book. There are, as we have discussed, two different views of what party identification is, and how much it can and does change. One side—the Michigan school—sees party identification as a strong, stable, and enduring predisposition that influences just about every other political attitude Americans hold.[14] The other side—the Downsian model—believes that party identification is more

---

[14] Green, Palmquist, and Schickler 2002; Campbell et al. 1960.

malleable, rational, and responsive.[15] We suspect that both views are right part of the time with at least part of the public. But what we have shown here puts us much closer to the Downsian model. We see major shifts in aggregate partisanship from quarter to quarter, a massive shift from Democratic Party dominance to Republican Party resurgence over time, and perhaps most noteworthy, changes in aggregate and individual partisanship responding rationally to real-world events and individual issue positions.

Our results also speak to the debate about media and framing. Laboratory tests often find substantial media and framing effects, but studies in the real world usually suggest that these effects are minimized by the counterarguments, time lags, and noise that almost inevitably occur outside the lab. Contrary to the minimal effects literature, we find that even in the real world, the media has a powerful impact on white macropartisanship. Negative framing on immigration in the media over the last thirty years is closely linked to subsequent shifts among the white public away from the Democratic Party and toward the Republican Party. These results demonstrate two things. First, the media plays a critical part in driving the immigrant threat narrative and the political reaction to immigration. Second, framing can alter core political attachments. Framing is important enough to help shape the balance of political power in the nation. What explains the uniqueness of our framing findings? We believe—but have far from proven—that immigration is a unique issue in that it is easy to understand, salient, and most of all largely lopsided. The media and political elites seldom highlight the benefits of immigration. Because Americans are much more likely to be exposed to negative accounts of immigration, framing effects are possible. This suggests that under the right circumstances, framing can matter in the real world.

Another lesson learned is that Latinos, as previous scholars have asserted, have agency.[16] Although Latinos are often targeted and disadvantaged in the battle over immigration and policy, there is reason to believe that as their numbers increase, they will have more influence in the political process. In our analysis of state policy, it was clear that whites regularly mobilized against a growing Latino threat, and such mobilization tended to end with policy outcomes that favored whites over nonwhites. But it was also evident that once the Latino population passed a certain threshold, Latinos' voices were heard and policy began to shift back to be closer to their preferences. In states

---

[15] Erikson, MacKuen, and Stimson 2002; Fiorina 1981; Downs 1957.
[16] See Garcia Bedolla 2005.

like California, where Latinos make up over a third of the population and where whites are now in the minority, recent years have seen policy outcomes that expand as opposed to detract from the rights and interests of the immigrant population. Under the right circumstances, Latinos and other minorities can have their interests heard at the state level.[17]

The Racial Divide in the United States

Throughout this book, we have typically told only one side of the immigration story—the white side. There is no doubt that our lack of attention to the views and voices of immigrants along with racial and ethnic minorities represents our most significant omission. In concentrating on the movement of white Americans to the political right, we have ignored a parallel and equally significant change among the minority population. Over the last few decades, more and more racial and ethnic minorities have entered the country, more and more have become engaged in the political arena, and perhaps most important, they have spoken with an increasingly clear political voice. Beginning in the 1960s and continuing to the present, there has been a slow and uneven but inexorable shift of nonwhite America to the Democratic Party. African Americans, once evenly divided, are now firmly and almost unanimously on the Democratic Party's side. In 2012, 87 percent of African Americans identified with or leaned toward the Democratic Party.[18] Although reliable, long-term trend data on Asian American partisanship are not available, the last two decades have also witnessed a dramatic shift of Asian American partisanship. In the early 1990s, the Republican Party held a slight edge among Asian Americans, but by 2012, the number of Asian Americans Democratic identifiers more than doubled the number of Asian American Republicans.[19] Data for the Hispanic population indicate that in recent years, Latinos have overwhelmingly favored the Democratic Party. Latino Democratic identifiers now outnumber Latino Republican identifiers by more than two to one.[20]

The end result of this movement of minorities to the left and whites to the right is a nation sharply divided by race. As figure C.1 depicts, the gap between white Americans who gave 59 percent of

[17] Rouse 2013.
[18] Ansolabehere and Schaffner 2012.
[19] Hajnal and Lee 2011.
[20] Ibid.

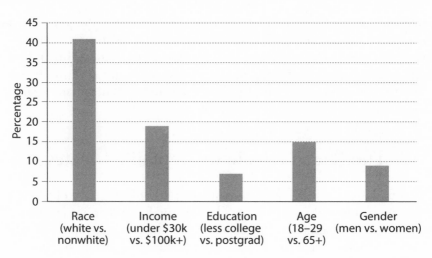

Figure C.1 Demographic Divides in US Politics, 2012 House Vote
Source: New York Times 2012.

their votes to Republican congressional candidates in 2012 and non-white Americans who bestowed only 18 percent of their votes on Republican candidates is a whopping 41 percent.[21] Minorities overwhelmingly oppose the party that is dominant among whites. That is not a gap. It is effectively a racial chasm.

That racial divide dwarfs divisions across class and other demographic characteristics that are supposedly central to the political arena. As figure C.1 shows, the racial divide in 2012 was more than twice that of any other demographic divide. Class and growing income inequality have recently been receiving a tremendous amount of attention in the media and among scholars, but at least from this one data point, it seems apparent that race has replaced class as the primary dividing line in US politics. Race is far bigger than education. It is far bigger than income. Likewise, race trumps gender and age in the vote. Moreover, these patterns are not peculiar to the 2012 house elections. The last presidential election was by some calculations the most racially divided presidential contest in US history. That contest pitted 93 percent of blacks, 71 percent of Latinos, and 73 percent of Asian Americans on one side against the clear majority of whites (59 percent) on the other. And while the racial divide may have reached an apex in 2012, the racial gap has dominated other demographic divides in almost all recent national electoral contests. Lest observers think

[21] In the 2012 house elections, Democrats garnered the support of 91 percent of blacks, 73 percent of Asian Americans, and 68 percent of Latinos (*New York Times* exit poll 2012).

that this large racial gap is somehow simply a function of the partisan nature of these contests, Zoltan Hajnal and Jessica Trounstine have found that race outweighs all other demographic divides in nonpartisan local elections as well.[22]

The implications of all this are surely distressing. While many have hoped for the end of large-scale racial tensions, and some have even acclaimed Obama's election as the first sign of a postracial United States, the politics of the nation seems to be moving in the opposite direction. In the political sphere, immigration and other factors appear increasingly to be pitting the declining white majority against the growing nonwhite minority. All this has made the Republicans the party of white America, and the Democrats the party of racial and ethnic minorities.[23] Division is a normal and healthy part of democracy, but when the core dividing line in a nation becomes closely aligned with race and ethnicity, larger concerns about inequality, conflict, and discrimination emerge. In short, when race becomes the primary determinant of political decision making, the nation's population is in danger of being driven apart.

The Future of US Politics

What does all this mean for the future of race and US politics? A reflexive response to the patterns we have illustrated is to boldly claim that the future is clear. A rapidly expanding racial and ethnic minority population will win out over a declining white population. That will mean more racial strife as the diminishing white majority struggles against the rising minority tide. That scenario will also bring about the demise of the Republican Party. Pundits and prognosticators, and maybe even most social scientists, tend to support this view.[24] We agree that all this is a real possibility.

In this final section, though, we seek to add nuance to our predictions, and introduce much greater uncertainty about the United States' electoral and racial futures. We note several underlying features of the US polity that suggest the potential of an alternative future path.

In thinking about the future, the first point to recognize is that the Republican Party is likely to play a key role in determining the path

[22] Hajnal and Trounstine 2014.
[23] Fully 91 percent of Republican identifiers are now white; slightly under half of all Democratic identifiers are now nonwhite (ANES 2012).
[24] Gimpel 2014.

the nation takes. As the party with both the clearest position on immigration and bleakest future, Republicans face an incredibly consequential choice. They can continue to use immigration to appeal to the white majority or can moderate their tactics on immigration to try to appeal to a more diverse audience. How they deal with that choice is likely to determine whether we continue to go down a path of increasingly racialized politics, or shift to an alternate one that incorporates more compromise on immigration and less racial division.

Over the short term, it is far from obvious what the Republican Party will do. Although pundits often lambast the Republican Party for its restrictive position on immigration, it is important to understand that the strategy has in many ways been relatively successful so far. Republicans have lost most of the minority vote as well as the last two presidential elections. But with the help of white voters, they control most of the governor's mansions (twenty-nine states), they control far more state legislators than do the Democrats (twenty-six versus eighteen), they are the majority in Congress and the Senate. For the time being, many incumbent Republicans and perhaps the party as a whole gain from a white immigration backlash.

But what happens when whites cease to be a majority of the population sometime around the midpoint of the century? If the current strategy begins to fail, can Republicans alter course and resurrect their fortunes? There is, we believe, every reason to think that they can and will be able to adjust their strategy as well as reverse the decline.

The history of immigration politics in the United States is particularly instructive here. Although immigration has sparked a number of popular nativist movements throughout US history, none of them has ever led to the demise of a major party.[25] In every instance, if the electoral advantage of immigration accrued overwhelmingly to one political party, the other party adapted and changed course. For example, in the years following the Civil War, Republicans looked favorably on immigration, recognizing its contributions to economic growth in the North and free labor in the West. But intense partisan pressures led Republicans in California and elsewhere to renounce their previous positions on immigration, and adopt a decidedly Sinophobic platform.[26] That shift ultimately led to Republican support of the Chi-

---

[25] Nativism also led to the birth and growth of several independent political organizations. It helped create the Know-Nothings, American Party, Workingmen's Party, Immigration Restriction League, and other prominent organizations. In each case, though, the movement either eventually faded away or was appropriated by one of the two major parties.

[26] Tichenor 2002.

nese Exclusion Act of 1882. In US history, immigration has had a powerful but short-lived impact on US partisan politics.

Both parties have also at different times chosen to reverse their stances on immigration. The Democrats of the 1950s were decidedly anti-immigrant in their tone and actions, but by 1965 were instrumental in passing the Hart Cellars Act, which repealed national origin quotas and instituted an immigration system based largely on family reunification. The Republican Party platform on immigration has been equally fluid in the past. As late as the Reagan presidency, the Republican Party was decidedly split on the issue of immigration, and only in the last two decades have Republican leaders put forward a clear, anti-immigration platform.[27] There is little reason to expect Republicans to fail to adjust their strategy in the future if the electoral incentives to do so become acute enough.

If the Republican Party does choose to embrace a more proimmigrant stance, there is a real chance that this strategy will be successful. Democrats have made enormous strides with minority voters in recent decades, yet their hold on them—especially with respect to Latinos and Asian Americans—is tenuous. When Latinos and Asian Americans vote, they strongly favor Democratic candidates. Similarly, when Latinos and Asian Americans choose to affiliate with a party, they generally choose the Democratic Party. But all this ignores the fact that nearly a majority of Latinos and Asian Americans do not vote, and when given the option, most choose not to identify with any major party. When asked in national surveys, most Latinos and Asian Americans say that they do not fit into a party at all. As table C.1 shows, the clear majority of both populations—56 percent of Latinos and 57 percent of Asian Americans—identify either as Independents, or nonidentifiers claiming that they do not think in partisan terms or refusing to answer the question altogether.[28]

Surveys also suggest that if Republicans change tactics on immigration reform, they can make major inroads with the Latino population. A recent Latino Decisions poll asked Latino respondents "if they would be more or less likely to vote for a Republican candidate in the future if the Republicans take a leadership role in passing comprehensive immigration reform including a pathway to citizenship." Forty-three percent of Latinos who had previously supported Obama said that they would be more likely to vote for the Republican candidate.[29]

---

[27] Wong 2013; Jeong et al. 2011; Miller and Schofield 2008; Gimpel and Edwards 1998.

[28] Hajnal and Lee 2011.

[29] The same poll asked Latinos whether they would support a Republican candidate who supports a pathway to citizenship for undocumented immigrants over a Democrat who opposes

TABLE C.1
Weak Partisan Ties among Latinos and Asian Americans

	Latinos	Asian Americans
Nonpartisans		
Nonidentifiers	38%	36%
Independents	17%	20%
Partisans		
Democrats	34%	30%
Republicans	10%	14%

Source: Latino National Survey 2006; National Asian American Survey 2008; adapted from Hajnal and Lee 2011.

There is no similar data available for Asian Americans, but experimental studies show that emphasizing or de-emphasizing racial discrimination can induce large shifts in Asian American partisanship.[30] All this suggests that both pan-ethnic groups are still very much up for grabs politically.

African Americans represent a far tougher case for the Republican Party.[31] But even among African Americans, there are signs of ambivalence toward the Democratic Party. Many African American commentators have expressed frustration with the Obama administration and party's lack of action on reducing racial inequality.[32] In surveys, almost 30 percent of blacks feel that the Democratic Party does not "work hard for black interests."[33] Many racial and ethnic minorities are not particularly enthralled with the Democratic Party.

History also suggests that racial and ethnic minorities are not blindly loyal to one party. Their allegiances will shift when partisan programs shift. As Michael Dawson has aptly demonstrated, African Americans have generally offered their support to the party that presented the most racial liberal policy agenda and have shifted in mas-

---

citizenship. Sixty-one percent of Latino survey respondents who voted for President Obama in the past reported that they would lend their support to the proimmigration Republican candidate. http://ccis.ucsd.edu/2013/05/what-the-gop-has-to-gain-and-lose-%C2%ADamong-latinos-when-it-comes-to-immigration-reform/ (accessed July 13, 2014).

[30] Kuo, Malhotra, and Hyunjung Mo 2014.

[31] Dawson 1994.

[32] Paul Frymer (2010) contends that African Americans have effectively been "captured" by the Democrats. Because there is no viable, attractive alternative, Democrats need and indeed have not made a real effort to enact a pro-black agenda.

[33] Authors' analysis of 1994 National Black Politics Study.

sive numbers when the two parties reversed their stances on race.[34] More recently, in 2004, Latinos offered up a historic 40 percent of their votes to Bush when he advocated for comprehensive immigration reform.

On this point it is also instructive to look north of the US border. After losing two out of every three elections in the twentieth century, the Conservative Party has "turned the tables by embracing immigration and reaching out to Canada's immigrant communities."[35] A historical transformation occurred in the 2011election when the Conservatives outperformed their rivals among foreign-born voters. And those gains have been solidified as the party has continued to reach out to immigrants.

Critically, the Republican Party may be able to attract minority support without realizing overwhelming losses among white Americans. It is true, as we have repeatedly mentioned, that large segments of the US public express strongly negative views on immigration. Yet as we have also highlighted, white Americans are far from universally fearful of immigration. Many hold ambivalent views on immigration. They admire immigrants and recognize some of the benefits that immigrants provide the nation. But they are deeply concerned about other aspects of immigration. And many others have generally positive feelings about immigrants.[36] This heterogeneity in white preferences means that Republicans may be able to retain a substantial amount of support from them even if they shift to more immigrant-friendly policies.

Republican leaders are of course not blind to the political imperatives of immigration and demographic change. Members of the Republican Party are already engaging in active debate about immigration.[37] A number of Republican senators—most notably Marco Rubio—have recently signaled a desire to move to the center on immigration. More moderate voices in the party have begun to push for comprehensive immigration reform and are now willing to support some form of amnesty.[38] Even house speaker John Boehner has sig-

---

[34] Dawson 1994.

[35] Alden 2013.

[36] Notably, younger whites appear especially favorable to immigration and less susceptible to the immigrant threat narrative. We found that across all our surveys, younger whites held significantly less negative views on immigration. Additional tests showed that perspectives on immigration were less influential in predicting the partisan choices of younger white Americans.

[37] Preston 2012.

[38] Ibid.

naled that "a comprehensive approach is long overdue."[39] But the conservative wing of the party remains adamantly opposed to these efforts. As we write this book, Republicans are blocking any attempts to bring a comprehensive immigration bill to the house floor for debate. Many incumbent elected officials who have benefited from the current strategy are understandably resistant to change. Other Republican strategists fear that the naturalization of millions of undocumented immigrants will only serve to do further damage to the Republican Party's electoral fortunes.[40]

We do not yet know what the outcome of this intraparty battle will be. We do believe, however, that the outcome will have enormous implications. As we have tried to show in this book, immigration has far-reaching effects that touch on nearly every aspect of the political behavior and attitudes of white Americans. We suspect that the issue is just as consequential for racial and ethnic minorities. The United States faces two radically different futures. In one scenario, the Republican Party alters its stance on immigration, it garners more votes from the nation's expanding racial and ethnic minority population, the worrisome racial divide between an almost exclusively white Republican Party and disproportionately nonwhite Democratic Party shrinks, and wide-ranging racial conflict is averted. In a more ominous scenario, though, the Republican Party continues to fuel a white backlash against immigrants and minorities, an increasingly anxious and aggrieved white population fights against the rising tide of minority voters, they in turn flock in every larger numbers to the Democratic Party, the racial divide in US party politics expands to a racial chasm, and the prospects for racial conflict swell.[41] That is a future we hope not to see.

---

[39] Ibid., A3.

[40] Gimpel 2014.

[41] Although partisan polarization has grown faster on immigration than almost any other issue, there is room still for immigration to push more whites to the Republican Party (Pew Research Center 2012). Some 58 percent of Democrats feel that we "should restrict and control people coming to live in our country more than we do" (ibid.).

References

Abrajano, Marisa A., and Michael Alvarez. 2010. *New Faces, New Voices: The Hispanic Electorate in America*. Princeton, NJ: Princeton University Press.

Abrajano, Marisa A., R. Michael Alvarez, and Jonathan Nagler. 2008. "The Hispanic Vote in the 2004 Presidential Election: Insecurity and Moral Concern." *Journal of Politics* 70 (2): 368–82.

Abramowitz, Alan I. 1994. "Issue Evolution Reconsidered: Racial Attitudes and Partisanship in the US Electorate." *American Journal of Political Science* 38:1–24.

Abramowitz, Alan I., and Kyle L Saunders. 1998. "Ideological Realignment in the U.S. Electorate." *Journal of Politics* 60 (3): 634–52.

Abramson, Paul R., John H. Aldrich, Jill Rickerhauser, and David W. Rohde. 2007. "Fear in the Voting Booth: The 2004 Presidential Election." *Political Behavior* 29 (2): 197–220.

Achen, Chrisotpher H. 2002. "Parental Socialization and Rational Party Identification." *Political Behavior* 24 (2): 141–70.

Adams, Greg D. 1997. "Abortion: Evidence of an Issue Evolution." *American Journal of Political Science* 41 (3): 718–37.

Alba, Richard, and Victor Nee. 2005. *Remaking the American Mainstream: Assimilation and Contemporary Immigration*. Cambridge, MA: Harvard University Press.

Albritton, Phyllis M. 1990. "Access to Health Care: A U.S. Congressional Staffer's Perspective on a National Problem." *Henry Ford Hospital Medical Journal* 38 (2–3): 108–9.

Alden, Edward. 2013. "What Canada Can Teach GOP on Immigration." http://www.cnn.com/2013/05/08/opinion/alden-canada-conservatives-immigration/ (accessed July 17, 2014).

Alesina, Alberto, Reza Baqir, and William Easterly. 1999. "Public Goods and Ethnic Divisions." *Quarterly Journal of Economics* 114 (4): 1243–84.

Alesina, Alberto, and Howard Rosenthal. 1989. "Partisan Cycles in Congressional Elections and the Macroeconomy." *American Political Science Review* 83 (2): 373–98.

Allport, Gordon W. 1954. *The Nature of Prejudice*. Menlo Park, CA: Addison-Wesley.

Almaguer, Tomas. 1994. *Racial Fault Lines: The Historical Origins of White Supremacy in California*. Berkeley: University of California Press.

Alvarez, R. Michael, and Lisa Garcia Bedolla. 2003. "The Foundations of Latino Voter Partisanship: Evidence from the 2000 Election." *Journal of Politics* 65 (1): 31–49.

Alvarez, R. Michael, and Jonathan Nagler. 1995. "Economics, Issues, and the Perot Candidacy: Voter Choice in the 1992 Presidential Election." *American Journal of Political Science* 39 (3): 714–44.

———. 1998. "Economics, Entitlements, and Social Issues: Voter Choice in the 1996 Presidential Election." *American Journal of Political Science* 42 (4): 1349–63.

Anand, Prerna. 2012. "Winners and Losers: Correction and Higher Education in California." http://cacs.org/research/winners-and-losers-corrections-and-higher-education-in-california/ (accessed July 14, 2014).

Anbinder, Tyler. 1992. *Nativism and Slavery: The Northern Know Nothings and the Politics of the 1850s*. New York: Oxford University Press.

ANES (American National Election Studies). 2008. Time Series Study [data set]. Stanford University and University of Michigan [producers]. www.election-studies.org (accessed July 14, 2014).

———. 2010. Time Series Cumulative Data File [data set]. Stanford University and University of Michigan [producers and distributors]. www.electionstudies.org (accessed July 14, 2014).

———. 2012. Time Series Study [data set]. Stanford University and University of Michigan [producers]. www.electionstudies.org (accessed July 14, 2014).

Ansolabehere, Stephen, and Brian Schaffner. 2012. "CCES Common Content." http://dx.doi.org/10.7910/DVN/24416 (accessed July 14, 2014).

Ansolabehere, Stephen, and Charles Stewart III. 2009. "Amazing Race: How Post-Racial Was Obama's Victory?" http://www.bostonreview.net/Ansolabehere -amazing-race (accessed July 14, 2014).

Archibold, Randal C. 2010. "Arizona Enacts Stringent Law on Immigration." *New York Times*, April 23, A1.

Arzheimer, Kai. 2009. "Contextual Factors and the Extreme Right Vote in Western Europe, 1980–2002." *American Journal of Political Science* 53 (2): 259–75.

Ayers, John W., and C. Richard Hofstetter. 2008. "American Muslim Political Participation Following 9/11: Religious Belief, Political Resources, Social Structures, and Political Awareness." *Politics and Religion* 1 (1): 3–26.

Bartels, Larry M. 1988. *Presidential Primaries and the Dynamics of Public Choice*. Princeton, NJ: Princeton University Press.

———. 2002. "Beyond the Running Tally: Partisan Bias in Political Perceptions." *Political Behavior* 24 (2): 117–50.

———. 2008. *Unequal Democracy: The Political Economy of the New Gilded Age*. Princeton, NJ: Princeton University Press.

Baumgartner, Frank R., and Jeffrey C. Talbert. 1995. "Interest Groups and Political Change." In *The New American Politics: Reflections on Political Change and the Clinton Administration*, edited by Bryan D. Jones, 95, 108. Boulder, CO: Westview Press.

Bean, Frank D., and Gillian Stevens. 2003. *America's Newcomers and the Dynamics of Diversity*. New York: Russell Sage Foundation.

Bentele, Keith Gunnar, and Erin O'Brien. 2013. "Convincing Evidence That States Aim to Suppress Minority Voting." http://www.scholarsstrategynetwork.org/policy -briefs/9%2B23%2B24%2B25%2B26%2B27%2B28 (accessed July 17, 2014).

Berry, Jeffrey M., and Sarah Sobieraj. 2014. *The Outrage Industry: Political Opinion Media and the New Incivility*. New York: Oxford University Press.

Berry, William D., Evan J. Ringquist, Richard C. Fording, and Russell L. Hanson. 1998. "Measuring Citizen and Government Ideology in the American States, 1960–93." *American Journal of Political Science* 42 (1): 327–48.

Black, Earl, and Merle Black. 1973. "The Wallace Vote in Alabama: A Multiple Regression Analysis." *Journal of Politics* 35:730–36.

———. 2002. *The Rise of Southern Republicans*. Cambridge, MA: Harvard University Press.

Blalock, Hubert M. 1967. *Toward a Theory of Minority-Group Relations*. New York: Wiley.

Bobo, Lawrence D. 2001. "Racial Attitudes and Relations at the Close of the Twentieth Century." In *America Becoming: Racial Trends and Their Consequences*, edited by Neil J. Smelser, William Julius Wilson, and Faith Mitchell, 264–301. Washington, DC: National Academy Press.

Bobo, Lawrence D., and Michael C. Dawson. 2009. "One Year Later and the Myth of a Post-Racial Society." *Du Bois Review* 6 (2): 247–49.

Bobo, Lawrence D., and Devon Johnson. 2000. "Racial Attitudes in a Prismatic Metropolis: Mapping Identity, Stereotypes, Competition, and Views on Affirmative Action." In *Prismatic Metropolis: Inequality in Los Angeles*, edited by Lawrence D. Bobo, Melvin L. Oliver, James H. Johnson Jr., and Abel Valenzuela Jr., 81–163. New York: Russell Sage Foundation.

Bobo, Lawrence D., Melvin L. Oliver, James H. Johnson Jr., and Abel Valenzuela Jr., eds. 2000. *Prismatic Metropolis: Inequality in Los Angeles*. New York: Russell Sage Foundation.

Bobo, Lawrence D., and Camille L. Zubrinsky. 1996. "Attitudes on Residential Integration: Perceived Status Differences, Mere In-Group Preferences, or Racial Prejudice?" *Social Forces* 74:883–909.

Borjas, George J. 2001. *Heaven's Door: Immigration Policy and the American Economy*. Princeton, NJ: Princeton University Press.

Bowler, Shaun, and Amihai Glazer. 2008. *Direct Democracy's Impact on American Political Institutions*. New York: Palgrave Macmillan.

Bowler, Shaun, Stephen P. Nicholson, and Gary M. Segura. 2006. "Earthquakes and Aftershocks: Race, Direct Democracy, and Partisan Change." *American Journal of Political Science* 50 (1): 146–59.

Bowler, Shaun, and Gary Segura. 2012. *The Future Is Ours: Minority Politics, Political Behavior, and the Multiracial Era of American Politics*. Thousand Oaks, CA: CQ Press.

Brader, Ted, Nicholas A. Valentino, and Elizabeth Suhay. 2008. "What Triggers Public Opposition to Immigration? Anxiety, Group Cues, and Immigration Threat." *American Journal of Political Science* 52:959–78.

Branton, Regina, and Johanna Dunaway. 2009. "Spatial Proximity to the U.S.-Mexico Border and Newspaper Coverage of Immigration Issues." *Political Research Quarterly* 62 (2): 289–302.

Branton, Regina, and Bradford S. Jones. 2005. "Re-Examining Racial Attitudes: The Conditional Relationship between Diversity and Socio-Economic Environment." *American Journal of Political Science* 49 (2): 359–72.

Brimelow, Peter. 1995. *Alien Nation: Common Sense about America's Immigration Disaster*. New York: Random House.

Bureau of Justice. 2012. "Prisoners in 2011." Washington, DC: Bureau of Justice.

Burns, Peter, and James G. Gimpel. 2000. "Economic Insecurity, Prejudicial Stereotypes, and Public Opinion on Immigration Policy." *Political Science Quarterly* 115:201–25.

Cameron, Charles, David Epstein, and Sharyn Halloran. 1996. "Do Majority-Minority Districts Maximize Substantive Black Representation in Congress?" *American Political Science Review* 90 (4): 794–812.

Campbell, Andrea, Cara Wong, and Jack Citrin. 2006. "'Racial Threat,' Partisan Climate, and Direct Democracy: Contextual Effects in Three California Initiatives." *Political Behavior* 28 (1): 129–50.

Campbell, Angus, Philip E. Converse, Warren Miller, and Donald Stokes. 1960. *The American Voter*. Chicago: University of Chicago Press.

Carmines, Edward G., and James A. Stimson. 1980. "The Two Faces of Issue Voting." *American Political Science Review* 74 (1): 78–91.

———. 1989. *Issue Evolution: Race and the Transformation of American Politics.* Princeton, NJ: Princeton University Press.

Carpini, Michael X. Delli, and Scott Keeter. 1996. *What Americans Know about Politics and Why It Matters.* New Haven, CT: Yale University Press.

Carsey, Thomas M., and Geoffrey C. Layman. 2006. "Changing Sides or Changing Minds? Party Identification and Policy Preferences in the American Electorate." *American Journal of Political Science* 50: 464–77.

Casellas, Jason P. 2001. *Covering Immigration: Popular Images and the Politics of the Nation.* Berkeley: University of California Press.

———. 2008. *The Latino Threat: Constructing Immigrants, Citizens, and the Nation.* Palo Alto, CA: Stanford University Press.

———. 2011. *Latino Representation in State Houses and Congress.* New York: Cambridge University Press.

CCES (Cooperative Congressional Election Study). 2012. "Cooperative Congressional Election Study." http://projects.iq.harvard.edu/cces/home (accessed July 14, 2014).

Chong, Dennis, and Jaime N. Druckman. 2007a. "Framing Public Opinion in Competitive Democracies." *American Political Science Review* 101 (4): 637–55.

———2007b. "Framing Theory." *Annual Review of Political Science* 10:103–26.

———. 2013. "Counterframing Effects." *Journal of Politics* 75 (1): 1–16.

Cisneros, J. David. 2008. "Contaminated Communities: The Metaphor of 'Immigrant as Pollutant' in Media Representations of Immigration." *Rhetoric and Public Affairs* 11 (4): 569–601.

Citrin, Jack, Donald P. Green, Christopher Muste, and Cara Wong. 1997. "Public Opinion toward Immigration Reform: The Role of Economic Motivations." *Journal of Politics* 59:858–81.

Citrin, Jack, Amy Lerman, Michael Murakami, and Kathryn Pearson. 2007. "Testing Huntington: Is Hispanic Immigration a Threat to American Identity?" *Perspectives on Politics* 5 (1): 31–48.

Citrin, Jack, Beth Reingold, and Donald P. Green. 1990. "American Identity and the Politics of Ethnic Change." *Journal of Politics* 52 (4): 1124–54.

Citrin, Jack, and John Sides. 2008. "Immigration and the Imagined Community in Europe and the United States." *Political Studies* 56 (1): 33–56.

Clark, William A. V. 1992. "Residential Preferences and Residential Choices in a Multiethnic Context." *Demography* 29 (3): 451–66.

Cohen-Marks, Mara, Stephen A. Nuño, and Gabriel R. Sanchez. 2009. "Look Back in Anger? Voter Opinions of Mexican Immigrants in the Aftermath of the 2006 Immigration Demonstrations." *Urban Affairs Review* 44 (5): 695–717.

Converse, Philip E. 1964. "The Nature of Belief Systems in Mass Publics." In *Ideology and Discontent*, edited by David Apter. Glencoe, IL: Free Press of Glencoe.

Corzine, Jay, James Creech, and Lin Corzine. 1983. "Black Concentration and Lynchings in the South: Testing Blalock's Power-Threat Hypothesis." *Social Forces* 61:774–96.

Craig, Maureen, and Jennifer Richeson. 2014. "On the Precipice of a 'Majority-Minority' America: Perceived Status Threat from the Racial Demographic Shift Affects White Americans' Ideology." *Psychological Science* 25 (6): 1–9.

Dancey, Logan, and Paul Goren. 2010. "Party Identification, Issue Attitudes, and the

Dynamics of Political Debate." *American Journal of Political Science* 54 (3): 686–99.

Dancygier, Rafaela M. 2010. *Immigration and Conflict in Europe*. New York: Cambridge University Press.

Daniels, Roger. 2004. *Guarding the Golden Door: American Immigration Policy and Immigrants since 1882*. New York: Hill and Wang.

Dawson, Michael C. 1994. *Behind the Mule-Race and Class in African-American Politics*. Princeton, NJ: Princeton University Press.

de la Garza, Rodolfo O., Louis DeSipio, F. Chris Garcia, John Garcia, and Angelo Falcon. 1992. *Latino Voices: Mexican, Puerto Rican, and Cuban Perspectives on American Politics*. Boulder, CO: Westview Press.

de la Garza, Rodolfo O., Angelo Falcon, and F. Chris Garcia. 1996. "Will the Real Americans Please Stand Up? Anglo and Mexican-American Support for Core American Values." *American Journal of Political Science* 40 (2): 335–51.

DeSipio, Louis. 1996. "Making Citizens or Good Citizens? Naturalization as a Predictor of Organizational and Electoral Behavior among Latino Immigrants." *Hispanic Journal of Behavioral Sciences* 18 (2): 194–213.

Dimitrova, Daniela V., Linda Lee Kaid, Andrew Paul Williams, and Kaye D. Trammell. 2005. "War on the Web: The Immediate News Framing of Gulf War II." *Press/Politics* 10:22–44.

Dixon, Jeffrey C. 2006. "The Ties That Bind and Those That Don't: Toward Reconciling Group Threat and Contact Theories of Prejudice." *Social Forces* 84 (4): 2179–204.

Dixon, Jeffrey C., and Michael S. Rosenbaum. 2004. "Nice to Know You? Testing Contact, Cultural, and Group Threat Theories of Anti-Black and Anti-Hispanic Stereotypes." *Social Science Quarterly* 85 (2): 257–80.

Downs, Anthony. 1957. *An Economic Theory of Democracy*. New York: Harper and Row.

Druckman, James N. 2004. "Priming the Vote: Campaign Effects in a US Senate Election." *Political Psychology* 25 (4): 577–94.

Druckman, James N., and Kjersten R. Nelson. 2003. "Framing and Deliberation: How Citizens' Conversations Limit Elite Influence." *American Journal of Political Science* 47 (4): 729–45.

Dunaway, Johanna, Regina P. Branton, and Marisa A. Abrajano. 2010. "Agenda Setting, Public Opinion, and the Issue of Immigration Reform." *Social Science Quarterly* 91 (2): 359–78.

Durr, Robert H., John B. Gilmour, and Christina Wolbrecht. 1997. "Explaining Congressional Approval." *American Journal of Political Science* 41 (1): 175–207.

Dustmann, Christian, and Ian P. Preston. 2001. "Attitudes to Ethnic Minorities, Ethnic Context, and Location Decisions." *Economic Journal* 111:353–73.

Dyck, Joshua J., Gregg B. Johnson, and Jesse T. Wasson. 2012. "A Blue Tide in the Golden State Ballot Propositions, Population Change, and Party Identification in California." *American Politics Research* 40 (3): 450–75.

Edsall, Thomas Byrne, and Mary D. Edsall. 1991. *Chain Reaction: The Impact of Race, Rights, and Taxes on American Politics*. New York: W. W. Norton and Company.

Ellison, Christopher G., Heeju Shin, and David L. Leal. 2011. "The Contact Hypothesis and Attitudes toward Latinos in the United States." *Social Science Quarterly* 92 (4): 938–58.

Enos, Ryan D. 2012. "The Persistence of Racial Threat: Evidence from the 2008 Election." Paper presented at the American Political Science Association annual meeting, Chicago, August 31–September 4.

Entman, Robert M. 1990. "Modern Racism and the Images of Blacks in Local Television News." *Critical Studies in Media Communication* 7 (4): 332–45.

———. 1992. "Blacks in the News: Television, Modern Racism, and Cultural Change." *Journalism and Mass Communication Quarterly* 69 (2): 341–61.

Erikson, Robert S., Michael B. MacKuen, and James A. Stimson. 2002. *The Macro Polity*. New York: Cambridge University Press.

Erikson, Robert S., and Kent L. Tedin. 2006. *American Public Opinion: Its Origins, Content, and Impact*. London: Pearson Press.

Erikson, Robert S., and Christopher Wlezien. 2012. *The Timeline of Presidential Elections: How Campaigns Do (and Do Not) Matter*. Chicago: University of Chicago Press.

Erikson, Robert S., Gerald C. Wright, and John P. McIver. 1993. *Statehouse Democracy: Public Opinion and Policy in the American States*. New York: Cambridge University Press.

Federico, Christopher M., and Jim Sidanius. 2002. "Sophistication and the Antecedents of Whites' Racial Policy Attitudes, Racism, Ideology, and Affirmative Action in America." *Public Opinion Quarterly* 66:145–76.

Fellowes, Matthew C., and Gretchen Rowe. 2004. "Politics and the New American Welfare States." *American Journal of Political Science* 48, no. 2 (April): 362–73.

Fennelly, Katherine, and Christopher Federico. 2008. "Rural Residence as a Determinant of Attitudes toward US Immigration Policy." *International Migration* 46 (1): 151–90.

Fetzer, Joel. 2000. *Public Attitudes toward Immigration in the United States, France, and Germany*. New York: Cambridge University Press.

Fiorina, Morris P. 1981. *Retrospective Voting in American National Elections*. New Haven, CT: Yale University Press.

Foner, Nancy. 1984. *Ages in Conflict: A Cross-Cultural Perspective on Inequality between Old and Young*. New York: Columbia University Press.Fossett, Mark A., and K. Jill Kiecolt. 1989. "The Relative Size of Minority Populations and White Racial Attitudes." *Social Science Quarterly* 70 (4): 820–35.

Fox, Cybelle. 2004. "The Changing Color of Welfare? How Whites' Attitudes toward Latinos Influence Support for Welfare." *American Journal of Sociology* 110 (3): 580–625.

———. 2012. *Three Worlds of Relief: Race, Immigration, and the American Welfare State from the Progressive Era to the New Deal*. Princeton, NJ: Princeton University Press.

Fraga, Luis, John Garcia, Rodney E. Hero, Michael Jones-Correa, Valerie Martinez-Ebers, and Gary M. Segura. 2012. *Latinos in the New Millennium: An Almanac of Opinion, Behavior, and Policy Preferences*. Cambridge: Cambridge University Press.

Frymer, Paul. 2010. *Uneasy Alliances: Race and Party Competition in America*. Princeton, NJ: Princeton University Press

Gamble, Barbara. 1997. "Putting Civil Rights to a Popular Vote." *American Journal of Political Science* 41 (1): 245–69.

Gamson William A., and Andre Modigliani. 1987. "The Changing Culture of Affirmative Action." In *Research in Political Sociology*, edited by Richard D. Braungart, 3:137–77. Greenwich, CT: JAI Press.

Garcia Bedolla, Lisa. 2005. *Fluid Borders: Latino Power, Identity, and Politics in Los Angeles*. Berkeley: University of California Press.

Garcia, F. Chris, and Christine Marie Sierra. 2004. "New Mexico Hispanos and in the 2000 General Elections." In *Muted Voices: Latinos and the 2000 Elections*. Lanham, MD: Rowman and Littlefield Publishers.

Gelman, Andrew, and Gary King. 1993. "Why Are American Presidential Election Campaign Polls So Variable When Votes Are So Predictable?" *British Journal of Political Science* 23 (4): 409–51.

Gerber, Elisabeth R., and J. Daniel Hopkins. 2011. "When Mayors Matter: Estimating the Impact of Mayoral Partisanship on City Policy." *American Journal of Political Science* 55 (2): 326–39.

Gilens, Martin. 1999. *Why Americans Hate Welfare: Race, Media, and the Politics of Antipoverty Policy*. Princeton, NJ: Princeton University Press.

———. 2012. *Affluence and Influence: Economic Inequality and Political Power in America*. Princeton, NJ: Princeton University Press.

Giles, Michael W., and Melanie A. Buckner. 1993. "David Duke and Black Threat: An Old Hypothesis Revisited." *Journal of Politics* 55 (3): 702–13.

Giles, Michael W., and Arthur Evans. 1986. "The Power Approach to Intergroup Hostility." *Journal of Conflict Resolution* 30:469–86.

Gilliam, Franklin D., Jr. 1999. "'The Welfare Queen' Experiment: How Viewers React to Images of African-American Mothers on Welfare." *Nieman Reports* 53 (2).

Gilliam, Franklin D., Jr., and Shanto Iyengar. 2000. "Prime Suspects: The Influence of Local Television News on the Viewing Public." *American Journal of Political Science* 44 (3): 560–73.

Gilliam, Franklin D., Jr., Shanto Iyengar, Adam Simon, and Oliver Wright. 1996. "Crime in Black and White: The Violent, Scary World of Local News." *Harvard International Journal of Press/Politics* 1 (3): 6–23.

Gimpel, James G. 1999. *Separate Destinations: Migration, Immigration, and the Politics of Place*. Ann Arbor: University of Michigan Press.

———. 2014. "Immigration's Impact on Republican Political Prospects, 1980 to 2012." https://cis.org/immigration-impacts-on-republican-prospects-1980–2012 (accessed July 17, 2014).

Gimpel, James G., and James Edwards. 1998. *The Congressional Politics of Immigration Reform*. New York: Longman.

Gimpel, James G., and Peter Skerry. 1999. "Immigration, Ethnic Competition, and Crime." Paper presented at the American Political Science Association annual meeting, Atlanta, GA, August.

Goren, Paul. 2005. "Party Identification and Core Political Values." *American Journal of Political Science* 49 (4): 881–96.

Graber, Doris A. 2009. *Mass Media and American Politics*. 8th ed. Thousand Oaks, CA: CQ Press.

Green, Donald P., and Bradley Palmquist. 1990. "Of Artifacts and Partisan Instability." *American Journal of Political Science* 34:872–902.

Green, Donald P., Bradley Palmquist, and Eric Schickler. 2002. *Partisan Hearts and Minds: Political Parties and the Social Identities of Voters*. New Haven, CT: Yale University Press.

Greenwood, Michael J. 1975. "Research on Internal Migration in the United States: A Survey." *Journal of Economic Literature* 2:397–433.

Griffin, John, and Brian Newman. 2008. *Minority Report: Evaluating Political Equality in America*. Chicago: University of Chicago Press.

Ha, Shang E., and J. Eric Oliver. 2010. "The Consequences of Multiracial Contexts on Public Attitudes toward Immigration." *Political Research Quarterly* 63 (1): 29–42.

Habyarimana, James, Macartan Humphreys, Daniel N. Posner, and Jeremy M. Weinstein. 2007. "Why Does Ethnic Diversity Undermine Public Goods Provision?" *American Political Science Review* 101 (4): 709–25.

Hainmueller, Jens, and Michael J. Hiscox. 2010. "Attitudes toward Highly Skilled and Low-Skilled Immigration: Evidence from a Survey Experiment." *American Political Science Review* 104 (1): 61–84.

Hainmueller, Jens, and Daniel Hopkins. 2014. "Public Attitudes toward Immigration." *Annual Review of Political Science* 17 (11): 1–25.

Hajnal, Zoltan L. 2006. "Black Exceptionalism: Insights from Direct Democracy on the Race vs Class Debate." *Public Opinion Quarterly* 71 (4): 560–87.

Hajnal, Zoltan L., Elisabeth R. Gerber, and Hugh Louch. 2002. "Minorities and Direct Legislation: Evidence from California Ballot Proposition Elections." *Journal of Politics* 64 (1): 154–77.

Hajnal, Zoltan L., and Taeku Lee. 2011. *Why Americans Don't Join the Party: Race, Immigration, and the Failure (of Political Parties) to Engage the Electorate*. Princeton, NJ: Princeton University Press.

Hajnal, Zoltan L., and Jessica Trounstine. 2010. "Who or What Governs? The Effects of Economics, Politics, Institutions, and Needs on Local Spending." *American Politics Research* 38 (6) 1130–63.

———. 2014. "What Underlies Urban Politics? Race, Class, Ideology, Partisanship, and the Urban Vote." *Urban Affairs Review* 50 (1): 63–99.

Hamilton, James T. 2004. *All the News That's Fit to Sell: How the Market Transforms Information into News*. Princeton, NJ: Princeton University Press.

Hanson, Gordon. 2005. "Why Does Immigration Divide America? Public Finance and Political Opposition to Open Borders." Working paper 129, Center for Comparative Immigration Studies, University of California at San Diego.

Hartz, Louis. 1955. *The Liberal Tradition in America*. New York: Mariner Books.

Hassell, Hans J. G. 2011. "Looking beyond the Voting Constituency: A Study of Campaign Donation Solicitations in the 2008 Presidential Primary and General Election." *Journal of Political Marketing* 10 (1): 27–42.

Hawley, George. 2013. "Issue Voting and Immigration: Do Restrictionist Policies Cost Congressional Republican Votes?" *Social Science Quarterly* 94 (5): 1185–206.

Hero, Rodney E. 1998. *Faces of Inequality: Social Diversity in American Politics*. New York: Oxford University Press.

Hero, Rodney E., and Robert R. Preuhs. 2006. "From Civil Rights to Multiculturalism and Welfare for Immigrants: An Egalitarian Tradition across American States?" *Du Bois Review* 3 (2): 317–40.

Hester, Joe Bob, and Rhonda Gibson. 2003. "The Economy and Second-Level Agenda Setting: A Time-Series Analysis of Economic News and Public Opinion about the Economy." *Journalism and Mass Communication Quarterly* 80 (1): 73–90.

Higham, John. 1985. *Strangers in the Land: Patterns of American Nativism, 1860–1925*. 2nd ed. New York: Atheneum.

Highton, Benjamin. 2004. "White Voters and African American Candidates for Congress." *Political Behavior* 26 (1): 1–25.

Highton, Benjamin, and Cindy D. Kam. 2011. "The Long-Term Dynamics of Partisanship and Issue Orientations." *Journal of Politics* 73 (1): 202–15.

Hill, Seth J., James Lo, Lynn Vavreck, and John Zaller. 2013. "How Quickly We Forget: The Duration of Persuasion Effects from Mass Communication." *Political Communication* (October): 521–47.

Hochschild, Jennifer L. 1981. *What's Fair: American Beliefs about Distributive Justice.* Cambridge, MA: Harvard University Press.

Hochschild, Jennifer L., Vesla M. Weaver, and Traci R. Burch. 2012. *Creating a New Racial Order: How Immigration, Multiracialism, Genomics, and the Young Can Remake Race in America.* Princeton, NJ: Princeton University Press.

Hood, M. V., III, Quentin Kidd, and Irwin L. Morris. 2012. *The Rational Southerner: Black Mobilization, Republican Growth, and the Partisan Transformation of the American South.* New York: Oxford University Press.

Hood, M. V., III, and Irwin L. Morris. 1998. "Give Us Your Tired, Your Poor . . . But Make Sure They Have a Green Card: The Effects of Documented and Undocumented Migrant Context on Anglo Opinion toward Immigration." *Political Behavior* 20 (1): 1–15.

———. 2000. "Brother, Can You Spare a Dime? Racial/Ethnic Context and the Anglo Vote on Proposition 187." *Social Science Quarterly* 81 (1): 194–206.

Hopkins, Daniel J. 2010. "Politicized Places: Explaining Where and When Immigrants Provoke Local Opposition." *American Political Science Review* 104 (1): 40–60.

Huckfeldt, Robert, and Carol Weitzel Kohfeld. 1989. *Race and the Decline of Class in American Politics.* Urbana: University of Illinois Press.

Huntington, Samuel. 2005. *Who Are We? The Challenges to America's National Identity.* New York: Simon and Schuster.

Hurwitz, Jon, and Mark Peffley, eds. 1998. *Perception and Prejudice: Race and Politics in the United States.* New Haven, CT: Yale University Press.

Iyengar, Shanto. 1987. "Television News and Citizens' Explanations of National Affairs." *American Political Science Review* 81:815–31.

Iyengar, Shanto, and Donald R. Kinder. 1987. *News That Matters: Television and American Opinion.* Chicago: University of Chicago Press.

Jackman, Mary R., and Marie Crane. 1986. "'Some of My Best Friends Are Black . . .': Interracial Friendship and Whites' Racial Attitudes." *Public Opinion Quarterly* 50:459–86.

Jeong, Gyung-Ho, Gary J. Miller, Camilla Schofield, and Itai Sened. 2011. "Cracks in the Opposition: Immigration as a Wedge Issue for the Reagan Coalition." *American Journal of Political Science* 55 (3): 511–25.Johnson, Martin. 2001. "The Impact of Social Diversity and Racial Attitudes on Social Welfare Policy." *State Politics and Policy Quarterly* 1 (1): 27–47.

Jurka, Timothy P., Loren Collingwood, Amber E. Boydstun, Emiliano Grossman, and Wouter van Atteveldt. 2012. "RTextTools: Automatic Text Classification via Supervised Learning." R package version 1.3.9. http://CRAN.R-project.org/package =RTextTools (accessed July 17, 2014).

Kaiser Family Foundation. 2004. Immigration in America. http://kff.org/other /poll-finding/immigration-in-america-toplines/ (July 14, 2014).

Kam, Cindy D., and Donald R. Kinder. 2012. "Ethnocentrism as a Short-Term Force in the 2008 American Presidential Election." *American Journal of Political Science* 56 (2): 326–40.

Keefe, William, and Marc J. Heterington. 2003. *Parties, Politics, and Public Policy in America*. Thousand Oaks, CA: CQ Press.

Keiser, Lael R., Peter R. Mueser, and Seung-Whan Choi. 2004. "Race, Bureaucratic Discretion, and the Implementation of Welfare Reform." *American Journal of Political Science* 48:314–28.

Key, V. O. 1949. *Southern Politics in State and Nation*. Knoxville: University of Tennessee Press.

Kim, Claire Jean. 2003. *Bitter Fruit: The Politics of Black-Korean Conflict in New York City*. New Haven, CT: Yale University Press.

Kinder, Donald R., and Cindy Kam. 2010. *Us versus Them: Ethnocentric Foundations of American Opinion*. Chicago: University of Chicago Press.

Kinder, Donald R., and Tali Mendelberg. 1995. "Cracks in American Apartheid: The Political Impact of Prejudice among Desegregated Whites." *Journal of Politics* 57 (2): 402–24.

Kinder, Donald R., and Lynn Sanders. 1996. *Divided by Color: Racial Politics and Democratic Ideals*. Chicago: University of Chicago Press.

King, Desmond S., and Rogers M. Smith. 2011. *Still a House Divided: Race and Politics in Obama's America*. Princeton, NJ: Princeton University Press.

Klinkner, Philip A., and Rogers M. Smith. 1999. *The Unsteady March: The Rise and Decline of Racial Equality in America*. Chicago: University of Chicago Press.

Kousser, Morgan J. 1974. *The Shaping of Southern Politics: Suffrage Restriction and the Establishment of the One-Party South, 1880–1910*. New Haven, CT: Yale University Press.

———. 1999. *Colorblind Injustice: Minority Voting Rights and the Undoing of the Second Reconstruction*. Chapel Hill: University of North Carolina Press.

Kousser, Thad. 2005. *Term Limits and the Dismantling of State Legislative Professionalism*. New York: Cambridge University Press.

Kuo, Alexander, Neil A. Malhotra, and Cecilia Hyunjung Mo. 2014. "Why Do Asian Americans Identify as Democrats? Testing Theories of Social Exclusion and Intergroup Solidarity." Working paper.

Lahav, Gallya. 2004. *Immigration and Politics in the New Europe: Reinventing Borders*. New York: Cambridge University Press.

Lakoff, George, and Sam Ferguson. 2006. "The Framing of Immigration." Rockridge Institute. http://academic.evergreen.edu/curricular/ppandp/PDFs/Lakoff%20 Framing%20of%20Immigration.doc.pdf (accessed August 1, 2012).

Lau, Richard R., and David P. Redlawsk. 2001. "Advantages and Disadvantages of Cognitive Heuristics in Political Decision Making." *American Journal of Political Science* 45 (4): 951–71.

Lax, Jeffrey R., and Justin H. Phillips. 2009. "Gay Rights in the States: Public Opinion and Policy Responsiveness." *American Political Science Review* 103 (3): 367–86.

Lay, Celeste. 2012. *A Midwestern Mosaic: Immigration and Political Socialization in Rural America*. Philadelphia: Temple University Press.

Layman, Geoffrey C., and Edward G. Carmines. 1997. "Cultural Conflict in American Politics: Religious Traditionalism, Postmaterialism, and US Political Behavior." *Journal of Politics* 59:751–77.

Layman, Geoffrey C., and Thomas M. Carsey. 2002. "'Party Polarization' and 'Conflict Extension' in the American Electorate." *American Journal of Political Science* 46:786–802.

Lazarsfeld, Paul F., and Robert K Merton. 1948. "Mass Communication, Popular Taste, and Organized Social Action." In *Mass Culture: Popular Arts in America*, edited by Bernard Rosenberg and David Manning White, 229–50. New York: Free Press.

Lecheler, Sophie, and Claes H. de Vreese. 2011. "Getting Real: The Duration of Framing Effects." *Journal of Communication*. 61 (5): 959–83.

Lee, Taeku. 2001. *Mobilizing Public Opinion: Black Insurgency and Racial Attitudes in the Civil Rights Era*. Chicago: University of Chicago Press.

Leighley, Jan E., and Jonathan Nagler. 2013. *Who Votes Now? Demographics, Issues, Inequality, and Turnout in the United States*. Princeton, NJ: Princeton University Press.

Lewis-Beck, Michael S., Charles Tien, and Richard Nadeau. 2010. "Obama's Missed Landslide: A Racial Cost?" *PS: Political Science and Politics* 43 (1): 69–76.

Lubbers, Marcel, Mérove Gijsberts, and Peer Scheepers. 2002. "Extreme Right-Wing Voting in Western Europe." *European Journal of Political Research* 41 (3): 345–78.

Lublin, David. 2004. *The Republican South: Democratization and Partisan Change*. Princeton, NJ: Princeton University Press.

Lupia, Arthur, and Mathew D. McCubbins. 1998. *The Democratic Dilemma: Can Citizens Learn What They Need to Know?* New York: Cambridge University Press.

MacKuen, Michael B., Robert S. Erikson, and James A. Stimson. 1989. "Macropartisanship." *American Political Science Review* 83 (4): 1125–42.

Malhotra, Neil, Melissa R. Michelson, Todd Rogers, and Ali A. Valenzuela. 2011. "Text Messages as Mobilization Tools: The Conditional Effect of Habitual Voting and Election Salience." *American Politics Research*. 39 (4): 664–81.

Markus, Gregory B., and Philip E. Converse. 1979. "A Dynamic Simultaneous Equation Model of Electoral Choice." *American Political Science Review* 73:1055–70.

Martinez-Ebers, Valerie, Luis R. Fraga, Linda Lopez, and Arturo Vega. 2000. "Latino Interests in Education, Health, and Criminal Justice Policy." *PS: Political Science and Politics* 33 (3): 547–54.

Massey, Douglas S. 2001. "Residential Segregation and Neighborhood Conditions in U.S. Metropolitan Areas." In *America Becoming: Racial Trends and Their Consequences*, edited by Neil Smelser, William Julius Wilson, and Faith Mitchell, 391–434. Washington DC: National Academy Press.

Massey, Douglas S., and Zoltan L. Hajnal. 1995. "The Changing Geographic Structure of Black-White Segregation in the United States." *Social Science Quarterly* 76 (3): 527–42.

Massey, Douglas S., and Magaly Sánchez R. 2010. *Brokered Boundaries: Creating Immigrant Identity in Anti-Immigrant Times*. New York: Russell Sage Foundation.

Masuoka, Natalie, and Jane Junn. 2013. *The Politics of Belonging: Race, Public Opinion, and Immigration*. Chicago: University of Chicago Press.

McCarty, Nolan, Keith T. Poole, and Howard Rosenthal. 2008. *Polarized America: The Dance of Ideology and Unequal Riches*. Cambridge, MA: MIT Press.

McClain, Paula D., Niambi Cater, Victoria DeFrancesco Soto, Monique Lyle, Jeffrey D. Grynaviski, Shayla Nunnally, Thomas Scotto, Alan Kendrick, Gerald Lackey, and Kendra Cotton. 2006. "Racial Distancing in a Southern City: Latino Immigrants' Views of Black Americans." *Journal of Politics* 68 (3): 571–84.

McClosky, Herbert, and Alida Brill. 1983. *Dimensions of Tolerance: What Americans Believe about Civil Liberties*. New York: Russell Sage Foundation.

McLaren, Lauren M. 2003. "Anti-Immigrant Prejudice in Europe: Contact, Threat Perception, and Preferences for the Exclusion of Migrants." *Social Forces* 81 (3): 909–36.

McManus, John H. 1994. *Market Driven Journalism: Let the Citizen Beware?* Thousand Oaks, CA: Sage.

Medina, Jennifer. 2013. "California Gives Expanded Rights to Noncitizens." *New York Times*, September 20, A1.

Mendelberg, Tali. 1997. "Executing Hortons: Racial Crime in the 1988 Presidential Campaign." *Public Opinion Quarterly* 61 (1): 134–57.

———. 2001. *The Race Card: Campaign Strategy, Implicit Messages, and the Norm of Equality*. Princeton, NJ: Princeton University Press.

Miguel, Edward, and Mary Kay Gugerty. 2005. "Ethnic Divisions, Social Sanctions, and Public Goods in Kenya." *Journal of Public Economics* 89 (11–12): 2325–68.

Miller, Gary, and Norman Schofield. 2008. "The Transformation of the Republican and Democratic Party Coalitions in the US." *Perspectives on Politics* 6 (3): 433–50.

Miller, Warren Edward, and J. Merrill Shanks. 1996. *The New American Voter*. Cambridge, MA: Harvard University Press.

Mutz, Diana C. 1995. "Effects of Horse-Race Coverage on Campaign Coffers: Strategic Contributing in Presidential Primaries." *Journal of Politics* 57 (4): 1015–42.

NAES (National Annenberg Election Survey). 2000. Annenberg School for Communication and Annenberg Public Policy Center of the University of Pennsylvania.

———. 2004. Annenberg School for Communication and the Annenberg Public Policy Center of the University of Pennsylvania.

National Asian American Survey. 2008. National Asian American Survey. http://www.naasurvey.com/ (July 14, 2014).

National Association of Hispanic Journalists. 2005. *The Portrayal of Latinos and Latino Issues on Network Television News*. Report, Austin, TX.

National Association of Latino Elected Officials. 2012. *National Directory*. Washington, DC: National Association of Latino Elected Officials.

National Association of State Budget Officers. 1993–2011. "State Expenditure Reports." http://www.nasbo.org/publications-data/state-expenditure-report (accessed September 20, 2012).

National Conference of State Legislatures. 2013. "State Laws Related to Immigration." http://www.ncsl.org/research/immigration/state-laws-related-to-immigration-and-immigrants.aspx (July 14, 2014).

National Election Pool Exit Polls. 2014. "National Election Pool Exit Polls." http://www.ropercenter.uconn.edu/elections/common/exitpolls.html (July 14, 2014).

National Survey of Latinos. 2006. "National Survey of Latinos." http://www.pewhispanic.org/2006/07/13/2006-national-survey-of-latinos/ (July 14, 2014).

Nelson, Thomas E., Rosalee A. Clawson, and Zoe M. Oxley. 1997. "Media Framing of a Civil Liberties Conflict and Its Effect on Tolerance." *American Political Science Review* 91 (3): 567–83.

Nelson, Thomas E., and Donald R. Kinder. 1996. "Issue Frames and Group-Centrism in American Public Opinion." *Journal of Politics* 58 (4): 1055–78.

New York Times. 2012. "National Exit Polls." http://elections.nytimes.com/2012/results/house/exit-polls (July 14, 2014).

Newman, Benjamin J. 2013. "Acculturating Contexts and Anglo Opposition to Immigration in the U.S." *American Journal of Political Science* 57 (2): 374–90.

Newton, Lina. 2008. *Illegal, Alien, or Immigrant: The Politics of Immigration Reform.* New York: New York University Press.

Nie, Norman H., Sidney Verba, and John R. Petrocik. 1979. *The Changing American Voter.* Cambridge, MA: Harvard University Press.

Niemi, Richard G., and M. Kent Jennings. 1991. "Issues and Inheritance in the Formation of Party Identification." *American Journal of Political Science* 35:970–88.

Nisbet Matthew C., Dominique Brossard, and Adrianne Kroepsch. 2003. "Framing Science: The Stem Cell Controversy in an Age of Press/Politics." *Press/Politics* 8:36–70.

Ngai, Mae. 2005. *Impossible Subjects: Illegal Aliens and the Making of Modern America.* Princeton, NJ: Princeton University Press.

Oliver, J. Eric, and Tali Mendelberg. 2000. "Reconsidering the Environmental Determinants of White Racial Attitudes." *American Journal of Political Science* 44 (3): 574–87.

Oliver, J. Eric, and Janelle Wong. 2003. "Intergroup Prejudice in Multiethnic Settings." *American Journal of Political Science* 47 (4): 567–82.

Olzak, Susan. 1992. *The Dynamics of Ethnic Competition and Conflict.* Palo Alto, CA: Stanford University Press.

Page, Benjamin I., and Calvin C. Jones. 1979. "Reciprocal Effects of Policy Preferences, Party Loyalties, and the Vote." *American Political Science Review* 73: 1071–89.

Pantoja, Adrian, Cecilia Menjivar, and Lisa Magana. 2008. "The Spring Marches of 2006: Latinos, Immigration, and Political Mobilization in the 21st Century." *American Behavioral Scientist* 52 (4): 499–506.

Parker, Frank R. 1990. *Black Votes Count: Political Empowerment in Mississippi after 1965.* Chapel Hill: University of North Carolina Press.

Passel, Jeffrey S., and D'Vera Cohn. 2009. "A Portrait of Unauthorized Immigrants in the United States." Washington, DC: Pew Hispanic Center.

Passel, Jeffrey S., Wendy Wang, and Paul Taylor. 2010. "Marrying Out: One-in-Seven New U.S. Marriages Is Interracial or Interethnic." Social and Demographic Trends Report. Washington, DC: Pew Research Center.

Pérez, Efrén O. 2010. "Explicit Evidence on the Import of Implicit Attitudes: The IAT and Immigration Policy Judgments." *Political Behavior* 32 (4): 517–45.

———. Forthcoming. *Unspoken: Implicit Attitudes and Political Thinking.*

Pettigrew, Thomas F., Oliver Christ, Ulrich Wagner, and Jost Stellmacher. 2007. "Direct and Indirect Intergroup Contact Effects on Prejudice: A Normative Interpretation." *International Journal of Intercultural Relations* 31 (4): 411–25.

Pew Research Center. 2006. "America's Immigration Quandary: No Consensus on Immigration Problem or Proposed Fixes." http://www.people-press.org/2006/03/30/americas-immigration-quandary/ (accessed July 13, 2014).

———. 2012. "Partisan Polarization, in Congress and among Public, Is Greater Than Ever." http://www.pewresearch.org/fact-tank/2013/07/17/partisan-polarization-in-congress-and-among-public-is-greater-than-ever/ (accessed July 21, 2014).

Polling Report. 2014. Immigration Polling Report. http://www.pollingreport.com/immigration.htm (July 14, 2014).

Poole, Keith T., and Howard Rosenthal. 1997. *Congress: A Political-Economic History of Roll-Call Voting.* New York: Oxford University Press.

Preston, Julia. 2012. "Republicans Reconsider Positions on Immigration." *New York Times*, November 9, A3.

Prior, Markus. 2005. "News vs. Entertainment: How Increasing Media Choice Widens Gaps in Political Knowledge and Turnout." *American Journal of Political Science* 49 (3): 577–92.

Quillian, Lincoln. 1995. "Prejudice as a Response to Perceived Group Threat: Population Composition and Anti-Immigrant and Racial Prejudice in Europe." *American Sociological Review* 60 (4): 586–611.

Ramakrishnan, S. Karthick. n.d. *The New Politics of Immigration in the United States*. Book manuscript.

Ramakrishnan, S. Karthick, and Tom Wong. 2010. "Partisanship, Not Spanish: Explaining Municipal Ordinances Affecting Undocumented Immigrants." In *Taking Local Control: Immigration Policy Activism in US Cities and States*, edited by Monica Varsanyi. 73–96. Palo Alto, CA: Stanford University Press.

Rivera, Michael 2013. "Immigration, Public Opinion, and State Policy Responsiveness." PhD diss., University of California at San Diego.

Roper Center. 2014. "Topics at a Glance: Immigration." http://www.ropercenter .uconn.edu/data_access/tag/Immigration.html (accessed July 14, 2014).

Rouse, Stella M. 2013. *Latinos in the Legislative Process: Interests and Influence*. New York: Cambridge University Press.

Santa Ana, Otto, ed. 2004. *Tongue-Tied: The Lives of Multilingual Children in Public Education*. New York: Rowman and Littlefield Publishers.

Scheve, Kenneth F., and Matthew J. Slaughter. 2001. "Labor Market Competition and Individual Preferences over Immigration Policy." *Review of Economics and Statistics* 83 (1): 133–45.

Schildkraut, Deborah Jill. 2005. *Press One for English: Language Policy, Public Opinion, and American Identity*. Princeton, NJ: Princeton University Press.

——. 2010. *Americanism in the Twenty-First Century: Public Opinion in the Age of Immigration*. New York: Cambridge University Press.

Schrag, Peter. 2011. *Not Fit for Our Society: Immigration and Nativism in America*. Berkeley: University of California Press.

Schuman, Howard, ed. 1997. *Racial Attitudes in America: Trends and Interpretations*. Cambridge, MA: Harvard University Press.

Sears, David O., and Jack Citrin. 1982. *Tax Revolt: Something for Nothing in California*. Cambridge, MA: Harvard University Press.

Severson, Kim. 2011. "Southern Lawmakers Focus on Illegal Immigrants." *New York Times*, March 25, A13.

Shafer, Byron E., and Richard Johnston. 2005. *The End of Southern Exceptionalism: Class, Race, and Partisan Change in the Postwar South*. Cambridge, MA: Harvard University Press.

Sharkansky, Ira, and Robert I. Hofferbert. 1969. "Dimensions of State Politics, Economics, and Public Policy." *American Political Science Review*. 63 (3): 867–79.

Shen, Fuyuan, and Heidi H. Edwards. 2005. "Economic Individualism, Humanitarianism, and Welfare Reform: A Value-Based Account of Framing Effects." *Political Communication* 55 (4): 795–809.

Sides, John, and Lynn Vavreck. 2013. *The Gamble: Choice and Chance in the 2012 Presidential Election*. Princeton, NJ: Princeton University Press.

Simon, Rita James, and Susan H. Alexander. 1993. *The Ambivalent Welcome: Print Media, Public Opinion, and Immigration*. Vol. 93. Westport, CT: Praeger.

Smith, James P., and Barry Edmonston, eds. 1997. *The New Americans: Economic, Demographic, and Fiscal Effects of Immigration*. Washington, DC: National Academies Press.

Smith, Rogers M. 1999. *Civic Ideals: Conflicting Visions of Citizenship in U.S. History*. New Haven, CT: Yale University Press.

Sniderman, Paul M., and Edward G. Carmines. 1997. *Reaching beyond Race*. Cambridge, MA: Harvard University Press.

Soss, Joe, Richard C. Fording, and Sanford F. Schram. 2008. "The Color of Devolution: Race, Federalism, and the Politics of Social Control." *American Journal of Political Science* 52, no. 3 (July): 536–53.

Soss, Joe, Laura Langbein, and Alan R. Metelko. 2006. "Why Do White Americans Support the Death Penalty?" *Journal of Politics* 65 (2): 397–421.

Squire, Peverill. 2007. "Measuring State Legislative Professionalism: The Squire Index Revisited." *State Politics and Policy Quarterly* 7 (2): 211–27.

Steele, Shelby. 2008. "Obama's Post-Racial Promise." *Los Angeles Times*, November 5. http://www.latimes.com/news/opinion/opinionla/la-oe-steele5–2008nov05-story.html#page=1 (accessed on July 12, 2014).

Stein, Robert M., Stephanie Shirley Post, and Allison L. Rinden. 2000. "Reconciling Context and Contact Effects on Racial Attitudes." *Political Research Quarterly* 53 (2): 285–303.

Sulzberger, A. G. 2010. "Growing Anti-Immigrant Sentiments in an Unlikely State." *New York Times*, October 2, A16.

Taylor, Marylee C. 1998. "How White Attitudes Vary with the Racial Composition of Local Populations: Numbers Count." *American Sociological Review* 63 (August): 512–35.

Tesler, Michael, and David O. Sears. 2010. *Obama's Race: The 2008 Election and the Dream of a Post-Racial America*. Chicago: University of Chicago Press.

Tichenor, Daniel J. 2002. *Dividing Lines: The Politics of Immigration Control in America*. Princeton, NJ: Princeton University Press.

Tocqueville, Alexis de. 1966. *Democracy in America*. Edited by J. P. Mayer and Max Lerner. New York: Harper and Row.

Tolbert, Caroline J., and Rodney E. Hero. 2001. "Dealing with Diversity: Racial/Ethnic Context and Social Policy Change." *Political Research Quarterly* 54 (3): 571–604.

Tolbert, Caroline J., Daniel Lowenstein, and Todd Donovan. 1998. "Election Law and Rules for Using Initiatives." In *Citizens as Legislators: Direct Democracy in the United States*, edited by Shaun Bowler, Todd Donovan, and Caroline J. Tolbert, 186–201. Columbus: Ohio State University Press.

Tomz, Michael, Jason Wittenberg, and Gary King. 2003. "CLARIFY: Software for Interpreting and Presenting Statistical Results." *Journal of Statistical Software* 8 (1): 1–30.

US Census Bureau. 2000. www.census.gov (accessed July 16, 2014).

———. 2003. www.census.gov (accessed July 16, 2014).

———. 2005. www.census.gov (accessed July 13, 2014).

———. 2008. www.census.gov (accessed July 16, 2014).

———. 2010. www.census.gov (accessed July 21, 2014).

———. 2012. *Statistical Abstract of the United States*. http://www.census.gov/compendia/statab/2012edition.html (July 21, 2014).

———. 2014. "Foreign-Born Population of the United States." http://www.census.gov
/population/foreign/data/cps.html (accessed July 21, 2014).

US Census of Government Finances. 2012. State Government Finances. http://www
.census.gov/govs/state/ (July 21, 2014).

Valentino, Nicholas, Ted Brader, and Ashley E. Jardina. 2013. "Immigration Opposition among U.S. Whites: General Ethnocentrism or Media Priming of Attitudes about Latinos?" *Political Psychology* 34 (2): 149–66.

Valentino, Nicholas, and David Sears. 2005. "Old Times There Are Not Forgotten: Race and Partisan Realignment in the Contemporary South." *American Journal of Political Science* 49 (3): 672–88.

Varsanyi, Monica. 2010. *Taking Local Control: Immigration Policy Activism in US Cities and States*. Palo Alto, CA: Stanford University Press.

Verba, Sydney, Kay Scholzman, and Henry Brady. 1995. *Voice and Equality: Civic Voluntarism in American Politics*. Cambridge, MA: Harvard University Press.

Voss, D. Stephen. 1996. "Beyond Racial Threat: Failure of an Old Hypothesis in the New South." *Journal of Politics* 58 (4): 1156–70.

Winter, Nicholas. 2008. *Dangerous Frames: How Ideas about Race and Gender Shape Public Opinion*. Chicago: University of Chicago Press.

Wong, Tom K. 2013. "The Congressional Politics of Interior Immigration Enforcement." Working Paper.

Wong, Janelle. 2007. "Two Steps Forward." *Du Bois Review: Social Science and Research on Race* 4 (2): 457–67.

Wong, Janelle, S. Karthick Ramakrishnan, Taeku Lee, and Jane Junn. 2011. *Asian American Political Participation*. New York: Russell Sage Foundation.

Wright, Matthew, and Jack Citrin. 2011. "Saved by the Stars and Stripes? Images of Protest, Salience of Threat, and Immigration Attitudes." *American Politics Research* 39 (2): 323–43.

Wu, Frank H. 2003. *Yellow: Race in America beyond Black and White*. New York: Basic Books.

Zaller, John. 1992. *The Nature and Origins of Mass Opinion*. New York: Cambridge University Press.

Zolberg, Aristide. 2009. *A Nation by Design: Immigration Policy in the Fashioning of America*. Cambridge, MA: Harvard University Press.

Zucchino, David. 1997. *Myth of the Welfare Queen: A Pulitzer Prize-Winning Journalist's Portrait of Women on the Line*. New York: Scribner.

Index

NOTE: Page numbers followed by *t* indicate a table; those with *f* indicate a figure.

racial politics, 20–21; black-white divide in, 72–77, 80, 81n56, 85–86, 100–101, 200; categories of immigrants and, 17–18, 52, 86; of diversity, 122n21; future of, 211–16; historical overview of, 25–26, 33; influence on policy debates of, 12–13; issue evolution approach to, 8; of partisan shifts, 44–45; of partisanship, 8–9, 207–16; party composition and, 42–43; in public opinion of Latinos *vs.* Asian Americans, 54–55; of racially-divided election outcomes, 15–16, 100–101, 209–11; racial threat narratives and, 5, 7, 12–13, 58–59, 117–18; in state and local policy decisions, 198–99; of welfare debates, 37–38; of white backlash, 121–22

racial resentment scale, 73

Reagan, Ronald, 40, 175

Republican Party, 2–3, 5; economic policies of, 10; electoral outcomes for, 91–110, 139t, 141–44, 212; future policies on immigration of, 211–16; immigration policies of, 39–43, 44n98, 64, 89–90, 102–8, 155, 160; interest group ratings of, 40–41; Latino identification with, 41–42; nativist politics in, 7–8; predicted demise of, 16, 211–12; racial composition of, 42–43, 209–11; social policies of, 10; Southern strategy of, 80, 85–86; in states with large Latino populations, 139t, 140–41; white migration to, 8–10, 13–14, 19, 27, 45, 109, 170–73, 202, 216. *See also* electoral politics; transformation of white partisanship

responses to immigration: in electoral politics, 10–11, 15–16, 19, 88–111, 139t, 141–44; evidence of, 9–13, 206–9; racial threat narratives as, 5, 7, 12–13, 32n36; scholarship on, 3–4, 28, 57–59, 118, 121–22; transformation of white partisanship as, 2–4, 13–18, 63–87; underlying causes of, 49–51, 58–59. *See also* consequences of immigration attitudes

Richeson, Jennifer, 3n9, 59n147

Romney, Mitt, 39, 89–90

Roper Center's Public Opinion archives, 169n55

Rowe, Gretchen, 187n14

Rubio, Marco, 89, 215

Sanders, Lynn, 66n23, 100

Save Our State initiative of 1994. *See* Proposition 187 (California)

Scheve, Kenneth, 151

Schofield, Norman, 39–40

Segura, Gary, 3n9

selective migration, 128–29

senatorial elections, 91–92, 103–6, 109

Sensenbrenner Bill (HR 4437), 166n50

Slaughter, Matthew, 151

slavery, 25–26

social welfare policies, 35, 37–38, 50n116, 51, 58n144; African Americans and, 37–38, 58–59, 158, 196; implicit link to immigration of, 183, 196; Latino demographic contexts of, 120–21, 130–34, 145, 197n41; news media coverage of, 167n53

Soss, Joe, 187n14, 196

South Carolina: Illegal Immigration Reform Act of 2008 in, 48, 116, 198; immigrant population of, 116, 197

Sowell, Ken, 63

spending decisions, 184; in direct democracy states, 204–5; rates of growth of Latino populations and, 197–98; size of Latino populations and, 189, 191–94, 196–97

Squire, Peverill, 190

state and local policy outcomes, 28, 35–37, 183–200; on criminal justice, 35–36, 120–21, 130, 134–37, 145, 150, 167, 183, 186–87, 197n41; on education, 36, 130, 137–38, 184, 186–87, 204n7; empirical analysis of, 129–31; growth of immigrant populations and, 144–49; on health care, 36, 120, 130, 134–37, 150, 183–84, 186–87, 197n41; ideological identification and, 138–40, 144–45; on immigration policy, 196, 205–6; on jobs and employment, 37, 116, 161; Latino demographic contexts of, 115–16, 119–21, 125–53, 183; macropartisanship and,